FATE Presents

PLANET
BIGFOOT

R. Crumb's famous Bigfoot cover for FATE, N0vember 2000.

FATE Presents

PLANET BIGFOOT

Compiled & Edited by
Rosemary Ellen Guiley

Visionary Living Publishing/Visionary Living, Inc.
New Milford, Connecticut

FATE Presents Planet Bigfoot

Compiled and edited by Rosemary Ellen Guiley

Copyright 2019 by Visionary Living, Inc.

Front cover design by April Slaughter
Back cover and interior design by Leslie McAllister

ISBN: 978-1-942157-60-1 (pbk)
ISBN: 978-1-942157-61-8 (epub)

Published by Visionary Living Publishing/Visionary Living, Inc.
New Milford, Connecticut
www.visionarylivingpublishing.com

TABLE OF CONTENTS

INTRODUCTION

Bigfoot did not enter modern Western awareness much before the 1950s though stories of encounters in America go back to colonial and pioneer times. Prior to that, stories of huge hairy hominids were largely confined to the wilds of Eurasia—the yeti or abominable snowmen—and to hairy wild men of earlier legend and lore. The idea of a species of hairy hominids living among human beings in all parts of the world was yet to evolve. Yes, the Native Americans had their lore about Sasquatches, but again, it was hard to accept the existence of such beings as a contemporary phenomenon.

One of the events to ignite interest in the field was the 1967 Patterson-Gimlin film of an alleged Bigfoot striding in the woods in northern California. It is still the subject of controversy—was it hoaxed or not? Probably the only film dissected and analyzed more over the ensuing years was the Zapruder Kennedy assassination film.

Since then, the Bigfoot research field has expanded considerably. Thousands of photographs, plaster cast footprints and hair and spoor samples have been collected, but none have offered conclusive proof of the existence of Bigfoot. It seems the most compelling evidence to date remains the eyewitness encounter.

Meanwhile, other avenues of intriguing evidence have opened: Bigfoot exhibits paraphysical abilities and has an undeniable connection to UFOs. Nonetheless, opinions remain sharply divided as to whether Bigfoot is a "lost" flesh and blood species that has managed to remain well hidden, or has some other, perhaps interdimensional origins.

My own opinion is that the "Forest People," as they are also known, have been on this planet a long time. They possess extraordinary abilities and powers and are intelligent beings. They have the capability to manipulate energy fields and perhaps even interdimensional openings. They have connections to extraterrestrials.

FATE began covering abominable snowmen and Bigfoot in the 1950s, and coverage has expanded over the decades. In this volume, experts in the cryptid field report and weigh in on Bigfoot from a variety of perspectives. The book is divided into six main sections. This volume is much larger than most FATE anthologies, so I will not summarize each section—but a glance at the table of contents will whet your appetite to dive in, and perhaps even join the ranks of researchers yourself.

Photos and illustrations original to the articles are included in many cases. Not all original articles included author bios.

I would especially like to thank Lyle Blackburn for preparing material on the Fouke Monster of Boggy Creek and the Lake Worth Texas Monster just for this volume.

– Rosemary Ellen Guiley

HISTORICAL ROOTS

BIGFOOT: MADE IN AMERICA

Mark Chorvinsky

Bigfoot, as we now know it, was born in 1958. For almost a decade, the media had publicized the Abominable Snowman of the Himalayas, and some Americans wanted a hairy hominid of their own.

Residents of the Pacific Northwest still remember the Mount St. Helens "apes" of the 1920s, which proved to be a hoax. While alleged encounters with hairy humanoid monsters in the Pacific Northwest date back to the 1800s, the term "Bigfoot" actually was coined in late August 1958, when the *Humboldt Times* in Eureka, California ran a cover story on a huge footprint found at a construction site 20 miles north of Klamath, California.

In the appendix to Loren Coleman's book, *Tom Slick and the Search for the Yeti*, I surveyed the 1950 Yeti films. They introduced the notion of Yeti existence to the American public. The Yeti films of 1954-1957 brought the idea of hairy hominid existence to a larger public and helped create fertile conditions for the birth, growth and flourishing of societal awareness of Bigfoot.

Bigfoot's cultural origin in the Yeti is exemplified in the title of Roger Patterson's 1966 book *Do Abominable Snowmen of America Really Exist?* Likewise, Ivan T. Sanderson's 1959 *True* magazine article that "made" Bigfoot famous to the crowd that would be first-generation Bigfoot hunters was entitled, "The Strange Story of America's Abominable Snowman."

In his 1961 classic *Abominable Snowmen: Legend Come to Life*, Sanderson wrote that: "In 1958 I received a number of reports of an ABSM [Abominable Snowman] in California. At first, this sounded quite balmy even to us—and we are used to the most outrageous things..."

Sanderson was the US-based expert at this time, and the notion of a hairy man-monster in Northern California sounded crazy to him. Sanderson wrote elsewhere that, "This [account] I frankly refused to believe, mostly because I rather naturally assumed that the location as given (California) must have been a complete error or misquote. It is all very natural to have abominable creatures pounding over snow-covered passes in Nepal and Tibet... But, a wild man with a 16-inch foot and a 50-inch stride tromping around California is a little too much to ask even Californians to accept."

Those of us who have grown up with Bigfoot do not realize that just 35 years ago Bigfoot was virtually unknown in the American popular consciousness. Bigfoot has become such a fixture on the cryptozoological scene, with thousands of alleged sightings throughout the US, that it is hard to imagine that when Sanderson wrote his book in 1961, the claim that there was a newly-dubbed monster, Bigfoot, in the US, was a unique and startling event. Bigfoot has since come to be sighted in every state except Rhode Island and Hawaii. *[Editor's note: Bigfoot is now reported in all US states.]*

Bigfoot's importance in the American cultural landscape belies the monster's relative youth.

The birth of Bigfoot

In August 1958, the Wallace Construction Company was creating a new road along the western wall of a valley that surrounds the now-famous Bluff Creek, which was to be the location nine years later of the Patterson film, considered by many to be the strongest evidence for the existence of Bigfoot. A bulldozer operator named Gerald (Jerry) Crew was fairly new on the job. New guys are often the butt of practical jokes, a sort of initiation rite. Sanderson, who interviewed Crew, noted that according to Crew, "his fellow workers liked a harmless joke as much as any man."

Crew claimed to have found a series of footprints that led to his tractor, circled it, and walked away from the machine. The 16-inch-long prints were of naked humanoid feet, with a 46 to 60-inch stride, almost twice that of most people. Later print discoveries and other odd events led to the story being carried across the country via the AP news wires, and the American Bigfoot was born.

Numerous key points which seriously taint the birth of Bigfoot have been ignored or overlooked. Jerry Crew was a bulldozer operator for the Wallace Construction Company, owned and operated by one Ray Wallace and at the time subcontracted through Block and Company for the National Park Service to clear roads near the borders of Humboldt and Del Norte Counties, California.

The connection between the Bigfoot birth case and Ray Wallace has rarely been discussed and is effectively ignored by Bigfoot enthusiasts, but it may be the most significant aspect of the case. John Green, in *Sasquatch: The Apes Among Us*, devotes hundreds of pages to obscure Bigfoot accounts, and manages to ignore Ray Wallace completely. In Dr. Grover Krantz's recent book *Bigfoot Prints*, Wallace is not even mentioned. But from 1959 until the late 1970s, Wallace claims to have seen Bigfoot himself—and many members of his clan—hundreds of times and has allegedly filmed the creatures on dozens of occasions. While other researchers have spent decades searching for Bigfoot, Ray Wallace claims to see the man monsters on a regular basis.

The early Wallace Bigfoot films

Ray Wallace took a number of little-known Bigfoot films long before the famous Patterson film was shot. John Napier, in *Bigfoot: The Yeti and Sasquatch in Myth and Reality*, devotes one paragraph to Wallace, noting that it is claimed that Bigfoot has been filmed three times—the first by Ray Wallace, who alleges that he took his film of the creature in 1957. As Napier correctly writes, Wallace's claim to have filmed Bigfoot so early in the game was only announced to the press in late November 1970, and must be considered a retroactive case, with a lower credibility quotient than a current case. According to Napier, Wallace is said to have 15,000 feet of Bigfoot film. Napier's assessment of the case: "I do not feel impressed with Mr. Wallace's story." This immense amount of footage supposedly includes Bigfoot throwing stones, eating frogs, and so forth. The short films that have been exhibited in the past by Wallace are generally held in low esteem by those who have viewed them. Many viewers have felt that the films show a man in a fur suit, though Wallace maintains that they are authentic.

The fact that Ray Wallace and his brothers were intimately connected to the birth of Bigfoot and that he is also a noted creator of questionable cinematic Bigfootage casts a pall over the birth. In addition, the Humboldt sheriff's office investigated the series of sightings and other strange occurrences surrounding the Wallace's road crew, and allegedly made accusations that Roy Wallace, one of Ray's two brothers, had "perpetrated a hoax on his own construction job." (The *Humboldt Times*, October 14, 1958.)

Rant Mullens, a resident of Wallace's hometown of Toledo, Washington, claimed he carved several pairs of huge, fake wooden footprints—which Wallace used to prepare casts for display.

Post-partum depression

Mark Opsasnick describes the situation after the birth of Bigfoot: "The romantic notion of stalking this giant monster was publicized through newspaper coverage and men's magazines (like *True*, *Saga*, and *Argosy*) and attracted a small group of Bigfoot hunters, banded together by a strong will to believe and the inevitable thoughts of financial prosperity. By 1959, Texas millionaire oilman Tom Slick financed the Pacific Northwest Expedition, a group of men including Bob Titmus, Ivan Marx, Rene Dahinden, and John Green—a group of men still prominent in the field today—who were commissioned to capture the beast."

The men's magazine genesis of America's favorite monster has rarely been acknowledged, but the Bigfoot field has been strongly influenced by its origin in this distinctive literary genre. Roger Patterson's obsession with Bigfoot began with the December 1959 *True* magazine article by Ivan T. Sanderson on Bigfoot. Because of the obvious pressures, including funding from Slick and macho peer group expectations, there was a great need to produce some type of tangible evidence. Opsasnick continues, "Titmus, the taxidermist, uncovered dozens of the mysterious five-toed footprints, but the group as a whole did little else but argue and eventually disbanded."

The Patterson film

Nine years later, in Bluff Creek, California, on the afternoon of October 20, 1967, a rodeo rider named Roger Patterson and his accomplice Bob Gimlin allegedly captured a Bigfoot on film, an event hailed by many as the single most important example of proof that the creature exists. The film has often been said to be one of the pillars of evidence for the existence of Bigfoot. Few know that Ray Wallace claims to have told Roger Patterson exactly where to go to shoot his film on that fateful day. Did Wallace, whom Patterson held in high esteem, also know of Patterson and Gimlin's prior agreement that they would not shoot at a Bigfoot if they found one?

Many have suggested that a man in a suit would have been taking a big chance going out into the woods to hoax Patterson and Gimlin since he would take a chance of being shot by them. Perhaps this objection is not valid. Wallace's involvement in the Patterson film is not public knowledge.

In his self-illustrated book, Patterson drew a picture of the woman Bigfoot that he would film a year later! Was this illustration, which closely resembles the creature that Patterson filmed—down to its pendulous breasts—used as a design for the creation of the Patterson Bigfoot? Is this drawing a storyboard for the film he would take shortly thereafter? Patterson's creature was made in Patterson's image of the creature. As scientists have pointed out, female hominids don't have hair on their breasts, but Roe, from whom Patterson got his ideas about women Abominable Snowmen, didn't know that, nor did Patterson.

Bigfoot is a mystery of huge proportions. Despite its checkered origins, it has captured the imagination of many thousands of enthusiasts and is certain to be one of the world's most enduring monsters.

Mark Chorvinsky (1954-2005): Former FATE *columnist and consulting editor and founding editor of* Strange *magazine.*

FATE July 1993

SASQUATCH GOTHIC

Joe Fex

Part I

The North American wilderness may seem somewhat uneventful and dull in this modern age of technology. Nowadays it seems that our society is just as deeply rooted in the securities of technological convenience as our forefathers were in life in the wilderness. In those days of early discovery, survival in the wilds was considered preferable by many settlers to the politics and oppressions of their own "modern world."

Most people today think there is no wilderness left and that everything has been discovered and tamed. They feel that "adventure" is only to be found in books, films, television, or the oft-misguided Internet. Such concepts could not be further from the truth.

The objective of this article is to focus not only on the continuous, steady stream of historical record throughout these past 1,000 years of recorded Sasquatch observation, but also to display the repetition of basic elemental data contained within these records. After all, most researchers would agree that such repetition in modern witness reports is the very foundation that supports the reality of these mysterious beings. Without the corroborative witness statements, there would not be much to support the idea that the Sasquatch is anything more than a modern legend or the mythology of primitive peoples.

It is intended to mainly focus on the social and cultural changes or evolutions of thought and perception that took place prior to general recognition of the Sasquatch phenomenon beginning around 1958. In those days accounts of these phantoms of the forest were confidential, low-toned whispers lest one be perceived as mad.

Our limited view from the shelter of our structured societies is far too often taken for granted. In paranormal matters, we often opt for simply downloading information given to us by would-be researchers and adopting the views of the favored researcher and/or scientist. What intimidates the minds of most who deny the reality of the paranormal is that it tends to remove us from the artificial illusions and securities—and control—of technology. We are clearly not in control of our world, our society, our universe, or even ourselves.

The monumental contributions of such minds such as psychologist Dr. R. Leo Sprinkle, journalist John A. Keel, physicist Dr. Claude Swanson, or NASA/Westinghouse Mercury mission engineer Dr. John F. Scheussler may not sound as appealing or exciting as "Giant Hairy Monsters" in deep dark places, but these gentlemen have had a careful eye on our big, hairy friends for many years. Although the Sasquatch enigma is not their respective field of expertise per se, they have much insight to offer as well as an unfiltered view not readily available to the standard conditioned researcher. After many private conversations on the topic with some of these gentlemen, I have discovered not only a wide range of scientific interest in the Sasquatch phenomenon, but a wealth of lessons in the ethics and disciplines required for a truly critical understanding of these most mysterious and perplexing phantasms that haunt us so deeply.

Perhaps Dr. Sprinkle's theory of the paranormal element in our experience as a possible educational, evolutionary, and/or even disciplinary mechanism of a cosmic-consciousness conditioning program, as outlined in his *Soul Samples,* should be considered. We need to integrate the spiritual perceptions of primitive tribes now lost to the old world, superstitious way of thinking to the great new world frontier regarding the Sasquatch enigma and translate them into a more comprehensive definition of the modern experience.

This current state of public consciousness is what I consider to be one of the most detrimental elements in any paranormal field. Simply put, the public and research communities should carefully consider all points of view, not just the convenient or "agreeable" ones, and ultimately make up their own minds. All who truly seek any sense of wisdom at all would do well to avoid this carbon copy intelligence.

Echoes of the past: AD 1000

More than 1,000 years ago, there roamed upon this land, while it was still in a primordial state, many races and tribes of Neolithic natives. They left their mark upon the land with standing stones and astrological calendars of stone and wood.

As with our Native American counterparts, it is suspected that these Neolithic tribes were integrated with, or co-existed with, the Sasquatch on a fairly common basis. Perhaps the creatures even assisted in the erection of some of the mysterious stone monuments. Many of these Neolithic burial mounds were excavated or even plowed over to level farming fields, revealing human-like skeletons of colossal size and structure. Since these tribes of our prehistory often practiced sacred ritual interment in mounds as well, it would seem that the giants that roamed these lands during the same age most likely shared a common spiritual, cultural, and social reality with their native counterparts. Their native co-inhabitants deified them or considered them sacred, thus interring them like their own holy shamans and tribal elders.

All that's clear about our Neolithic North American past is that we have been deceived as to the truth of our history. But these matters are not only restricted to North America. These monuments that defy what we know of our origins can be found anywhere around the globe, and they persist in constantly exposing our structured assembly of higher intelligence as a mere fraud. Guesswork and often blind assumption are passed off as truth and fact.

There is far too much data in the fascinating field of lost civilizations and hidden histories to elaborate here. The point is that the Sasquatch is in no way new to this continent. Evidence would suggest that they have been an element of the human experience longer than our historical records can account for.

In 2003 I was delivering a lecture on the nature of paranormal phenomena in one of the most mysterious locations in the United States, a place where all manner of phenomena both natural and unnatural have been occurring frequently as far back as records can be traced. It was the desert sands of the San Luis Valley in Hooper, Colorado, cattle mutilation capital of the world as well as a major hub of frequent UFO and occasional Bigfoot activity. There are few accommodations available for miles, so my stay required a few days camping out on the desert floor. It was while winding down the lecture activities that I met an interesting gentleman attending the lectures named Lonnie Brummit.

He related to me an event that took place around 1970 while he was in service in the Navy. His best friend in the service was an amateur archaeologist, now an established professor of archaeology who does not wish his identity revealed. While his friend was on leave near the Clinch River in Tennessee, he searched through the wilderness for areas of old native occupation or signs of hunting grounds where he could discover more Native American relics for his collection. He stumbled across a curious mound of earth that was unnatural to the immediate terrain. He started to explore the base of the mound and began to uncover several fragments of primitive pottery. His curiosity piqued, he explored deeper into the mound and collected a handful of odd fragments. When he realized that this was an ancient Indian burial mound and recognized that he'd discovered something of significance, he contacted the University of Tennessee. The site was excavated...minus one small piece of a bowl that had been pocketed by the discoverer of the mound.

He'd brought the curious fragment, estimated to be 700–750 years old, to Brummit when he returned to duty. They studied the curiosity at length, perplexed as to why Neolithic Indians would create the image of an ape when there were no known species of apes or even monkeys in North America. They wrote to *Argosy* magazine, which carried many Bigfoot-related stories at the time, for their opinion of it in regard to Sasquatch and or other anomalous relics, but never received a reply.

I asked Brummit if he was still in touch with his old Navy buddy and if he still possessed the artifact. Brummit said he hadn't spoken to him since the mid-1970s, after their duties in Viet Nam. However, they had hired a photographer to create detailed photos of the artifact and he thought he still had some of the pictures. I asked him if he would contact me if he ever ran across any of them or heard from his friend.

Nearly a year later Brummit would do just that and produce for me not only over 40 detailed original photos of the artifact but an original copy of their letter to *Argosy's* editors as well. I passed along the data and photos to Dale A. Drinnon, former anthropology consultant and colleague of the Society for the Investigation of the Unexplained (S.I.T.U.), founded and operated by foremost scientific paranormal pioneer Dr. Ivan T. Sanderson.

He responded, "I am fairly certain the pottery fragment's affiliations will prove to be Hopewellian," and although it was difficult to say without actual firsthand examination of the piece, his estimate was that it was at least 1,000 years old.

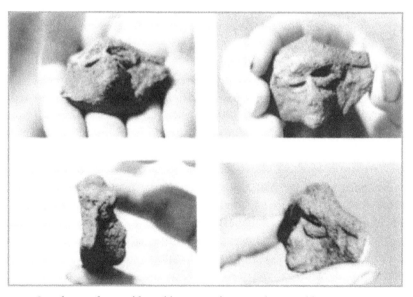

One-thousand-year-old ape-like pottery fragment discovered by an amateur archeologist in 1970, found in Neolithic native shaman's burial mound in Central Tennessee, presumed to be from an effigy bowl. The location of the sacred burial mound was less than 50 miles from Mary Green's contact area, and a large burial mound was also observed near the Coy site.

13

What was so curious about the relic, outside of the fact that no natives should have had any reference or familiarity with apes of any kind in North America 1,000 years ago, was that this ape image was slightly different from a typical ape or gorilla. It bore the usual characteristics: heavy brow ridge above the eyes, sagittal crest at the top back of the head, full sloping-forward, protruding mouth—but the nose was distinctly human in structure. An ape's nose is very short to the skull, not long and narrow like our noses are. An ape's nose is generally located more closely to the orbital sockets (eyes) where the cartilage of a human's nose begins. This ape clearly has a long, narrow-bridged nose, with the nostril openings much lower and closer to the palate of the mouth.

There is only one apelike creature that I know of that has a long, narrow-bridged, human-like nose, and that is the Sasquatch. It's entirely possible, although not very likely, that this ancient Indian shaman took part in communions with the Sasquatch peoples to maintain peace and harmony between their tribes, and that the effigy bowl this fragment came from was used for offerings to initiate such sacred meetings.

New World, new fears: 1200–1700

For the majority, brave new lands beyond the comforts of collective society represented dark, new fears of the unknown and restored deep-seated horrors and superstitions of the old world.

Along with the truly alien foreign cultures imported into this New World, entirely new concepts in psychology were imported as well. To most of the indigenous tribes, the realm of the unknown or paranormal reality has always been an intricate, important, and functional facet of their spirituality and culture. It is co-existed with instead of weighed, argued, believed, denied, or otherwise wrestled with as it is in our modern technological culture. Unfortunately, the same would not be true for their European counterparts. In fact, a near polar opposite of perceptions regarding such matters would be held by the European settlers.

Unlike the native cultures, the European settlers had come from a heritage of devastating plagues which in turn stimulated a grim frenzy of homicidal madness that would forever scar the history books with the age of the witch hunts. The psychology of modern man as a whole still has not fully recovered from this event. The paranoia and gripping fear of demonic manifestation was still fresh in the minds of most of the newcomers to the New World, and superstitions ran deep as they faced the great unknown. Anything of a paranormal nature was perceived by most as a demonic force at work. As with all paranormal experiences of the age, such things were neither discussed nor recorded lest one become suspect of cavorting with demonic agents or in league with the devil. As history has proven, so much as even a whisper of such activity could stimulate a mob mentality with deadly consequences.

Undoubtedly, the early settlers and colonists had at minimum some experiences with the Sasquatch, but to what extent, we may never know. Few records of such encounters are likely to exist. Any experience of the screaming wails of the Sasquatch, piercing, red-glowing eyes in the darkness of the forest, or apparitions of gigantic, hairy, man-like phantasms of the woods could have only been seen as demons in the minds of the early settlers. Any presence of the Sasquatch could only have fed fuel to the flames of superstitious beliefs. Even today there are many who still believe all things paranormal are demonic manifestations.

1750

When the first wave of brave wilderness frontiersmen such as Daniel Boone (1734–1820), the first settler of Kentucky, ventured into the great unknown, they would discover unsurpassed beauty, bountiful virgin lands, wondrous native cultures, and unforeseeable deadly perils. Upon close examination, one finds that a great number of our nation's earliest explorers either encountered the Sasquatch or recorded details about them as told by their native contacts and guides.

Daniel Boone was known to repeat stories of the wild men, or "Yahoo" as he called them. It is also noted by historians that Boone himself claimed to have shot and killed a 10-foot-tall hairy giant on one occasion. Although the seriousness of Boone's claim is debatable, as he was also known for enjoying folklore and tall tales, he was also a highly accomplished, dedicated, and serious pioneer. It is interesting to note the few descriptive details involved, as they conform well to modern descriptions of the Sasquatch. According to folklorist and historian Leonard Roberts, as he noted in the *Journal of Western Folklore* published in 1957, Boone had documented several versions of "a curious and strange legend" from the occupants of remote regions of the Kentucky mountains. There was said to be a group of huge, hair-covered wild men living in the wilderness of that region. Even the *Skeptical Inquirer* recognized Boone's historical account but did their best to explain it away. Hugh Trotti speculated that Boone simply borrowed the concept from the classic Jonathan Swift book *Gulliver's Travels,* of which Boone was known to be a fan. Boone most likely borrowed the term "Yahoo" from Swift's book. But the account of killing a similar being as repeated by Boone is far less easily confirmed. Daniel Boone did indeed make the claim to have shot a hairy giant in a region still known to be inhabited by the Sasquatch and state it as truth with all seriousness, more than 100 years before the native traditions of hairy giants would receive any serious recognition from modern white civilization.

Boone is known to have been familiar with many Native American tribes. It's possible that he became familiar with the concept of giant, hairy wild men through native oral tradition and then spun a tall tale from those legends. But if Daniel Boone had indeed shot and killed a Sasquatch, why did he not study its features and catalog the creature along with his other wildlife discoveries? Did he document the Sasquatch only for the data to be suppressed by governing offices?

Standing alone, this fragment of history might not appear very relevant, but a steady stream of wilderness frontiersmen has supplied a great number of similar accounts. Rest assured Boone was not the last accredited explorer to encounter the Sasquatch.

Home of the brave and (almost) fearless: 1811

The famous and celebrated Canadian explorer and geographer David Thompson would also record several curious notes in his journals in 1811. Thompson, widely known as the greatest geographer in North American history, mapped over 3.9 million square kilometers of this continent. Having developed bad relations with the Blackfoot tribes by unknowingly trading guns to their enemies, Thompson inadvertently forfeited their good graces, leaving him unable to complete his route through the mountains via the North Saskatchewan River. He was forced to venture north through the valley of the Athabasca, near Jasper, Alberta, where he observed the first perplexing trail of huge tracks. He wrote:

I saw the track of a large animal—has four large toes about 3 or 4 inches long and a small nail at the end of each. The ball of his foot sank about 3 inches deeper than his toes—the hinder part of his foot did not mark well. Very much resembles a large bear's track. It was in the Rivulet in about 6 inches of snow...

Then on January 7, 1811, as his party neared Jasper, Thompson entered this in his journal:

I now recur to what I have already noticed in the early part of last winter, when proceeding up the Athabasca River to cross the mountains, in company with... men and four hunters, on one of the channels of the river we came to the track of a large animal, which measured fourteen inches in length by eight inches in breadth by a tape line. As snow was about six inches in depth the track was well defined, and we could see it from a full hundred yards from us, this animal was proceeding from north to south. We did not attempt to follow it, we had not time for it, and the hunters, eager as they are to follow and shoot every animal, made no attempt to follow this beast, for what could the balls of our fowling guns do against such an animal? Report from old times had made the head branches of this river, and the mountains in the vicinity the abode of one, or more, very large animals, to which I never appeared to give credence; for these reports appeared to arise from that fondness for the marvelous so common to mankind: but the sight of the track of that large a beast staggered me, and I often thought of it, yet never could bring myself to believe such an animal existed, but thought it might be the track of some Monster Bear.

Three points can be assessed from these notes: there was fear and apprehension among Thompson and his men, including his hunting party, who had absolutely no interest in pursuing such a tremendous quarry. Thompson himself admittedly wrestled with the implications of the track and tried his hardest to rationalize it and convince himself that it was something even remotely explainable, such as a monster bear. It was so large and profound that Thompson could not fathom it in his scope of reality.

But most importantly, Thompson noted his familiarity with old legends that he'd heard telling of such a massive beast in this region but that he had never believed. This element of a psychological "wake-up call" in the face of one's own firsthand encounter is still prevalent today. A good number of modern witnesses of phenomena of all kinds previously did not accept the reality of it until confronted with it. Many years later David Thompson would reminisce this event in more detail when he was preparing his notes for publishing his narrative:

> ... the hinder part of the foot did not mark well, the length fourteen inches, by eight inches in breadth, walking from north to south, and having passed about six hours. We were in no humour to follow him: the Men and Indians would have it to be a young mommoth [sic] and I held it to be the track of a large old grizzled bear; yet the shortness of the nails, the ball of the foot, and its great size was not that of a Bear, otherwise that of a very large old Bear, his claws worn away; this the Indians would not allow.

Again, it is apparent that Thompson truly struggled to define these tracks to himself but was not gaining much support from his men or from his native guides, all of whom unanimously insisted that they were made by some "mommoth" of the mountains. All these historic frontiersmen and their native companions were all well versed with wildlife, yet the colossal size of Thompson's discovered tracks was beyond his own comprehension.

1839

Then in 1839, a stunning article was printed in the *Ottawa General Advertiser* (picked up from the *Boston Times*) detailing the live capture of an adult male Sasquatch and two adolescents. It reported the bizarre story of how Robert Lincoln, an engineer for a lumber company, was scouting locations for sawmill construction and logging operations when two of his men reported a giant, hairy wild man. A pursuit ensued with the assistance of several Native American guides, and when, at first opportunity, the beast was shot in the thigh with a blast of buckshot, it was subdued and transported into captivity. Shortly after securing the strange creature, two very young adolescents approached and though the adult cried out in rage at them, the two young cubs were apprehended without struggle. The authors and representatives of the Boston newspaper felt that their association with Lincoln (a native of Boston) allowed them a private viewing of the creature in question, who was distinctly described as humanlike but definitely nonhuman. It was transported live to the city. Just as these documents detail mysterious gigantic humanlike skeletons, the trail of events by document runs cold and the fate of these fantastic subjects is still unknown. It was stated that Lincoln intended to exhibit them, but no record of this has yet come to light.

Given the fact that many of our early frontier explorers did not act in any official capacity, kept no journals, or lacked basic educational skills such as reading or writing, it is interesting to note that elements of the Sasquatch mystique are fairly common.

1847

By 1847, renowned Irish-Canadian artist Paul Kane was living among several native tribes and traveling the country preserving scenes of untouched lands and native peoples in oil paintings. He found himself inspired to make a sketch at the base of Mount St. Helens, where he noted in his journal:

> *When we arrived at the mouth of the Kattlepoutal [Lewis] River, twenty-six miles from Fort Vancouver, I stopped to make a sketch of the volcano, Mt. St. Helens, distant... about thirty or forty miles. This volcano has never been visited by either Whites or Indians; the latter assert that it is inhabited by a race of beings of a different species, who are cannibals, and whom they hold in great dread; they also say that there is a lake at its base with a very extraordinary kind of fish in it, with a head resembling that of a bear more than any other animal.*

Here Kane makes note of a familiar Sasquatch theme in native traditions; they are feared and dreaded by the local inhabitants because of their cannibalistic nature... In short, they like to eat Indians! Why the native tribes are divided between those who integrated with the Sasquatch and revered them as a source of wisdom and spiritual enlightenment, while others greatly feared them because of aggressive behaviors, kidnapping, and cannibalism, is still a perplexing mystery. Are we dealing with two distinctly different beings, very similar in appearance but greatly different by nature?

Bigfeet and monkeyshines

Perhaps this division of perception is the source of conflict within the Bigfoot research community today. Perhaps it is entirely possible that the phenomenon is both a physical anthropoid or hominid with apelike and manlike evolutionary lineage as well as a quasi-physical manifestation that occupies both physical and non-physical states of being.

The concept of transmogrification may seem foreign to the Bigfoot community, but it is an old and familiar concept to studies within occult, ufological, ultraterrestrial, and religious studies. To these fields, it represents the highest order of theorem. Most Sasquatch researchers do not have any experience exploring these fields, but perhaps it would be beneficial if they did.

As with ufology and ultraterrestrial visitations, the Sasquatch are not really avoiding us at all. They are just intent on meeting us on their terms, not ours. We are clearly not reasonable, trustable, or responsible. They are indeed fully intent on manifesting before us, often for the purpose of confounding our experiences and challenging our beliefs. I contend that the Sasquatch are promoting contact, persistently tempting our pursuit, but like the UFO, patiently awaiting the right individuals to welcome the challenge. But for the most part, the Sasquatch struggles to get our attention while we struggle to ignore their existence.

Part II

In the mid-1850s, a young, prominent pioneer and newspaper correspondent, Myron Angel, migrated westward from New York to the Sierra Nevada region. There he spent years collecting and documenting what he believed to be a lost tribe of gigantic Indians, from old records, early Spanish documents, local legends, and the oral traditions of rapidly diminishing Native American tribes. He collected an archive throughout the entire region from California to Nevada and portions of the Rocky Mountains.

He served as one of the primary contributors in the first assembly of Nevada history, *History of Nevada* (1881).

The Sierra Mountains have a long history of Bigfoot activity that persists to this day.

What became of Myron Angel and his archive is still unknown. Somewhere out there, perhaps in some dusty old collection, Angel's invaluable data may still be awaiting discovery. I discovered a reference to him and his work in an article by Princess Daria Troubetskoi in a stack of 1940s *Atlantean Research* journals.

It is highly beneficial to obtain stacks of old science and exploration journals of all kinds and carefully and systematically run through them looking for key elements like "wild men" or "giant skeleton," etc. There are tons of hidden history awaiting our rediscovery, but it takes patience to find it.

Sandstone footprints

On February 14, 1879, the *Eureka Daily Leader* reported that Captain Joseph Walker, a well-established mountaineer, trapper, and guide, had produced a large slab of sandstone that contained a preserved humanlike footprint bearing four toes and measuring 14 inches long, six inches wide, and an inch deep. Walker had retrieved it from a new quarry he was working on near the mouth of New York Canyon. The fact that this distinctively Sasquatch footprint was preserved in sandstone substantiates a prehistoric presence in North America. This would not be the last we would hear of the Sasquatch in Eureka, California.

In December of 1883, in New Lisbon, Ohio, two hunters would experience what would become one of the single most common BF encounter scenarios. According to the *New York Tribune,* while Bob Bradley and Henry Rauch were hunting in an area near Spruce Vale, "they heard a noise near a rugged cliff, and saw a huge hairy object, apparently half man and half beast, spring from behind the cliff, and start for the woods, running with the speed of the wind. Mistaking it for an animal, one of the hunters fired at it. The shot appeared to take effect in the arm; for, with a scream of pain, the creature halted, tapped the wound, and turning, charged its pursuers, who with empty guns in hand dared not measure strength with the foe. Dropping their guns, both sought safety in flight."

This typical scenario or variations thereof could just as well have taken place last week or any other period of the white man's occupation of North America.

Teddy Roosevelt's story

Many are familiar with Theodore Roosevelt's account in *Wilderness Hunter* (1892). An elderly guide, Bauman, told how, in his younger years, he and another beaver trapper had encountered a terrifying bipedal beast in a forest considered haunted by the natives. Shots were fired at it, the men decided to leave, and while Bauman collected the traps, he left his companion alone to pack up camp. When Bauman returned, he found his counterpart dead with a broken neck and puncture marks from a bite on his throat. He also found marks on the ground that indicated the killer approached from behind and rolled on the ground with his lifeless victim as if in a frenzy of violent glee. Roosevelt even noted the nervousness and trembling of the old man at certain points of the tale. Roosevelt was well known for his stout, no-bull attitudes and was not prone to believing (or tolerating) wild or ridiculous tales. He believed this one.

The Old Man of the Crater

Founder of the historic Washington Alpine Club and among the earliest adventurers to achieve the summit of Mt. Rainier, Maj. E. S. Ingraham wrote about an encounter with a bizarre Bigfoot-like creature deep within an icy passage of the mountain during one of his climbs. Mt. Rainier, like Mt. St. Helens, has a long history of UFOs, water and mountain monsters, and phantasms of all kinds. It was also the historic birthplace of the modern UFO phenomenon when pilot Kenneth Arnold observed several UFOs while searching for a downed plane in 1947. (Arnold's story was the cover of the first issue of FATE in the spring of 1948.)

Ingraham described a Sasquatch-type being he'd encountered while alone deep within a steam cave of the mountain. He described a trance-like state that came over him and stated, "The crown of its head was pointed with bristled hair pointing in every direction. The eyeballs were pointed too..." Was he describing slit reptilian or cat-like eyes?

"For an hour I received impressions from the Old Man of the Crater. It is a strange story I got from him. While the time was comparatively short, yet what he told me, not by voice or look, but by a subtle agency not known or understood by me, would fill a volume of many pages."

Without a doubt, Ingraham was receiving a telepathic communication.

"This is no myth. The old man told me of his abode in the interior, of another race to which he belonged and the traditions of that race; of convulsions and changes on the earth long, long ago..."

It is clear that the occasional reports of telepathic voices from Sasquatch are not without historical substantiation.

The Ape Canyon incident

The Jerry Crew incident in Eureka, California, is generally thought of as the first public introduction to the Bigfoot mystery, but the first widespread media introduction was in 1924. Five prospectors had a run-in with a group of unruly Sasquatch that attacked their cabin after one of the men shot one. Fred Beck shot a Bigfoot that was observing them across a ravine as they descended. It presumably fell to its death into what is now known as Ape Canyon in the Mt. St. Helens area. The prospecting party, who had a proven claim, owned the land, and had worked the mine for over two years, abandoned it completely after the assault, never to return.

Although this incident has often been reported, no one included Beck's whole account of the event. Beck was frustrated at this because he felt that these were not just apes or wild men as indicated by the many researchers who wrote about it, so he wrote a 21-page book, *I Fought the Ape-men of Mt. St. Helens*. This pamphlet detailed the event in its entirety, as well as his thoughts about it all. He detailed how the entire series of circumstances that placed these men there from beginning to end was surrounded with a wide range of paranormal activity, starting with the psychic contact. Beck never profited from the event, his account, or his publication. He simply wanted to ensure that the full story was told.

Early Mountain Devil Hunters investigating 1924 Ape Canyon Incident. Left to right, back to front: Burt Hammerstrom, Bill Welch, Frank Lynch, and Spirit Lake forest ranger Jim Huffman. Fred Beck's cabin is at the left. They confirmed the event took place.

After many years to reflect upon his experiences, which actually began in childhood, Beck expressed with utmost confidence and sincerity how he'd long been immersed in the psychic world, that he was a clairvoyant, and that it was through these means that he and his party would become familiar with the spirit beings that would manifest into the physical world and guide the men to the claim through real-time holographic-like psychic visions. He said that "a large Indian dressed in buckskin appeared to us and talked to us. He was the picture of stateliness itself." He never told the men his name, but they called him "The Great Spirit" for lack of a better definition and addressed him by such a title. He responded, "The Great Spirit is above me. We are all of the Great Spirit, if we listen when the Great Spirit talks…" Another contributor to leading them to the claim was "more in the role of a comforting friend," a female Indian spirit apparition whom they would later name the claim Vander White, after her last name.

The male guide led them through the wilderness and directed their attention. Beck recounts: "The big Indian told us there would be a white arrow go before us. Another man who was not present during the attack in 1924, could see the arrow easily and clearly at all times. And I could see it nearly as well."

For four days it would soar up in the sky and hover over an area until they located it again, and it would continue until they reached their destination near the north cliff of Ape Canyon. During the journey the men were plagued with an inexplicable hollow thudding, like a drumming sound, following them. The sound was coming from underground.

Beck was later convinced it was the Sasquatch watching them, but at the time one of the men lost patience with the length of the journey and the strangeness of it all. The result was an outburst of verbal frustration and accusations that the large Indian had deceived them, leading them on a wild goose chase.

After finally reaching their destination, Beck said, "We all saw the image of a large door open, and the big Indian appeared in front of it. He spoke: 'Because you have cursed the spirit leading you, you will be shown where there is gold, but it is not given to you.' With those words, he disappeared. Then we saw the door slowly close. There was a huge lock and latch, but as the door shut, it did not latch. And that is just the way our gold mine turned out—closed but not locked."

But there were many other elements to lend credence to Beck's statement. "I was always conscious that we were dealing with supernatural beings—they are not entirely of the world." And the supporting details are more familiar to mainstream Bigfoot research than one might presume.

At some point during their excursion they discovered tracks in a sandbar that started from nowhere and then continued into nowhere after 160 feet. There was nowhere on the sandbar that any other steps could have been taken without leaving more tracks, but there was no trace of any to be found.

"For six years all had been peaceful. We were simple men and hardworking men, and an aura of good spirit or spiritual power surrounded us. We had all seen the tracks, but the makers of them had left us alone. No one was worried about the tracks as regarding any threat to our safety. But after one of us had lost his temper and denounced the spirit as a liar, from that time on, a quiet apprehensiveness settled over us. We continued working our claim, but down deep we felt it would avail to no good end. We had outbursts of enthusiasm but no success. And yet we did have success, because we learned. Nothing can replace experience as a teacher."

For Bigfoot researchers at all levels of expertise and standing, it is almost unanimous that the Fred Beck Ape Canyon event did indeed occur. So why is it that none seem to have paid any attention to the wealth of supposedly unrelated paranormal elements that Beck provided? We must expand our examination of the Sasquatch to encompass all possibilities. The phenomenon is of unknown origin and nature, so we must not be too quick to identify anything when we have such limited firsthand knowledge. We cannot force it into known science with no other considerations.

Newspaper reports

The now famous Ape Canyon incident of 1924 sparked reactions from newspapers across the United States that received the news over the then-new wire. Wire transmission was an important factor in the public's knowledge of paranormal events (and news in general) because people could see that the same types of beings and experiences were not isolated to their respective locale. Newspapers mostly carried the general run-of-the-mill story of the assault on the cabin with occasional slight variations and the usual uninformed, unprofessional, and often moronic commentary that is still prevalent within the news media today. However, some newsrooms were fascinated by the confirmation of these strange ape men by the authorities involved and took it one step further. They considered listening to local native sources.

On August 3, 1924, Marion K. Gould of the *Houston Dispatch* published an extensive article inspired by the Ape Canyon event. She revealed the results of her inquiries with the Challam tribe, a Salish division on the coast. She had spoken to George Totsgi, who gave her many leads to other tribes that could corroborate the tradition of these mysterious giants. Thus, she gained further insight from other Salish tribes of the region. Gould wrote:

Among the Sanpoil people, who are another part of the Salish division, there are several tales told of the hairy men. So much detail is included that there must be a foundation for the legends and the recent report links with the ancient in a surprising manner.

Most of the article is presented in the context of native lore and fable intended to carry historical tradition as well as important social lessons for tribal youths. The Native Americans believed that the hairy giant legends were real. Although most of the Salish tribes believed them to be extinct or that they had migrated to Texas, they still feared and dreaded their presence.

A Sasquatch by any other name

As you read the following portion of the Salish legend as it originally appeared in Gould's article, the nature of the hairy giants and native perceptions thereof are most important. These fables parallel traditional lore of many African tribes regarding ogre legends.

The Indian legend: Karnecher, the granddaughter of the official storyteller of the Sanpoil tribe, not only has told some of the stories in which the Chi-wah-ni-tum (as the Sanpoil call the hairy-ape-men), but she has drawn their likeness from descriptions given her by aged members who have imprinted it clearly upon her mind. Her talent is purely primitive and its result is unusual. One tale she tells is of the time when these creatures roamed the forest and the Indian children were cautioned in regard to them. Here is the tale as it was told to the writer.

Long ago in the forest lived a grandmother and her two little grandchildren. One day when they went out to play, the grandmother said, "Do not go far from the tipi because the Chi-wah-ni-tum has been seen near here and he will catch you and eat you. Stay within sight of the tipi door and I will protect you."

They played hide-and-seek among the trees and forgot that they must not shout so loud with laughter. Suddenly they heard a sound and looked around. A great hairy man was coming toward them. The little boy, Quat-

cha-wea, was almost paralyzed with fright, but his sister, who was older, slipped behind a tree. When the Chi-wah-ni-tum was almost ready to grab him, he turned and ran for his life. The hairy man ran after him. Quat-cha-wea stumbled over a log and fell, and as he did so, the long arm with its cruel hand and sharp nails, reached for him. He scrambled up as fast as he could, but the nails raked three long scratches down his back and when the scars healed, they left three dark marks that made him known as "Chipmunk" to this day. He darted in and out among the trees until he could run straight into the tipi door. "Hide me! Hide me!" he cried to his grandmother. "The hairy man is coming after me."

The old woman looked around. Quat-cha-wea had popped into a basket that was nearby. His back hurt so that he was not able to keep still and the basket wobbled all over the floor. That would never do. The hairy man would have him at once when he arrived. So the grandmother took him out and put him into a bag and drew the strings. He whimpered and trembled so she knew it would be seen immediately, so she took him out and put him into a clam shell—one of the large shells found in the Columbia River. He crept into it and became so much smaller in size that she tucked him into the front of her buckskin dress. "Be still," she said softly.

The hairy ape-man was not long behind. He pulled open the flap of the tipi and strode in. "Where's the boy?" he demanded. Grandmother was not afraid of him because she had power over many things. She shook her head without a word. The hairy man looked in the basket. He looked in the bag and nothing was there. He went outside and met the sister of the little boy.

"Go and find where your brother is and I will give you these," he said holding up a string of seed beads he had strung. She looked at the beads and admired them. She went into the tipi and asked where her brother was. Her grandmother patted the front of her dress. "He is here in my bosom," she said.

The girl went outside. "Look in the bosom of grand-mamma," she told the ape-man and immediately she was changed into a meadowlark and flew up on top of the tipi. "I'm sorry, I'm sorry," were the words she tried to say but the song sounded as if it was, "Wah-weech-qua-Ia," over and over and that is why the Indians call the meadowlark wah-weech-qua-la to this day.

Going back into the tipi the hairy man jerked open the buckskin dress and took poor little Chipmunk in his hand. As he did so, he saw the smooth soft skin of the old woman and he asked: "What makes your skin so smooth? It is not like mine."

Grandmother thought for a moment. "I will show you," she said. She took a piece of pine pitch and held it in the fire, the hot pitch dropped in great drops and she let one fall on the arm of the hairy man. Then she pulled the blister off and the smooth place that showed underneath pleased him although he winced with the pain. "Could I be like that all over?" he inquired.

"Yes, if you let me put the hot pitch on," said the old wily woman. "I could dip you all at once and you would never feel it."

"All right," said the hairy man, and he went with her to gather the pitch from the trees. They gathered wood and a great fire was made and the pitch was put into a stone pot. When the pitch was bubbling, the old woman and the ape-man and little Chipmunk danced around and around the hole where the fire was with the pot upon it. As they were circling nearer and nearer and the ape-man followed them, the old woman gave him a push and he went head first into the pitch-pot. So he never felt anything again, and the little boy played in the forest in safety.

Here we have a wonderful example of traditional native storytelling that, like most legends, might be based in a real event but has been molded into a fable to teach the new generations of the tribe important lessons vital for survival in the wilderness. Demonstrating that one should not wander, lest the hairy giants catch you and eat you; one should exhibit reverence and not announce your presence in the wilderness, lest you attract predatory attentions; listen to your elders, lest you stray your path; one should not betray confidence or trust, lest it backfire to your disadvantage; one should remember the origins of things (such as the meadowlark story) as they preserve culture and information as well as teaching that one should utilize cunning and ingenuity to resolve one's problems in life. There are literally hundreds of names among the various tribes of North America that describe our mysterious woodland friends. I prefer Sasquatch. It's more dignified, but most just call them Bigfoot.

The lettuce crate label

Coinciding with widespread media and newspaper reports and public availability, by the 1930s stories of the wild men and throw-back cavemen became more frequent. Locations, descriptions, and behavioral aspects from the Native American accounts of the phenomenon were detailed. In Alaska and British Columbia, such accounts became downright common.

In early 2002, I was approached by Dwayne Rogers, who is in the business of ephemera (collectible paper of antiquity). He asked me if there were any old Bigfoot reports that I knew of in Salinas, California. I casually responded that "California has had a long history of activity and it wouldn't be surprising at all, as Salinas has been a large vegetable-growing community for nearly a century, thus supplying a good amount of food for an obviously healthy Sasquatch population to steal away with in the night without being detected."

In reply, he showed me an unused lettuce crate label and asked, "Do you think this could be a Bigfoot?"

I was floored by what I saw. The art deco-style art on the label clearly depicted a large, muscular man with big feet, stealing a crate of lettuce from a growing field in the night—and he was covered with hair.

I purchased seven original, unused labels, one for archival preservation and the rest for Bigfoot research colleagues and correspondence contacts.

Though the media circus that would forever label these beings with the idiotic title of Bigfoot would not occur until 1958, it was clear that a growing company's representatives in Salinas were already well familiar with our big and hairy co-inhabitants in the 1930s.

1940s

I obtained a photograph of a purported Sasquatch. It was originally discovered by Ryan Emerson of the Museum of the Unexplained in the early 1990s. He obtained it from his lawyer, who took the four-by-four-inch photo (originally shot from about 50-60 yards away) from its frame and allowed Emerson to photograph a close-up image.

The lawyer told Emerson that he obtained it from the nephew of an old Oregon miner who'd had a claim. The miner had land there and complained that a few Bigfoot had been raiding his orchard. The lawyer handling the family's affairs kept the original while the miner's nephew kept the negative. Outside of his wife and the nephew who retrieved the photo and negative from the trash, the miner's descendants did not take his stories of hairy giants seriously.

*Is this the face of the beast photographed by an Oregon
Miner in the early to mid- 1940s?*

After a closer examination of the photo, my colleagues and I found many earmarks of authenticity. All of the morphology of the subject in question seems to be accurate. A second-generation close-up of this nature is difficult study adequately, but a light-blast test revealed that the surface hair was devoid of any of the usual hoax elements that might suggest fur or artificial hair. The texture was what I'd expect from a Sasquatch living in the wilderness under less than sanitary conditions. Also, there were no indications of seams. After the enhancement, a slight hint was revealed of the right eye turned up. A light-blast test doesn't change the photo at all as computer enhancement often does.

Unfortunately, a definitive conclusion cannot be made without a study of the original photo and or negative, which we are still trying to track down. All things considered, it does appear to be authentic, as well as from the 1940s at minimum to early/mid-1950s at the latest.

Oregon has certainly had its fair share of miners, mountain devils, and Sasquatch, so this may be our earliest photographic record of a Bigfoot.

Newspapers have consistently documented accounts of Sasquatch-like beings, formerly known as bad Indians, Wild Men, or Mountain Devils. Old newspaper archives over the world are littered with these accounts. Also plentiful are accounts in the early explorer's journals, stories of the Native Americans, and the flood of modern reports.

After an examination of literally thousands of such descriptions and accounts, one can only conclude that there must be something to it. The next phase of rational examination is to determine the nature of the beast so to speak, and progress to exactly what it is that we are experiencing.

This leads us in two directions of thought: that it is merely a biological entity of primate or early man origin, or that outside phenomena accompanying Sasquatch encounters indicate a nonphysical or quasi-physical nature. Few have viable concepts at all.

The best research from the most disciplined minds will always be from those who present all sides of a phenomenon without restriction and examine all possibilities. We must promote a closer, more honest discipline in the face of the incomprehensible. We must look into the piercing eyes of what we fear most, into the dark unknown, with the undying hope that one day we can evolve into a more enlightened state of existence for ourselves and the universe around us enough to see the light of day through the darkness, into a new dawn from our troubled world of fear and ignorance. Into the dawn of the Sasquatch.

Joe Fex: Founder and curator of the former APE-X Research; longtime researcher of cryptids and the paranormal.

FATE September-October 2009 and November-December 2009

WUDEWASA: THE FURRY MEN OF EUROPE

Ivan T. Sanderson

A preliminary search through some bestiaries and other medieval European illuminated manuscripts has brought to light a number of illustrations of creatures called "woodhouses," wodehouses, Wudewasa, or simply "wild men."

They are shown completely covered with long hair or fur and having certain other specific characteristics. They are readily distinguishable from depictions of apes and monkeys on the one hand, and people in costumes playing the parts of these wild men in traditional, religious, or secular plays and carnivals on the other hand.

Because of the overwhelming number of illustrations known to exist of these wild men, because of the diverse historical periods and wide geographical distribution of the artistic depictions of them, and because of the basic similarities of these representations it seems quite certain that they once walked this earth, and perhaps not so long ago.

In the June 3, 1961, issue of the *Illustrated London News*, there appeared a reproduction of a plate from an English bestiary that was being put up for sale at Messrs. Sotheby's. The four creatures depicted were: "an ostrich, a ram, a wolf and a 'wyld man.' This last has his body covered in hair."

This "wyld man" holds a snake in his right hand and a rough club in his left hand; his hands and feet are "naked" or hairless; he sports long curly hair and a very generous mustache and beard. The hairiness of his body is formally represented by wavy lines, and he wears a belt so that it looks as if he were clothed in an overall, tight-fitting, fur garment.

This depiction shows certain points of similarity to some early Mongolian brush drawings of *Hunguressu*, namely the *Gin Sung* or "Bear Man" of the Chinese, or the *Dzu-Teh* of the Nepalis—in other words, the largest of the three types of those creatures which have come to be called "Abominable Snowmen" and are alleged to exist in the eastern part of Eurasia.

There are other collections, including one entitled *Dyson Perrins*, a reproduction of which we found in New York's Pierpont Morgan Library.

Although the individual figures in all these depictions have been fully catalogued by scholars, they apparently have not been critically examined by anthropologists or zoologists with full knowledge of the literature pertaining to the field of what we have been constrained to call "ABSMS"—stemming from the inappropriate but now firmly established nickname "abominable snowmen." As a result, some very significant features of a number of these depictions of wild men, and of a number of others stated to be of apes and monkeys, have been missed.

Critical examination seems to make clear that Dark Age and Middle Age European artists knew a great deal more about the anatomy and external morphology of primates than has been supposed, and that they went to particular pains to differentiate between seven distinct categories of primates: lemurs, monkeys, apes (they knew only the orangutan), "woodhouses" or Wudewasa, simple "wild men" or wild humans, such as troglodytes, people dressed in costumes in imitation of Wudewasa, and finally human beings per se.

While much that is depicted by these artists is allegorical or has mythological connotations, the artists seem to have made a careful distinction between fact and fancy. One example will suffice.

The crude clubs carried by the Wudewasa types are invariably of the same form and size and are nearly always carried in the left hand, even if the right hand is free. Even more convincing than this detail is the care with which they depict the feet of each of the different categories. The form of the feet is of greater significance than any other anatomical detail in distinguishing between hominid and pongid anthropoids.

There are several significant points in the illustration from the *Dyson Perrins Folio*. First, at the top are men in then current dress, hunting a stag with dogs. However, the two figures on the left are smaller, apparently naked, hairy, and armed with a bow and arrow and a spear respectively. These figures are shown on an open down. To the right is a river shown in very fine perspective running from a gap in these downs, the other bank of which is heavily forested. Three wodehouses are shown running down this river bed to a foreshore, immediately off which a fourth, mounted astride a large bird with a doubly-hooked beak and prominent narrow tongue, defends himself with a wooden club and an exceedingly crude shield of most significant construction.

The clubs carried by the wodehouses are carefully shown to be crude logs with rounded ends, of somewhat lesser diameter at the end held by the hand. The "shield" is composed of two laths of wood, presumably held together by crosspieces, but arranged so that the holder may peer between the two slats. Such shields may be found today among the exceedingly primitive Hill Batuks of Sumatra. Similar shields seem to be portrayed in Spanish Stone Age cave paintings such as those in the Cuevas del Civil near Albocacer, Castellon.

After reviewing hundreds of reports by persons who say they have observed the various ABSMs, it transpires that nobody claims they ever carried anything made of other than wood; while we have constant reference to crude wooden clubs, and primitive wooden bows and arrows.

The external morphology of the wodehouses in this illustration is even more significant than the implements they are carrying. They are small of stature with short legs and long arms. They have comparatively large heads with massive but shortish hair and fringe beards *under* their chins. The brow ridges are pronounced and "beetle"; the nose is large; the mouth wide and full, and the naked face is shown to be black but very shiny. Most important of all, the artist went to great pains to draw no less than seven hands and two feet of these creatures in great clarity. These feet, like the hands, are *completely hominid* with a fully *opposed* great toe. In other words, despite the very animalistic features of their overall morphology, these wodehouses are depicted as decidedly human on two counts—the use of offensive and defensive weapons; and the form of their feet. The importance of the latter fact cannot be too greatly stressed.

The last point of real significance in this depiction is the contemporary written mention of "wodehouses." This name has an increasingly precise meaning as one goes backward through Wodehouse to Woodwose, Wodwose, Wodewose, Wodewese, and Wodwos to the late Anglo-Saxon Wudewasa (which remained current till at least the 15th century) and thence to *Wudu Wasa*. The first of this combined term is the Late Old English for a "wood"; the word *wasa* is discreetly described as obscure but is frankly unknown. However, in combination *Wudu Wasa* means "Wild Man of the Woods." Later, it also was applied to a person dressed to represent such a being in a pageant. One suggestion has been made as to the origin of *wasa*; namely, that it originally derived from *vu'asear*, from *assir, aesir*, Asia-Man, or Asiatics. The implication then would be that the mediaeval artists knew of "Wild Men of the Woods" armed only with primitive wooden weapons that lived in Asia and attempted to defend it from knights in armor coming to the mouths of rivers from the sea—allegorically depicted at the bottom of the *Dyson Perrins Folio*.

Monkeys and the orangutan, as the only ape known to mediaeval artists, are a fairly common item in depictions from the earliest phases of illumination in Europe. They seldom are confused with Wudewasa by these early artists.

Critical analysis, consistent with a prior knowledge of the literature on ABSMs, shows most of these creatures to be careful, detailed depictions. One example, in Janson's *Apes and Ape Lore*, displays two anthropomorphic figures apparently dancing and holding hands but naked and shown to be fully haired all over by formalized lines. The faces are humanic but low-browed and almost chinless; the head is very short. The hands are completely human but very long-fingered; the feet, however, are completely humanoid with fully *apposed* big toes, and shown in four different positions and from four different angles. There can be no doubt at all that these are meant to be hominids as opposed to pongids for the very simple reason that all pongids are shown with widely *opposed* big toes.

The most enlightening illustration is captioned "Fortitude Transfixing Ape" from *Fons memorabilium*, Oxford, Baliol College. In this we see "Fortitude" in the guise of an entirely human, though naked and furred figure with curl-peaked helmet and a thin lance, standing over a prone "ape" through the head of which he has driven the lance. The former's feet are completely humanoid and have *opposed* great toes; the latter has hand-like feet with a fully *opposed* great toe.

By the 16th century, memory of the original Wudewasa seems to have become dimmed. Considerable confusion has arisen in the minds of naturalists and artists alike due to the importation of many more kinds of primates from Africa and the Orient (and even from the N Neotropical region), and to an ever increasing infusion of legend, mythology, and hearsay from the past, combined with a growing skepticism fostered by strict adherence to the Biblical version of creation. However, hairy hominids were considered, up till the 15th century, to be perfectly valid former inhabitants of Europe. Evidence of this is to be found in a delightful little depiction in the British Museum, appropriately called "a drollery" in Queen Mary's Psalter, of the 14th century. This shows a very hairy wild man with perfectly human hands and feet pursued by one dog and confronted by two more.

From these and other examples it is plain that while monkeys and apes were not initially very well known or at all times realistically depicted, they were from the earliest times recognized as such while an entirely different class of beings—namely wild, fully-haired humanoids or hominids—were also generally accepted as either still existing (at least in central Eurasia) or presumably, to have previously existed in the western part of that continent—i.e. Europe.

The belief in trolls, satyrs, fawns, and their small counterparts the pixies, elves, and gnomes, has persisted until today in various forms and by various names in all the mountainous countries of Europe. In Scandinavia country folk in the far north adjacent to the montane forests assert that some of these Wudewasas still exist; while the Academy of Sciences of the U.S.S.R. treats similar reports from the Caucasus with the utmost consideration and now has sent several expeditions to that area to search for evidence of them, called there *Kaptar* or *Kheeter*.

Further confusion in depictions of hairy men in mediaeval art arises because of the frequent occurrence of persons dressed in fur costumes in imitation of Wudewasa for pageants, plays and other performances. Such figures form the basis of Bernheimer's studies. And it is interesting to note that author Janson adopts the thesis that most, if not all, such depictions are of what he calls apes, and implies that all those which are manifestly *not* of apes or monkeys are men in costumes.

The third alternative, namely that some of them are of a specific creature, the Wudewasa, or even that the costumes are imitative of such a creature does not appear to have occurred to either of these scholars.

Let us repeat: the single most distinguishing feature of the true wild man or Wudewasa is the form of the foot, with particular regard to the size, form and disposition of the great toe. It is rapidly becoming recognized that the only constant and valid feature for differentiating hominids from pongids is the first toe; being in hominids apposed and in pongids opposed.

All other characteristics put forward to distinguish between the two groups have in time broken down. This includes both anatomical characteristics like the simian self, brain size, tooth size and structure; and cultural characteristics like the use of implements, interpretable vocalization, and so on. Hairiness is really no criterion though we do not know of any race of fully haired hominids living today. This, however, makes the early depictions of the Wudewasa, bestial as they may be in other features, the more convincing, for the human type foot and first toe pronounce them to be hominids (*not* pongids) and proclaim also the artists' great care in so depicting them.

From detailed studies of these medieval depictions combined with those of some earlier depictions on pottery, and later illustrations in early natural histories, we are forced to the conclusion that a type or types of primitive, fully-furred or haired human beings with long arms, beetling brows, dark skins, and possessed only of wooden implements, were known to these early artists. Further, this knowledge was very widespread throughout central and northern Europe until the 14th century, though it seems to have died out in the Mediterranean area during middle Roman times.

It has long been taught that the Neanderthalers disappeared from Europe at the end of the last ice advance and, it is implied, at the hand of Cro-Magnon man. However, Cro-Magnon man appeared rather abruptly on the extreme western fringe of the continent, and it would seem that the other peoples in the late Paleolithic and Mesolithic stages of advance also spread into the Mediterranean from the west, ending with the appearance of the Iberians.

Even today there remain considerable areas in northern Sweden and the Caucasus that have not been explored. Settlement followed by civilization spread northwards into Europe from the Mediterranean basin but took several thousand years to reach the ultimate peripheries of the continent. During this period post-glacial conditions continued undisturbed in many places until the 14th century.

The Aurochs lingered on till that century in the Black Forest; the Wisent still clings precariously to survival in western Russia.

Neanderthalers and other primitive humanoids or submen were not exterminated overnight by Cro-Magnon nor any other race of modern men. In some areas they appear to have been absorbed rather than exterminated. In other areas they just removed themselves, probably back into the forests. Not being tribalized, the Neanderthalers undoubtedly did not fight unless attacked and cornered individually or in family groups.

For these reasons it may be inferred that the Neanderthalers disappeared from Europe very gradually and over a very long period; and that some of them remained in central Europe till medieval times, and some may still survive in the two extreme limits of that continent—in northern Sweden and the Caucasus.

There is no valid or conclusive argument against Neanderthalers being fully furred or clothed in hair. There is some concrete evidence that they were so clothed, and it would seem logical that they should have been for they dwelt in cold climates, even right up to the ice front.

And they only "disappeared" when modern men appeared in each locality, in turn. So there is nothing extraordinary about modern man at the dawn of civilization first in the Mediterranean (see Etruscan depictions), then in central Europe, and finally around its fringes, and right up to medieval times knowing these creatures—knowing what they looked like, what weapons they used, how they deported themselves, and that their feet were just like ours. The difficulty in grasping this concept is due entirely to the gap between the end of the Dark Ages and current anthropological thinking: a gap that was filled with skepticism combined with outright lack of knowledge and progressive suspicion of ancient traditions and accounts.

It is our contention, therefore, that the Wudewasa are detailed and accurate descriptions of Neanderthaloids—maybe of more than one type—that lingered on in Europe north and east of a line drawn through central Ireland, Britain, Germany, Austria and the Balkans to the Dardanelles, until comparatively late dates and progressively later as you travel from the extreme southwest to the north and east.

There is today growing evidence of such Wudewasa in the Caucasus and the mountains of northern Iran, and thence via the Pamirs to the whole of the great Mongolian upland massif of eastern Eurasia. Reports even more recently have been received (Porshnev, B.F.; private communication) that they are also spread over the forested areas of easternmost Siberia.

The most pertinent argument against the notion that the Wudewasa and other wild men were Neanderthalers is that this group of primitives or submen were creators of very fine stone implements and therefore, had graduated from the dendritic phase long ago, while these latter-day creatures seem never to possess anything but wooden implements. However, there is evidence that primitives dispossessed of their territory and forced to retreat into forests where stones may be rare or entirely unknown over great areas between watercourses, give up the use of all instruments of any complexity except for wooden ones.

Finally, as to the disappearance of the Neanderthalers or other primitives which give rise to the Wudewasa tradition, it should be pointed out that small relic groups of low culture, especially if untribalized, once split up and confined to limited and shrinking territories invariably appear to dwindle in numbers due to a progressive deterioration of their fertility. Thus, it was first the dissection and then the clearing of the forests that brought about the dissolution and extinction of the Wudewasa rather than any deliberate massacre by more advanced races.

But the forests on the fringes of Europe even now have not been finally cleared, especially in mountainous districts. The Wudewasa could well have still existed in many large areas up till medieval times.

[Note: illustrations referenced did not appear with this article; Sanderson relied on description.]

Ivan T. Sanderson (1911-1973): Scottish biologist who became a naturalized U.S. citizen and was best known for his books and articles on cryptid and paranormal topics; he influenced the work of his friend and colleague John Keel.

FATE November 1962

EARLY AMERICAN MOUNTAIN BIGFOOT

Preston Dennett

Mount Rainier towers 14,410 above sea level, making it the tallest mountain in Washington State. This massive mountain has long been the source of strange and mysterious stories. Early Native Americans believed that the mountain was inhabited by evil spirits and refused to climb it. It was first summited in 1870 by Stevens and Van Trump, who were actually misled by their Native American guide in an attempt to keep them off the mountain. In 1947, Kenneth Arnold sighted his famous flying disks while flying over Mt. Rainier, marking the beginning of the modern UFO era. One of the most persistent mysteries pertaining to the mountain is the presence of Bigfoot high on its slopes.

Beyond the line of death

As all climbers know, there is a zone on the top of all mountains affectionately known as the "death zone." High above the tree line, the temperatures are so severe and the air so thin that slopes become totally devoid of life. In this zone, climbers have often found the stiff and frozen bodies of small animals such as rodents, birds, and insects. There are some well-verified sightings of out-of-place animals in Rainier's "death zone"—creatures that had no right to be there.

One early climbing party claimed to have encountered a large black bear on the crater rim. It was assumed that they had either misperceived, hallucinated or hoaxed the report. Then, on July 17, 1948, three climbers observed a porcupine climbing up the mountain at 14,000 feet. They even photographed the animal and signed affidavits attesting to the sighting. In 1967, a climbing guide saw a golden-mantled ground squirrel on the summit with a white-footed mouse in its mouth. Ravens have also been seen. In 1951, a climber claimed that he was harassed by a small swarm of bumblebees at the incredible altitude of 14,000 feet.

For the most part, however, the upper slopes and summit harbor no kind of life whatsoever—except Bigfoot.

Stories of Bigfoot encounters in and around Mt. Rainier have abounded for decades. In fact, the area is the one of the world's leading locales for such stories. One of the earliest and most interesting of these accounts may be the only one in which a Bigfoot-like creature was seen on the summit of the mountain. What makes this account particularly amazing is the identity of the main witness.

The man and the mountain

Major E. S. Ingraham was an outstanding figure in the history of Mt. Rainier. He was founder of the Washington Alpine Club and one of the pioneering explorers of the region. He made several ascents to the summit in the 1880s through the 1910s. Even in his 60s, he continued to climb and was often the leader of his climbing group. His influence was such that many geological features of the mountain have been named in his honor, including Ingraham Glacier and Ingraham Disappointment Cleaver. He was also given the honor of naming other features himself. He named "Gibraltar Rock" at the summit and gave the name "Camp Muir" to the high base camp.

Ingraham wrote extensively about Mt. Rainier, detailing the best climbing routes, the climate, the wildlife and much more. His numerous accomplishments earned him a trusted reputation as an expert in all things pertaining to the great mountain.

In 1895, Ingraham put his sterling reputation on the line and stunned the world when he published his account of "The Old Man of the Crater," which detailed his fantastic encounter with what appears to have been Bigfoot. Ingraham's account is one of the earliest and strangest accounts of an extensive Bigfoot encounter. He tells his story with incredible detail, insisting that everything really happened.

The Old Man of the Crater

Ingraham wrote: "While my companion and I were exploring the steam caves at the time of my second visit to the crater of Mt. Rainier, I noticed peculiar marks and scratchings on the floor of the cave. In some places the ground appeared as though it had been the scene of a conflict between some maddened beasts, so extensive was the disturbance. In other places there were depressions that might have been made by some flatfooted animal pawing in the earth. My curiosity was deeply excited. The lower we descended the cave, the more frequent but less marked became those scratchings. As the sunlight from without became dim, I noticed a peculiar, soft glow in the atmosphere of the cave, hardly perceptible, that might have been produced by either light or heat, but it was probably brought about by the presence of some force more subtle than either. I also felt a peculiar sensation of the body, such as a person feels when standing upon an insulated stool with his hand holding the pole of an electrical machine slightly charged. Whether my companion noticed these startling phenomena I do not know. If he did, he, like myself, remained silent upon the subject. The situation was extremely interesting to one of a scientific turn of mind and invited investigations; but I suggested to my companion a return to the outer world. Within my own mind I had decided to revisit the cave alone later.

"Late in the night, when my three bedfellows were sound asleep, I cautiously crawled from under my scanty covering and was soon in the cave again. While it was intensely dark within and cold without, the warmth of the steam cave soon restored my benumbed body to an unusual degree of comfort and my sleepy senses resumed an unwonted activity. Slowly groping my way along the floor of the cave I was soon within the influence of the mysterious glow I had noticed upon my first descent. The situation was weird and startling."

The encounter

Ingraham crept farther into the cave, when he heard a strange noise. "I had reached a point where another passage joined, or more properly separated from the one I was following when I was startled by a noise, followed by several stones rolling down the tributary passage. Had my companion of the first visit noticed the mysterious things that I had, and was he, like myself, seeking to discover their cause?

"I quickly stepped within a recess in the wall of ice on my left and awaited developments. I had not long to wait, for almost immediately there came, now rolling, now making an attempt to crawl, a figure of strange and grotesque appearance, down the passage. It stopped within a few feet of me, writhing and floundering very much as a drowning man would do, when drawn from the water as he was about to sink for the last time. Its shape was nearer to that of a human being than of any other animal. The crown of its head was pointed, with bristled hair pointing in every direction. The eyeballs were pointed too; and while they appeared dull and visionless at times, yet there was an occasional flash of light from the points, which increased in frequency as the owner began to revive. The nails of its fingers and toes were long and pointed and resembled polished steel more than hardened cuticle. I discovered that the palms of its hand and the soles of its feet were hard and calloused. In fact the whole body, while human in shape, except the pointedness I have mentioned, seemed very different in character from that of the human species. There was nothing about the mysterious being, however, that would make it impossible that its ancestry of long ages ago might have been human like ourselves. Yet by living in different surroundings and under entirely different conditions, many of its characteristics had changed."

Ingraham watched in fascination as the creature revived itself by rubbing its hands and feet against the cave floor. Ingraham then imitated the movements, and to his shock, he found himself in telepathic rapport with the creature. "...We were in communication. There, in that icy passage connecting the unknown interior of this earth with the exterior, by means of a new medium, or rather an old medium newly applied, two intelligent beings of different races were enabled to communicate, imperfectly at first of course, with each other."

Telepathic communication

"For an hour I received impressions from the Old Man of the Crater. It is a strange story I got from him. While the time was comparatively short, yet what he told me, not by voice or look, but by a subtle agency not known or understood by me, would fill a volume of many pages. Finally expressing doubt at what he communicated, he commanded me to follow him. I had anticipated such a demand and was ready to resist it. So when he turned to descend to the hot interior of the earth as I verily believe, by a superhuman effort I broke the spell and hastened upward and back to my sleeping companions.

"This is no myth. The old man told me of his abode in the interior, of another race to which he belonged and the traditions of that race; of convulsions and changes on the earth long, long ago ..."

Ingraham's claims may be fanciful, or perhaps it was an attempt to perpetuate some of the Native American legends about evil spirits, or perhaps, as he insists, he really did encounter a Bigfoot-type creature. As he writes, "This is no myth."

Interestingly, the details he describes turn up often in other Bigfoot accounts, including the bizarre appearance of the creature and the telepathic rapport with the witness.

Whatever the case, Ingraham's story remains an intriguing chapter in the mystical history of Mt. Rainier.

Preston Dennett: Field investigator for the Mutual UFO Network (MUFON); author and researcher of mysterious phenomena and creatures, and UFOs.

FATE May 2001

PRESIDENTIAL BIGFOOT

Gary W. Hemphill

Just over 100 years ago, Theodore Roosevelt was the country's chief executive and favorite son. His personality was larger than life. His exploits captured people's imaginations worldwide. After the death of his first wife in 1884, Roosevelt spent two years as a rancher and hunter on his ranch in the Badlands of Dakota Territory. He climbed down from the saddle long enough to pen three books during this period. In 1893, he published a lengthy and most entertaining narrative entitled *The Wilderness Hunter: An Account of the Big Game of the United States and Its Chase with Horse, Hound, and Rifle*, a memoir of sorts of his days in the territories. Among the stories recorded here is what seems to have been a 19th-century Bigfoot encounter.

The frontiersman's tale

The report came to Roosevelt from the lips of a grizzled old mountain man named Bauman, who had spent the entirety of his very long life on the frontier. As he recollected the details of the event, Bauman had difficulty controlling his emotions. The event was very real to him.

President Theodore Roosevelt.

Bauman was a trapper as a young man. His strange encounter occurred sometime between 1810 and 1840 when he and a partner were trapping in an area around the forks of the Salmon and Wisdom rivers in the Bitterroot Mountains, near the border of Idaho and Montana. The trapping business was rather lean, so the two frontiersmen decided to try their skills in a remote area around a small mountain stream that seemed to have a lot of beaver signs.

This area had a rather sinister reputation. A year earlier, a lone hunter had wandered into the area and been slain by a wild beast. His half-eaten remains were discovered by a prospector. People who knew of the strange killing gave that area a wide berth, but this did not deter the two adventuresome trappers.

Bauman and his partner rode to within a four-hour hike of the area where they were going to trap. They hobbled their mountain ponies in a beaver meadow and set off on foot into the underbrush of the Bitterroot Range.

The trappers hastily erected a lean-to where they stowed their packs, then hurried upstream to set a few traps and explore for signs before nightfall. When they returned to their makeshift camp at dusk, they made an unpleasant discovery. Their packs had been vandalized, and their gear thrown in every direction. Whatever attacked the camp had been vigorous in its assault, churning up the ground and destroying the lean-to.

Such vandalism was completely out of place. Frontiersmen knew of the hardship of survival. Lean-tos might stand for years as hunter after hunter used them and passed on their way. Packs were far too valuable to be recklessly strewn on the ground; they might be purloined by the unscrupulous, but never vandalized. Bears and other creatures might be drawn to food, but this was evidently not the case. It appeared someone was bent on destroying their packs.

As the unfortunate trappers gathered up their possessions, they noticed footprints in the ground that were "quite plain." The urgency of salvaging their goods and rebuilding the lean-to required their immediate energies. The footprints, plain or otherwise, would have to wait.

Two long nights

When the camp was restored, Bauman began cooking a meal while his partner examined the footprints by torchlight. Returning for another firebrand, he remarked that the attacker walked on two legs. Bauman broke into laughter at the idea of a marauding bear walking upright as it demolished the camp. His partner insisted the bear must have walked on its hind legs, and he took a larger firebrand to examine the tracks in more detail. The prints clearly indicated that they were made by a creature that walked upright, having been made by two paws or feet.

Around midnight, Bauman was awakened by a noise. An awful stench filled his nostrils, the strong odor of a wild beast. By the opening of the lean-to, he saw the menacing shadow of a great body lurking in the darkness. He fired his rifle. The shot either missed its intended mark or did little harm to the towering form, but whatever it was ran off. The curtain of night could not obscure the sounds of something very large forcing its way through the thick underbrush surrounding the camp.

The second half of the night passed slowly as the trappers watchfully tended the fire. Nothing more of the great thing was heard, seen, or smelled that night.

When daylight came the two men set out to check their traps and make additional sets. Both were experienced mountain men, but instead of separating and covering twice as much area, they worked together all day. The events of the previous night obviously impacted them enough to alter their behavior.

As the last light of the afternoon began to give way to the ensuing night, the men reached their camp. It was déjà vu: again, the camp had been destroyed. All their possessions had been rummaged and tossed about. The earth was churned up, indicating a great deal of furious activity. In the soft, damp earth near the stream were found clear footprints as crisp as if made in snow. The tracks were made by a creature that was obviously bipedal.

As darkness surrounded them, the trappers restored their camp as best they could, concentrating their efforts on building a roaring fire. That night, they could hear branches breaking in the underbrush, indicating that it was near. Occasionally it emitted long, drawn-out groans and moans, sounds that proved to be terrifying to the two men.

With the arrival of the new day came a decision. Although the area showed signs of an abundance of game, very little had been taken so far. Combined with the harassment of the unwelcome camp follower, the trappers decided to leave.

As the two men collected the traps they had set the day before, they felt the presence of someone or something watching them, dogging them. Their awareness of this phantom seemed to intensify their resolve to leave the area.

A fatal decision

But the light of day began to work on their manhood. They felt embarrassed about sticking so close together. Both men were experienced in wilderness survival. Both had faced danger from man, beast, and the elements before and had prevailed. Perhaps this reasoning influenced their next move. They decided to separate. Bauman was to check the remaining traps while his partner returned to camp and pack. They would meet at the camp and move somewhere else.

Fortune blossomed at the wrong time: each of the three remaining sets had caught a beaver. One of the poor creatures had fought with the trap and tangled the chain in a beaver lodge, requiring extra time to untangle. By the time Bauman had skinned the beaver carcasses and stretched the pelts, most of the afternoon was gone. As the last moments of daylight were disappearing, he neared the camp.

An eerie silence seemed to envelop the site. No birds could be heard. Bauman's steps were muted by the pine needles and even the perpetual breeze of the mountains was still. He whistled, expecting a reply from his partner. No acknowledgement was heard. All was silent.

Within sight of the camp, Bauman saw that the fire was out, a thin blue smoke trailing from the dying embers. His partner's lifeless body lay stretched on the ground by the trunk of a fallen tree. The body was still warm. The poor man's neck had been broken. Four fang-like incisions marked the throat. Footprints indicated the attack was from an animal that walked on two legs.

Upon completion of packing, the unfortunate trapper must have sat on the tree trunk facing the fire waiting for Bauman to return. Reaching out from behind the resting man, the unknown creature must have wrenched the trapper's neck. Evidence indicated that whatever killed the lone trapper had thrown the body about and rolled on it.

Bauman abandoned the camp, taking only his rifle. He made his way down the mountain pass to the hobbled ponies in the beaver meadow, then rode beyond the point of pursuit.

Roosevelt noted that Bauman was of German ancestry and would have heard many a ghost and goblin story as a child. In his years on the frontier he would have heard tales of the unexplained and of the magic of the Indian medicine man. As a hunter and trapper, he would have learned the track of every animal in the area. Roosevelt did not doubt that an incident took place, but he gives the impression that a psychological explanation would account for the unexplainable part of the story.

According to this report, a large, foul-smelling creature that appeared to be bipedal repeatedly attacked two young frontiersmen in the region of the Bitterroot Mountains. What was it? Roosevelt did not say. However, something about the story of the old mountain man must have impressed the future president deeply for him to include it in his great narrative of the frontier West.

FATE January-February 2009

EVIDENCE

BIGFOOT: THE NEW EVIDENCE

Jerome Clark

At 11:30 on the morning of June 10, 1982, US Forest Service patrolman Paul Freeman was driving through the Blue Mountains in the Walla Walla Ranger District of the Umatilla National Forest, which stretches across southeastern Washington and northeastern Oregon. When he spotted some elk, he stopped his truck and got out to pursue the animals on foot; he wanted to see if there were any calves among them.

As he walked down the old logging trail called Tiger Canyon Road he certainly didn't realize he was approaching the most shattering event of his life, that he was about to spark new interest in one of this country's most enduring scientific mysteries and provide investigators with powerful new evidence for the reality of a creature that is not supposed to exist.

As Freeman rounded a bend he noticed a "stench" and at the other side of the turn saw something coming down a bank through thick vegetation.

When the figure stepped into the clearing, Freeman froze and stared in disbelief at an "enormous creature" which stared back at him.

For a few seconds the two studied each other at a distance of 150 to 200 feet, then fled in opposite directions.

Until that fateful meeting, Freeman, a veteran outdoorsman who had started working for the Forest Service only the month before, openly ridiculed Bigfoot reports. But the thing he had seen had an apelike appearance, stood about eight-and-a-half feet tall and was covered with reddish-brown hair. Its long arms stretched all the way to its knees. It had a "peaked crown" (sagittal crest) on its head. It matched in every particular the classic physical characteristics of the fabled hairy giant of the Pacific Northwest.

"I could see the muscles of his legs when he walked," Freeman told investigators soon afterwards. "I could see the muscles in the arms and shoulders. It just plain scared me, and I've never been scared in the woods before. This thing was real. It was big enough to tear the head right off your shoulders if it wanted to."

The encounter was especially frightening because the hair on the creature's neck and head stood up three times "like a dog's back," causing Freeman to fear "it was going to come at me."

He was positive it was not a bear. "I see bears all the time in the watershed," he said. "I just stand still and they walk off... I never saw anything like this in that area... I've been working in the wild all of my life and I know a bear or a man in a gorilla suit when I see one—and that's not what I saw. I still can't sleep at night thinking about it."

The badly shaken patrolman immediately notified his superiors in Walla Walla, Washington, and two hours later a group of Forest Service personnel arrived at the site, located in Oregon near the Washington border. They found 21 footprints measuring 14 inches long by seven inches wide. They took three casts and some pictures of the prints.

One member of the party, Fire Management Officer Wayne Long, has lived in Washington and Oregon forests for over three decades, but this was, he said, "the first time I've ever seen a foot like this. I don't think this thing is man-made. If it had been a single track or two tracks, I might dispute it. But 21 tracks?"

Even more impressive, however, was the fact that the prints were over an inch deep in the hard ground of the unpaved logging road.

On June 14 the Walla Walla station released a statement recounting the details of Freeman's sighting and remarking that "no determination can be made" concerning the creature's identity. The Forest Service said it had no further plans to investigate. Nonetheless, four days later it reported that on the 16th, Freeman and Patrolman Bill Epoch had discovered about 40 new tracks in the Mill Creek Watershed on the Washington side of the border. On the 17th, Joel Hardin, a US Border Patrol tracking expert, examined the prints and declared they were hoaxes. He pointed out that they showed evidence of dermal ridges, which animals don't have. Hardin did not mention that higher primates—monkeys, apes and human beings—do have such ridges on their toes and fingers.

Freeman, who accompanied Hardin to the site, disputed Hardin's conclusions. "I'm just as much a professional tracker as he is," Freeman said. "He's good at tracking people but I've been tracking animals for 30 years."

One problem with Hardin's hoax hypothesis is that the area in which the prints were found is a restricted site inaccessible to the public and cut off from any roads. A hoax would have been simpler to perpetrate in a place more easily accessible such as the Tiger Creek location where Freeman supposedly had his sighting.

But Freeman's colleagues are convinced that he told the truth and that the footprints associated with his report are genuine. District Office Resources Manager Randy Dohrmann and Fire Management Officer Long testify to his integrity and they recall how shocked and frightened Freeman had appeared to be. If the event was a hoax, Long insisted, it was a hoax on Freeman, not by him—but even so, how could a hoaxer in a Sasquatch suit leave inch-deep prints in hard ground?

The day after Freeman's sighting, the Umatilla County (Oregon) Sheriff's Department sent a five-person team of volunteers to the Tiger Creek area. The searchers were not looking for a Bigfoot but for the body of a boy who had disappeared the previous fall. They were brought to the site because the sheriff's officers noted Freeman's report of a "stench," which they thought might be from a decaying corpse. The sheriff did not even inform the searchers that the odor had been noted in association with a Bigfoot sighting. Although the team found neither stench nor body, it did make another discovery.

According to Art Snow, a MiltonFreewater, Oregon businessman who headed the team, the search party was able to follow the tracks beyond the 21 found by the Forest Service people. In fact, Snow claimed, tracks were discernible for three-quarters of a mile. The team made a cast of one of the better prints.

"It would not be possible to fake the tracks without a helicopter," Snow says. "We assumed Freeman was telling the truth and we could find no evidence whatsoever to contradict that assumption. I'm not saying that there is or is not a Bigfoot, but all evidence verifies his story."

In July, Paul Freeman, still distraught from his experience and upset at all the publicity it had received, resigned from the Forest Service.

At the time the Walla Walla Bigfoot incidents were occurring, anthropologist Grover Krantz was out of the country. One of the places he visited was China, where he met with scientists who are investigating reports there of "wildmen," apelike creatures somewhat akin to our own Bigfoot.

An associate professor of anthropology at Washington State University, Dr. Krantz, who has spent 15 years studying reports, tracks and other Bigfoot evidence, is America's leading scientific authority on the phenomenon. It is perhaps ironic that he was among the last to hear of what may well be the most important Bigfoot-related incident yet to occur.

Krantz learned of it shortly after his return to the United States when he visited the home of J. Richard Greenwell, secretary of the International Society of Cryptozoology, of which Krantz is a founding member. After Greenwell described the incident to him, Krantz promised to investigate it as soon as he got back to Washington.

Soon afterwards Wayne Long furnished Krantz with four casts from both the Tiger Creek and Mill Creek Watershed areas. Krantz also secured the print Art Snow had cast the day after Freeman's reported encounter.

Some weeks later, in a summary of conclusions from his investigation, Krantz wrote that the prints were from "two individuals." The first of these, represented by two casts, one of each foot, had a big toe larger than that in the average Bigfoot track. The second specimen had a "splayed-out second toe."

Aside from these distinguishing features, the prints were much alike and typical of those associated with Bigfoot reports. The feet were about 15 inches long and the toes were more nearly equal in size than a human being's toes would be. The arches were nearly flat and a "double ball" was visible at the base of the big toe.

Adding to the prints' credibility was the fact that there were no human prints around the Bigfoot tracks. The distance between them suggested that whoever made them had a *long* stride. Moreover, they were so deeply impressed into the ground that most investigators believed it would have taken over 600 pounds of force to make them; yet there was no evidence to suggest the presence of the kinds of mechanical devices necessary to fake this effect. The more likely explanation is that these were indeed the footprints of two huge, heavy figures.

But the most dramatic evidence of all came not from Krantz but from another specialist who studied the prints. Krantz had observed that because of the unprecedented clarity of the prints, dermal ridges, which are fine lines about half a millimeter apart in the skin of the feet, were visible—the first time this had ever happened on Bigfoot prints. The same kinds of ridges when found on the hand are called fingerprints.

Krantz presented this evidence to Benny D. Kling, a forensics expert at the Law Enforcement Academy in Douglas, Wyoming. Kling's examination revealed that the dermal ridge patterns were those of higher primates, but the foot and toe shapes were different from a human being's or an ape's. Some of the ridges were worn smooth in exactly the places one would expect from someone or something that had walked barefoot for a long time. The patterns of ridges and furrows were so intricate and so anatomically correct that in Kling's view a hoax was simply not possible.

At a press conference held at the University of British Columbia on October 22, 1982, Krantz reported the results of his and Kling's studies of the prints. "It is beyond the ability of anyone to fake these ridges," he declared. "These may be the best set of prints of a Sasquatch ever obtained."

On November 2, 1982, in a letter to a number of America's leading anthropologists, Krantz described briefly the results of his and Kling's work on the prints and solicited his colleagues' help in the continuing investigation. Subsequently Krantz sent copies of the letter to forensics specialists and fingerprint experts.

The response from the anthropologists has ranged from total rejection to cautious interest but none has volunteered his services. This is hardly surprising since anthropologists traditionally have been more interested in keeping their distance from Bigfoot than in considering the evidence for its existence. Many of the forensics specialists, on the other hand, have been impressed, even excited by the new evidence and some of the top people in the field are now actively involved in the research.

The prints, Krantz remarks wryly, "come from a higher primate that doesn't exist. So, we have an interesting problem here."

Meanwhile Paul Freeman, whose sighting started it all, has become a man obsessed. Stung by the ridicule to which he was subjected after his sighting was publicized, he is determined to prove that he told the truth about his experiences—and the way to do that, he reasons, is to prove Bigfoot exists. So, he spends most of his spare time with his son roaming the area where he had his encounter with the creature. He hopes to see it again. But this time he is armed, and he intends to supply the world with the only proof he thinks it will accept: a Bigfoot body.

Krantz seems to have something of the same idea. He plans to return to the site this summer in order, he says, to "obtain a specimen." Asked if this means he intends to kill one, he replies vaguely that the International Society of Cryptozoology has no policy on "hunting or not hunting."

In any case, it looks very much as if the long controversy over Bigfoot has taken a major new turn. Body or no body, a breakthrough may be imminent and all of us, scientists and lay persons, may be forced to live with a disquieting fact: that we share the North American continent with strange hairy animals which are uncomfortably close relatives of ours.

Jerome Clark: Former longtime FATE *columnist and contributor reporting on UFOs, cryptids and paranormal topics; author of several books.*

FATE May 1983

JEFF MELDRUM CHECKS BIGFOOT TRACKS

Tom R. Kovach

Dr. Jeff Meldrum, an anatomy and anthropology professor at Idaho State University, has been studying footprint castings he has collected from all over the United States. Dr. Meldrum feels that some of these prints show evidence that the legendary Bigfoot does indeed exist. To add credibility to his findings, Dr. Meldrum has the backing of a fingerprint expert from the Conroe, Texas, Police Department.

Police Officer Jimmy Chilicutt went to Idaho State University in the spring of 1999 to examine the footprint casts.

Chilicutt says that the ridge detail (fingerprint pattern) on the casts is neither man nor ape. While admitting that fakery is possible, Chilicutt points out that the faker would have to have an intimate knowledge of primate footprints—knowledge that didn't exist at the time the castings were made.

Chilicutt says he was interested when he heard about the Bigfoot castings in Dr. Meldrum's possession, but he was also skeptical and didn't care one way or another if Bigfoot existed.

However, one casting (made near Walla Walla, Washington in 1984) caught his interest. In this casting, the ridge pattern ran vertically along edges of the foot, then angled across underneath the toes (a pattern different from humans and apes, which have ridges running horizontally and at an angle across the food pad, respectively).

Not only that, the imprints showed splits in the feet, presumably where the ridges didn't realign perfectly when the skin healed after an injury.

The officer got another surprise when he checked a casting from Northern California which was made in 1967. In this casting the pattern was similar to the one in Walla Walla, although it was made from a smaller animal. Chilicutt says that for the two casts to be fake, the same person would have had to fabricate both prints—found hundreds of miles apart after an interval of 17 years.

This scenario seemed unlikely to Chilicutt, especially after he failed in an attempt to duplicate the castings. So, while some of Dr. Meldrum's scientist colleagues might still be a bit skeptical, Officer Chilicutt, a fingerprint expert, believes that something is going on here.

Could the 1967 and 1984 castings have been scratched to account for the different patterns? "When I went to Idaho State University last spring [1999] to examine the castings," said Officer Chilicutt, "I found that Dr. Meldrum had about 100 castings from all over the United States. Each cast was in a padded cabinet and had been well cared for. During my examination I only found four or five casts that had friction ridges visible."

Chilicutt is quite confident, based on his examinations of these castings, that there is a strange animal up in the Pacific Northwest—something we have never seen before.

Chilicutt should know what he is talking about. He started the study of primate fingerprints in the mid-1990s in hopes that this knowledge would help him in his criminal investigation work. He has more than 1,000 fingerprints from various primates in his computer data bank.

FATE November 2000

THE MYAKKA SKUNK APE PHOTOGRAPHS

Loren Coleman

Two remarkable new photographs of what may be a Florida Skunk Ape have been discovered through an interesting chain of events by Sarasota resident and animal welfare specialist David Barkasy. This article will overview how these photographs were taken, how this find surfaced, the first reactions and analyses, and some tentative conclusions.

Backyard pictures

The circumstances behind the photographs are intriguingly innocent. In early autumn 2000, an elderly couple living near 1-75 in Sarasota County, Florida, began to experience routine visits from an apelike animal. On one of these visits, the wife took two relatively clear photographs of the creature. The couple did not know what the animal was, but since her husband said it looked like an orangutan, they called it an orangutan.

The location of these events was near I-75, most likely east of Sarasota, which includes the Myakka River and Myakka State Park.

The woman describes the events leading up to the photographs being taken: "For two nights prior, it had been taking apples that my daughter brought down from up north off our back porch. These pictures were taken on the third night it had raided my apples."

She went out into her backyard after hearing deep "woomp" noises. She aimed her camera toward the hedgerow at the back of her property and was startled to see what her flash revealed. "I didn't even see it as I took the first picture because it was so dark. As soon as the flash went off for the second time it stood up and started to move. I then heard the orangutan walk off into the woods." She noticed that its "awful smell" lasted long after it had left her yard.

Reflecting on what had occurred, she said that the anthropoid "sounded much farther away than it turned out to be." She thinks she was about 10 feet away from it, and it looked like it was crouching, then standing. She notes it is hard to know how big it was, but she would "judge it as being about six and a half to seven feet tall in a kneeling position. As soon as I realized how close it was, I got back to the house." (Eyewitnesses regularly report larger sizes for animals which are hair-covered and seen in the dark.)

The woman photographer remarks: "It only came back one more night after that and took some apples that my husband left out in order to get a better look at it. We left out four apples. I cut two of them in half. The orangutan only took the whole apples. We didn't see it take them. We waited up but eventually had to go to bed." Then they placed a dog in their backyard, and the animal did not return.

The photographs surface

According to the evidence provided by the postmark on the envelope, on December 22, 2000, the woman mailed a letter signed "God Bless. I prefer to remain anonymous" to the Sarasota Sheriff's Department. They received the letter on December 29, 2000, although most people at the sheriff's office were unaware of it until after the holidays. According to the department's official report created later, the filing officer wrote: "I received an unusual letter addressed to the animal services of the sheriff's office. The letter told of an encounter with a monkey or ape and contained two photos. The letter was anonymous." The animal control officer read the letter which begins: "Enclosed please find some pictures I took... My husband thinks it is an orangutan. Is someone missing an orangutan?"

May 2001
USA $4.95   CAN $6.50

FATE

True Reports of the Strange & Unknown

Skunk Ape
Fact or Fiction?
Loren Coleman
Investigates

Haunted Lakes

46674   A Llewellyn Publication

Is this the alleged Myakka Skunk Ape?

The woman was especially concerned, and nothing about "skunk ape" or "Bigfoot" was mentioned in the letter. This was merely a normal person who had a remarkable encounter. She was worried about her grandchildren's safety and her own. She wanted to alert the police and requested clearly for them to "please look after this situation."

The matter in which it was treated in the department will be debated for years. Our understanding is that, initially, the letter and photographs were seen as merely an amusing thing to talk about around the office. No file was created; no permanent record was made. The photographs were passed around and there were joking asides.

This began to change when a member of the animal control division contacted David Barkasy, owner of the Silver City Serpentarium in Sarasota, Florida. He was informed that local authorities were matter-of-factly discussing the local "orangutan animal" problem and some interesting photographs had been sent to the department. On January 3, 2001, David was given details about the photographs and a black-and-white photocopy of them was shared with him.

Barkasy, who was aware of Florida's history of Skunk Ape reports due to his animal welfare interests, felt the photographs he was shown might be firm evidence of the local mystery anthropoids, which he understood were much different from the Pacific Northwest's Sasquatch and Bigfoot. That night, Barkasy contacted me because I was known as a cryptozoologist and author of several books on mysterious primate reports. He also contacted a Bigfoot email list moderator. Barkasy wanted assistance and opinions on what he had discovered, to explore possible hoaxing, and to make certain that anthropological, zoological, and photographic analyses could be brought to bear on this, if the photographs turned out to be authentic. (Since January 3 [2001], David Barkasy and I have talked frequently about the details of the ongoing investigation.)

On January 11, Barkasy was able to borrow photograph no. 2 (the one where the animal begins to pull up and away from the photographer). He made copies and high-quality scans on January 12, returning them to the department the same day. Barkasy was working on gathering all the information he could legally, within the non-official avenues, on the nonofficial photographs. (They did not have a file or case number and were only one day away from being discarded by the department.) He was gaining the trust of the department and getting closer to finding some answers to the who, what, and where of the photographs.

Meanwhile, unknown to Barkasy, someone behind his back independently contacted the department and demanded, as part of the open records laws, copies of the photographs. Barkasy was upset by this and talks of what impact it had on limiting his access to the department and his investigation: "[This person] knew I was in the process of getting copies of both of the pictures one at a time. I had already made copies of the picture with the apelike creature rising before he called the department. By him doing this, a friend of mine, who works for the department, was reprimanded for letting this happen. He put a good friend of mine's livelihood in danger for his own personal interest. It was an anonymous report which did not even have a file number at the time. After [his] intrusion, the photos were given a case number. I then had to have a Sheriff's Department Courier escort me to various copy houses to get copies of the remaining picture .... So much for letting me carry on with my investigation in peace."

When Barkasy was able to obtain high quality copies of photograph no. 1 on January 23, 2001, a file had been created on the incident, on January 18. Color photocopies on regular printer paper had also apparently been sent to the email list moderator by then. Barkasy noticed that staple holes, scratch marks, and other damage had occurred to the original photographs. This is an important detail, because later Internet analyses and critics of the photographs would begin to claim that many of these marks were evidence of hoaxing. (People would later see UFOs, running lights, and stars in the skies, but all of these were just scratches and staple holes.)

Although Barkasy's attempts to discover all the particulars of the photographs were frustrated by the unfolding events, his work led to the eventual surfacing of the photographs. Furthermore, officers were telling him of rumors of an animal bothering neighborhoods in east Sarasota County. Some of Barkasy's searches in the Myakka neighborhoods had some eventful and humorous outcomes—like the time in early February he was stopped by an officer and frisked to see if he was a burglar checking out homes.

Barkasy also found that no feral apes or lost pets had been reported or recovered. Finally, without talking to Barkasy or me, the moderator used his own small email list to publish the color-copied generations of the photographs on Sunday, February 4, with only the slightest of details on the circumstances of the report. A fuller telling appeared most appropriate at that time, and Barkasy requested that I release all the details as a coherent whole, versus the piecemeal way they were being presented. This article is part of that effort.

Perhaps someplace out there is one of the photographer's relatives or friends who could lead us, confidentially, to the source of these pictures.

The Myakka Ape photos

On February 5, 2001, an initial report was posted on www.lorencoleman.com entitled "The Myakka Ape Photographs" detailing an overview of the case. The photographs were said to perhaps be the first good, non-hoaxed photographs of a so-called Florida Skunk Ape, but further investigations must be ongoing. No claim to authenticity was made, but the reaction across the Internet was otherwise. For a point of reference, these photographs were designated the "Myakka Ape Photographs" until further analyses discover a definite identity for this cryptid.

On the 5th and 6th of February, email lists involved in cryptozoology and Bigfoot studies began to discuss the photographs. People outside of cryptozoology may feel there is a vast network of supportive followers, but what occurs is usually the opposite. In the first days when only color photocopies were being posted, when the quality of the scans was minimal (long before Barkasy or I wanted to present this story), the general consensus was that the photographs were (1) a cardboard cutout, (2) a dog, (3) a man in a mask, (4) an African American with an earring, (5) a man wearing a furry coat, and (6) a Photoshop or other computer-created image.

But with the posting later in the week, through Barkasy's scans of the original photographs and my posting and enhancements of them, the analyses shifted. With incomplete data, a few have already dismissed the photographs and the surrounding events. We have all had such experiences in our investigative lives. This is an understandable reaction.

The whole innocent and yet remarkable incident may be a hoax, a fraud, an escaped animal, an ape, a chimp, an orang, or a Skunk Ape. The object in the photographs reminded some of dogs or a prehistoric man off to the side. One individual said it was a black man with an earring. But in general, we do not know what these photographs demonstrate, only that they are for now linked to the Skunk Ape inquiries in Florida.

David Bittner, well-known videographic, photographic and film analyst, and partner of Pixel Workshop, Inc., notes that some caution must be given to any consideration of computer posted jpgs from photocopies of prints of photographs. Some critics of the posted images of what seems to look like an apelike creature in Florida have quickly noted the "photographs" appear as if they are, as one person put it, of a "possible cardboard prop." This could be true, but part of the problem is merely in the way these images appear because of the multiple generations of reproducing them.

While not commenting on the authentic nature versus possible faking of the Myakka photos, David Bittner told me: "There's definitely a whole collection of artifacts that color Xeroxing will introduce, including edge enhancement and color field flattening which contributes to a 'flat' look. As the infamous Crook/Murphy Bell incident taught us, you cannot rely on a color copy for pixel level analysis." After looking at the better scans provided by Barkasy, Bittner commented: "I'm pretty impressed with it so far, at least in terms of it being a real photograph, and not a compositing job or a cardboard cutout."

Newspapers in Florida and talk radio shows (from the BBC-News radio to Art Bell, Jeff Rense, and Bob Hieronimus & Co. programs) during mid-February, decided to discuss the Myakka photographs. The hope was that the woman photographer would be identified. In the meantime, in-depth analyses of the eye shine, the pupil diameter, the dentition, the tongue, hair color and exhibited behavior of this apparent primate is taking place.

Some tentative conclusions

The various analyses of the two photographs are holding up and there does not seem to be computer fakery or apparent hoaxing involved. Whether this is an escaped animal or a mystery primate remains to be seen, however. In terms of an investigation, we are still in the early stages, but with the interest running high, here are some preliminary thoughts.

The reported Florida animal matches the descriptions of the unknown anthropoids variously called Boogers, North American apes

(Napes), and Skunk Apes. It looks like what would be expected of an unknown primate in the underbrush in Florida, if it were authentic.

The Florida photographs seem less likely to be a hoax, but there are still a number of possibilities which must be explored:

(1) Early scans of the photocopied photographs seemed to show a much more chimpanzee-like animal, so it was possible that a masked chimpanzee *(Pan troglodytes verus),* with the older male display of white beard and distinctive lighter brow ridges, might have been involved. That appears less likely now.

(2) Another definite area to explore is whether or not this is a feral or escaped orangutan. The first two witnesses used this moniker, and the clearer the scans of the photographs, the more orangutan features we can see. Perhaps the Skunk Apes are feral orangutans (specifically the Sumatran subspecies *Pongo pygmaeus abelii*), perhaps they are an unknown, nocturnal orangutan relative, or perhaps we will discover an affinity to orangutans we could only have guessed. Nevertheless, my thoughts are returning to comparisons of the photographed Myakka apes with orangutans.

Concurrent with my thinking, Tony Scheuhammer, a biologist with the Canadian Wildlife Service, pointed out some features on a good photograph of an orangutan by Denise McQuillen. This is not to say the Myakka photographs are of an orangutan, but it certainly assists in identifying features that are found on a known anthropoid that appear to exist on this one too.

Furthermore, a few primate, Bigfoot, and cryptozoological students and scholars have sent in their insightful comments. One note reinforces something we had noticed ourselves, namely that the animal is displaying a characteristic "pant hoot" expression to the photographer. A hoaxer would need to be extremely familiar with the finer points of pongid behavior to include this aspect within a hoaxed scenario.

Jay O'Sullivan, a Ph.D. candidate at the University of Florida Department of Zoology and Florida Museum of Natural History, points out that eye shine is useful in determining whether this thing was alive or a mask. The expectation is that the pupils will contract in response to exposure to the first flash. The eyes would be wide open for the first photo, but smaller in the second. The pupils do appear to be smaller in the second shot. Based upon O'Sullivan's and our initial measurements (index of pupil size vs. orbit minus distance of withdrawal), the eye shine is about 40 percent larger in photograph 1 than in photograph 2.

We are assembling all comments from a variety of sources for future installments of our reports.

These Myakka photographs have refocused the debate on "types" of mystery primates in America back to the compelling evidence of Unknown Pongids in Florida. Some current critiques of the Myakka photographs have mentioned that the object does not look enough like a Bigfoot. Patrick Huyghe and I explored, in our field guide, the fact that the overuse of "Bigfoot" as an umbrella term has caused harm to research in this area. I refer people to that guidebook for more on that discussion.

Funny thing is that no one expects a Bigfoot in Florida. Unfortunately, the fakery of the 1980s-1990s from south Florida have resulted in people forgetting the great work of Ramona Clark (see her biography in my *Cryptozoology A to Z*) and others from the Sunshine State in the l950s-l970s. These early researchers gathered reports that described unknown anthropoids, not hominids. Even *Sports Illustrated* did an article on the "new" Skunk Ape reports from Florida in 1971. That article straightforwardly talked about these animals as more chimp-like than Bigfoot-like.

In my book *Mysterious America: The Revised Edition* (2001), I write of the classic Skunk Ape (versus the allegedly hoaxed south Florida images of Patterson Bigfoot clones seen on recent reality TV programs) in chapter 16:

"...1971 report from Broward County, Florida, involving a small brown-black 'skunk ape' (so called because of its foul smell) seen with a larger gray one with splotches and sores all over it ..."

"In 1965, following the late-night visit of a stooping figure in Hernando County, investigators discovered rounded tracks with 'one big toe stuck out to the side like a thumb on the hand.'"

"Control Officer Henry Ring, investigating sightings of two apes by the residents of the King's Manor Estates Trailer Court during August 1971, reported that he had 'found nothing but a bunch of strange tracks, like someone was walking around on his knuckles.' What Ring discovered was hardly 'nothing'—to the contrary, it was striking evidence of the presence of anthropoid apes in Florida. Whereas most quadruped mammals, as well as monkeys, 'walk on the flats of the hands, the gorilla, chimpanzee, and orangutan use the backs of the fingers to knucklewalk. Officer Ring's finding of knuckle prints is a vital clue in any effort to piece together the Napes puzzle."

The Myakka Ape Photographs are only the most recent of a long history of Skunk Ape and related mystery anthropoid reports. I have files and letters from people that lived along the east-central coast of Florida (mostly in the HolopawBrooksville area) who related to me their series of encounters with apelike animals, especially during the 1963-1968 period. The Everglades may not be the key to solving this mystery, but the Myakka area certainly could be.

Loren Coleman: Longtime former FATE *columnist and contributor; author and researcher of mysterious creatures.*

FATE May 2001

INTERVIEW WITH BIGFOOT HUNTER JOHN GREEN

Daniel Perez

In the annals of Bigfoot research and investigation, few people remain as steadfast in the pursuit as John Green, one of the true pioneers in the field. Green has been tracking Bigfoot for 40 years. In 1961, the late Ivan T. Sanderson described him as indefatigable, and Green, who turns 71 this month, shows no sign of letting up.

The British Columbia native has written such classics as *On the Track of he Sasquatch (1968), Year of the Sasquatch (1970), The Sasquatch File (1973),* and *The Definitive Sasquatch: The Apes Among Us (1978).* The six-foot-plus, slender Green has been at the scene of the classic Bigfoot events: the Patterson-Gimlin film, the Glen Thomas incidents, the Ruby Creek sighting, and the Albert Ostman abduction. One of his major career findings is that Bigfoot reports occur in areas where there is more than 20 inches of rain per year. Lately Green has been involved in computerizing his massive files, and he recently returned from a research

John Green with his collection of Bigfoot plaster foot casts.

trip to Russia. Bigfoot hunters hope his completed database will provide important clues about Bigfoot's existence.

Perez: Forty years ago "Bigfoot" had not yet been heard of, even in California, and "Sasquatch" was a British Columbia phenomenon. What was it presumed to be?

Green: The picture presented to the non-Indian community was of giant Indians wearing breech clouts, hairy only in that they had long hair on their heads; a wild tribe who had a language, lived in villages, and communicated with signal fires. The Indians knew what they really looked like but did consider them to be human.

Perez: When you began investigating, what did you learn?

Green: It very quickly became clear that first-person descriptions didn't match the popular concept. Witnesses told of creatures completely covered with short hair and looking more like erect apes than people. There was no mention of clothing, fire, or villages. Observations of behavior accumulated more slowly but were equally consistent. They added up to a creature that depended on physical abilities, not mental ones: They used no tools, had no language and no home, didn't form groups, and generally lived the same lives as bears.

Perez: What do you think is up and coming in the field of Sasquatch research?

Green: I hope DNA techniques will soon be able to establish if hair is from an unknown higher primate, and with camcorders so common someone should get a good video of a Sasquatch before long. But for a decisive conclusion someone has to get a Sasquatch, or part of one, which almost certainly depends on chance. A Sasquatch should have been collected by now. I have no explanation why that hasn't happened.

Perez: What might humans learn by collecting a Sasquatch?

Green: The study of another higher primate that has adapted to bipedal locomotion is bound to add a lot to human knowledge. It should also be useful to research the reasons our branch of the primate family was so insistent that this other branch must not exist.

Perez: Would you shoot one?

Green: I don't know, I don't hunt anything .... But there is no hope of protecting their habitat without first proving that they exist, and science has made it very clear that only physical remains will do that.

Perez: What is your computer study telling you?

Green: I don't think any computer study will enable anyone to make an appointment with a Sasquatch, as some claim. What my work does is give a quick access to the massive amount of information in my files so that I can answer questions and check theories against what has actually been reported. For example, the average height estimate is slightly more than seven and a half feet. Average footprint size is 16 inches long and seven inches wide. There are no patterns indicating that Sasquatch migrate. A powerful smell is reported in only about one third of close encounters, indicating that Sasquatch either control emission of the odor, or, like silverback gorillas, only emit it under stress.

Perez: How many reports do you now have on file?

Green: More than 3,000, counting both sightings and footprints. More than half are from eastern North America, and for most of those I have little specific information.

Perez: What might be a reasonable guesstimate as to how many Sasquatches are on the North American continent?

Green: For Sasquatches to be reported as widely throughout North America as they are, a reasonable estimate of their numbers has to be in the thousands, probably tens of thousands.

Perez: How do you explain the lack of fossil evidence?

Green: I don't consider the lack of fossils at all unlikely. Many fossil finds are of large creatures not previously known to exist, and I am told that there is as yet no fossil ancestor for gorillas.

Perez: What do Sasquatches live on?

Green: They have been reported eating many types of vegetation, including leaves, but also killing other animals, presumably for food. Evidence is mounting that they are major predators, easily able to catch and kill deer.

Perez: How do they survive in winter?

Green: Since there are no patterns in the accumulated information to suggest that they migrate, it seems probable that they hibernate. As predators they could obtain food in winter, but the scarcity of tracks in snow indicates that they aren't active.

Perez: Are they an endangered species?

Green: How could they be? There is no confirmed record of any being killed by humans, and they are reported almost everywhere in the world. North America, particularly, must have a thriving population, but some are suffering habitat destruction in places where wild areas are being cleared and subdivided.

Perez: Aren't they sometimes seen in groups?

Green: Very rarely. More than 90 percent of reports involve a single individual, and only two percent involve more than three.

Perez: What about mothers and young?

Green: Very few reports involved identifiable females, and there are almost none of females carrying small ones. Since higher primates can't travel on their own for years, it seems that females must be careful to avoid places where they might be seen.

Perez: If I pressed you for a definite yes or no with regard to the famous 1924 abduction of Albert Ostman by a family of Sasquatches in British Columbia, which way would you go?

Green: Given only that choice I have to say yes, but with no great assurance. I would reject a story like that today, because the information to fake it is now in circulation, but I came to know Albert Ostman well and heard him questioned by experts in ape anatomy and in cross-examination. I don't think he was lying.

Perez: What's your feeling about Forest Service patrolman Paul Freeman's 1982 sighting in Oregon, which resulted in *Newsweek* coverage and Freeman quitting his job, and the reported footprints with dermal ridges?

Green: I would have had little reason to question Paul Freeman's story of his original sighting had he not followed it up with an unbelievable number of further claims. As to the dermal ridge evidence, I find it interesting but not conclusive.

Perez: Do you think hoaxers are a lot more sophisticated today?

Green: The most sophisticated hoaxes I know of took place about 20 years ago, but there may well have been better ones since which have not been exposed.

Perez: The 1967 Patterson-Gimlin film was the red-letter event of Bigfoot studies. What's been your best case, minus that one?

Green: There may be a better "best case" than Patterson-Gimlin, namely Glen Thomas' story of Sasquatches digging out and eating hibernating rodents in a rock pile near Estacada, Oregon [in 1967]. A great range of behavior was observed with three very different individuals, and hard evidence—a pit in the rocks that neither bear nor human could duplicate—is still there.

Perez: There is now a new generation of scientists who grew up knowing about the Sasquatch question. Might this group be more successful in obtaining funding than past generations?

Green: The negative peer reaction toward scientists doing Sasquatch research has eased a lot in recent years. I think some of them may well be able to get funding soon.

Perez: So, do you think the search for the Sasquatch will be wrapped up within your lifetime?

Green: Probably not. I don't have another 40 years.

Perez: Well, if you knew in 1957 the Sasquatch mystery would not be resolved in 1998, would you have gotten involved?

Green: Do I regret becoming involved? No, I don't.

[John Green: 1927-2016. At the time of his death, Green's database included more than 3000 sighting and track reports. Known as "Mr. Sasquatch," he also authored several books on the subject.]

Daniel Perez: Director of the Center for Bigfoot Studies; editor of Bigfoot Times.

FATE February 1998

BIGFOOT'S WEIRD BLOOD

Jon-Erik Beckjord

There is precious little physical evidence for Bigfoot. Tracks, feces, dermal ridges are not physical evidence, but are marks of the beast. Parts of the beast have eluded researchers for centuries. Lacking these parts—physical evidence—zoologists are loath to grant a name to the creature, with good reason. Recently we cryptozoologists have gotten into deeper and more murky waters than if we had found some pieces of the beast that would be satisfactory to zoologists—Bigfoot blood. But the blood of Bigfoot appears to have anomalous characteristics.

In 1976, during a research expedition on the Lummi Indian Reservation near Bellingham, Washington, I was able to gather a blood sample smeared over broken glass from the window of a food storage room in a fisherman's house. A large creature of some kind had hit the house so hard one night in January that it woke the people inside. They initially thought that a car had struck the house. The dogs all tried to get into the house (possibly to hide), which was unusual behavior.

Checking the room where they heard the noise, they found broken, bloody glass and some batches of black hairs with white tips on them. The window was five feet off the ground. No bears had been seen in the area in 10 years.

I took the hairs to a number of forensic analysts, mainly Dr. Ellis Kurley and Dr. Stehpen Rosen at the University of Maryland, and also to a noted forensic biologist in a Western state (whose name is on file with FATE). The three independently determined that the hairs:

1. Matched three other unknown sets from three other states

2. Did not match any of 84 different North American mammals

3. Did not match any of the higher primates, including man, and

4. Came closest to gorilla, though not gorilla

The blood was tested by Dr. Vincent Sarich, at UC Berkeley, a noted blood analyst and anthropologist, and he was able to determine that the blood sample was of higher primate origin, but no more specific than that. Of course, using the corroboration of the hair sample, it is thus likely that the blood and the hairs came from the same unknown creature, and that thus the blood was also of a new, unidentified primate. Of interest is that during 1.5 years on this reservation, I made one sighting of what appeared to be a six-foot tall, black hair-covered, erect primatelike creature from 200 feet away, and I collected accounts from over 150 Indians and non-Indians, including some police, of sightings of what they felt was the Sasquatch, or Sasquatches.

The area was rife for several years with such sightings: a veritable Bigfoot flap. I also observed many instances of Bigfoot-type tracks that I do not believe were faked. Strange howls, not coyote, were also heard often, both by myself and by others in the area.

It was frustrating, however, to find that the techniques of 1976 were insufficient to verify the blood sample further to the species level. In 1989 I was directed to a Dr. Jerold Lowenstein, partly through a FATE article. I was encouraged to learn from him that by using a technique called radio-immunoassay or RIA, it was now possible to take very old blood, in quantities as minute as one billionth of a gram and test it down to the species level. Excited, I sent Dr. Lowenstein the remainder of the blood sample, preserved these many years for just such an event. He received them by registered mail and proceeded to test them.

To my surprise, and at first, disappointment, he wrote back later to inform me that the sample yielded "no immunological reactions whatever." He further suggested that if the sample really was of blood, then it should give some reaction, even in tiny dilutions, since "blood is highly reactive in my assay." There is no question in my mind that this sample was of blood, even if dried and small. The shards of glass were all photographed in 1976, and they all had some degree of red smears on them. Over time, these one-inch triangular pieces all faded to a dark brown and a white smear on different portions of the glass. I took the returned glass shards to Santa Monica College, and there, using a compound microscope, examined the glass at 400 power.

I found dried, smashed material, greenish to gray, that was in clumps. However, in several clumps, there were red round dots that one professor suggested might be hemoglobin. Red blood corpuscles might dry and disappear, but the hemoglobin seems to have remained.

The implications of this result

According to Dr. Vincent Sarich, with whom I consulted in March [1989], all normal blood samples, even if quite old, do and must provide some positive immunological reactions. It would be highly significant if a sample that is blood fails to provide such a reaction. Dr. Lowenstein stated much the same thing: for it to fail to react in the tests would indicate a very unusual result if the blood sample was actual blood. Being scientists with established reputations, they could not speculate on the implications any further than this, and this is proper.

In my own view, using logic added to my own experiences in the field for over 13 years, we can infer that the blood that reacted in 1976 and failed to react to the more sensitive test in 1989 is a highly unusual blood sample. Not only highly unusual, but I would venture to suggest that it is behaving with anomalous characteristics.

It is thus anomalous blood, evidence of an anomalous phenomena. It comes from a large primate-like creature that has unidentified primate-like hair. The creature itself, which we tend to name Bigfoot, (Sarich calls them Creature X, and George Schaller, the gorilla expert, also prefers that term) would therefore be an anomalous creature. If we wish to be conservative, we can call this an abnormal creature. On the liberal side, I might suggest that an anomalous creature, showing anomalous characteristics might be considered, or called, an alien creature, one of the "Alien Animals" referred to by Janet and Colin Bord, the English cryptozoologists.

How or from where they came, we do not know. But we do know that they have anomalous blood. This is the only physical evidence other than hair that exists for them today. Being internal, blood might be considered more significant.

Comments from FATE editor Donald Michael Kraig

Mr. Beckjord included copies of letters verifying the above information. However, it is possible to come to conclusions other than those of Mr. Beckjord. Dr. Lowenstein doubts that it is blood because it doesn't act like blood. Mr. Beckjord, however, has sworn that it is the sample he had collected. Dr. Sarich, as reported by Mr. Beckjord, says he could not identify it completely, even though he would guess that it was human. The hairs that were found included some that were not identifiable. Finally, in a note dated May 10, 1989, Mr. Beckjord has informed us that the Seriology Research Institute of Richmond, California, confirms that the sample is not blood.

Mr. Beckjord's honesty and integrity in this matter is above reproach. He has presented all possible information. About the information from the Seriology Research Institute he says, "While superficially disappointing, it is logical, for if it was blood per se, it would react like blood, and it does not. It is therefore a sample that behaved like blood in 1976, but not in 1989, and is therefore an anomalous body fluid."

Jon-Erik Beckjord (1939-2008): Well-known paranormal, cryptid, crop circles and UFO investigator; photographer. He believed Bigfoot and similar entities are interdimensional shapeshifters who manipulate the light spectrum to make themselves invisible.

FATE August 1989

Do Sasquatches have a Language?

Micah A. Hanks

Albert Ostman had been restricted to a sitting position for the better part of what he guessed was three hours, a prisoner inside his own sleeping bag. He could barely move and he had nearly passed out more than once already since the mouth of his bag was kept closed and he had been forced to recycle the same air since his strange journey had begun. As best as he could gather from the bouncing he'd felt since he awoke, something large had thrown him over its shoulder while he was sleeping and carried him off into the night.

Whatever was carrying Albert had taken him from his campsite in the mountains on Vancouver Island and though he wasn't sure what time it was, he could sense it was still dark as he and his captor traveled. Finally, all the motion stopped and he felt himself being lifted up, then gently placed on the ground. Albert could hear voices, but he couldn't understand any of the words he heard, though he could certainly tell that there were more than only the one that had brought him here. Crawling out of his sack, he tried to massage his legs, which were cramped from holding the same position for so long. In the faint moonlight, he could make out little more than the silhouettes of four figures around him.

The chattering continued and Albert remembered legends that the natives in the area had told him of creatures called sasquatches, a race of hairy giants that haunted the highest most inaccessible regions of the island. Though he couldn't yet see the things standing all around him, he knew now what they were.

He was a little frightened and finally asked them why they had brought him here. Only more chatter, this time a female voice expressing what Albert took as anger that he'd been brought to the sasquatch home. Dawn came slowly and as the dim light of morning began to fill the sky, he began to see clearly how hairy these "people" were, despite which they certainly looked like people. The large male waved his hands wildly, presumably relating the ordeal of bringing Albert back with him and drawing closer to him said something that sounded to Albert like *"sooka sooka."*

The young boy came near also and grabbed Albert's can of snuff, tasting a bit of it. He too spoke with his new prisoner proclaiming "ook" which Albert took as a request for a can of snuff from the young sasquatch.

If you think this sounds like the dialogue from a television show or a grade B horror flick, think again. This is actually a portion of a story dating back to the late 1920s describing how Albert Ostman, a construction worker looking for a lost mine near the head of Toba Inlet, Vancouver Island, was kidnapped by what he believed were sasquatches, the legendary beasts that haunt the mountains and forests of the Pacific Northwest. According to his account he was kept with the creatures at their home in the mountains for several days before he fed them snuff, on which they choked, allowing him to escape.

Stories like Ostman's about humans interacting with sasquatches may actually provide more than just entertainment and fuel for the fire of investigators in search of proof. There seems to be a recurring element in most tales where sasquatches are surprised by or are in regular contact with humans; they are often observed speaking and in a few odd cases, have actually said things that people were able to understand.

Albert Ostman being interviewed about his abduction.

Just what is speech?

Speech can be defined as verbal communication through air vibration. As far as science can prove, humans are the only creatures on Earth with a sophisticated verbal language based on this principle. It has been proved in recent years under lab conditions that some animals, including parrots and gorillas can learn to communicate with humans. You may have seen gorillas on television communicating by use of sign language not only with humans but with each other, and parrots have been able to learn human names for objects and solve puzzles with the air of verbal communication on about the level of a second grader.

Obviously, animals can communicate. We see them do it every day from dogs marking their scent to define territorial boundaries to bees directing other workers to a source of nectar with their dance. Animals can also communicate fairly successfully with humans. Just try surprising a rattlesnake on a warm day in the woods—I'm sure you'll know just what he means when he rears back and rattles his tail!

But wouldn't it be a little strange to try and call this form of communication a language? There obviously has to be more present before intelligent, comprehensive communication in the form of verbal speech can be recognized.

J.W. Burns and the Chehalis Indians

In the 1920s, a man named J.W. Burns began collecting odd stories of hairy giants that haunted the mountains, legends of the Chehalis Indians whose reservation was located near the southern end of Harrison Lake, British Columbia. Burns had worked for a number of years as the government Indian agent of the Chehalis reservation and had noted that the Chehalis people were reluctant to talk about their bizarre experiences with these hairy savages of the mountains.

Through years of inquiry, Burns began gathering tales from the natives on the reservation about their encounters with this entity. Many of these tales came from hunters or others who happened upon one of these creatures by chance while alone in the forest. These tales often ended with one or both parties fleeing from the scene. But in a few of the accounts gathered by Burns, some of the natives had actually said they heard the sasquatches speak and a few even claimed to understand what they were saying.

In one case Burns collected, an Indian named Charley reported coming across a sasquatch woman while on a hunting trip. While in the woods with his hunting dog, Charley heard what he thought was a bear crying from a hole inside a redwood tree. When his dog disappeared into the hole, Charley shot the first thing that came running out, which he said looked to him like a young Caucasian boy. The injury was only a flesh wound and Charley tried to comfort the boy who continued to cry out into the empty forest around them. Before long, a voice began answering from off in the distance and finally a large female sasquatch appeared. Charley was frightened already but his apprehension only increased when the creature turned to him and said, *"You have shot my friend."*

The Douglas Dialect

The interesting part about this is that in many similar cases related by the Indians of the Chehalis reservation about sasquatches speaking, the creatures are nearly always understood to be speaking in what is referred to as "the Douglas Dialect."

I first found mention of the Douglas Dialect in stories from Burns' collections. But there was little else said about it in these texts and I had a difficult time digging up much additional information on my own. Finally, thanks to a native British Columbian, I contacted a man named Ken Kristian. I learned that "Douglas" was reference to Salish Indians living in the area of Port Douglas at the north end of Harrison Lake. This particular band is known as the Douglas First Nation. Kristian also told me that the Chehalis band that Burns had worked for as an agent was located on the south end of Harrison Lake. Each band's dialect differs slightly from one to the next but as one could guess, there would obviously be recognizable trails between dialects just as well as the differences. The aforementioned Charley was said to be part Douglas himself.

But why has the Douglas Dialect been associated with sasquatch speech patterns? Although the region in which this dialect originates also happens to have been a hotbed for sightings over the last several decades, it still seems strange that there might be a specific Northwestern Indian dialect associated with this entity.

What if it were a regional variation on what is known to be the Douglas Dialect? Perhaps certain groups of sasquatches borrowed portions of an existing language from other people in the region.

Charley recounted the sasquatch calling the child her "friend." He took this to mean that the creature had probably kidnapped the Caucasian boy, hence "friend" supported the fact that the child wasn't her own. But could Charley have been mistaken in his interpretation? Could the sasquatch have meant "child" after all, but opted for this term because she didn't know the correct word?

Such speculation still leaves us with the question of how these creatures started speaking a language so similar to that of a particular group of humans. Might this suggest that the sasquatch and human races had common ancestors? It is said that Charley himself guessed that the sasquatches were somehow related to the Douglas band.

Into the modern era

At the current time, the field is simply too broad to even try and make guesses, at least until we are finally able to interact with a living specimen of Bigfoot.

I've spoken with a number of experts and researchers about the possibility that Bigfoot may be able to speak. The general consensus, it seems, is that they probably don't have language. Even when shown the stories of J.W. Burns, many people say that such tales are outdated and merely reflect the cultural beliefs of a secluded group of people.

But Native Americans are by no means the only people to report experiences in which sasquatches appear to be trying to communicate. A man named Alexander Katayev told of an experience he had in Russia in August 1974, where he witnessed two large hairy creatures eating together. He reported that one appeared male and other female, and that they seemed to speak to one another in voices that reminded him of how deaf people sound when speaking. At one point the female appeared to respond with laughter to something her male counterpart said. The creatures were also described using hand motions.

Arthur Buckley once said of his research, "They communicate orally. On two separate occasions with colleagues, we have surprised a small group in their base camp—who upon a hurried retreat have resorted to a jargon that has the phonetics of a language when we got close to them."

Another strange account from September 1955 is presented by J. Robert Alley in his book *Raincoast Sasquatch*:

> *Just as it was getting dark, we heard a noise coming from the far bank; it sounded like rising and falling series of barking chattering sounds. We answered back, but it waited a minute before answering and was moving along the edge of the trees. It was wailing and making different sounds, and I asked Ed, who had a lot of experiences down south with coyotes, if it was a coyote, but he said not. The sounds were all jumbled together, and it sounded as though whatever it was, were [sic] trying to put words of sorts together, like it was trying to communicate with us. This would go on every minute or so. Whatever it was*

circled around our camp in the forest without ever coming out. It sounded like it was trying to talk to us but didn't quite have the nerve to step out and let us see it. It wasn't real high pitched and was about as loud as us, like a man talking in a normal voice.

Even with as many accounts as there are, we'll never be certain as to whether or not people may actually be witnessing sasquatches performing anything close to speech as we know it until we can actually sit down with one and attempt to communicate verbally with it. The idea that we could share language with another species on this planet is fascinating for us as humans, no matter how far-fetched or even frightening it may be for some of us. Ultimately, such a discovery would certainly make this strange planet of ours feel a little smaller.

And besides, until proven under biological conditions, we may never know whether or not the sasquatch is really anything more than a figment of our collective imaginations. But for the time being, the more we can learn about them, the closer we may come to actually providing the hard evidence for which we've searched for so long. So, we might as well turn over every stone we can, no matter how strange the notion behind them. For all we know one day we may be able to learn much about the sasquatches from their "language" alone.

Micah A. Hanks: Freelance writer, cryptid researcher, and frequent contributor to FATE.

FATE October 2004

You Don't Know 'Squatch!

Robert Damon Schneck

It is 9:30 on a Saturday night in late April 1994. On a little-used road in the lonely foothills of Mt. Rainier, Washington, the lights of a solitary truck can be seen bouncing through the pine woods. Brian Canfield is at the wheel, sober as usual, and watching the patch of illuminated road as it disappears under the wheels of his pickup on his way home to the small settlement of Camp One, Washington.

He has just driven out of the forest and into a clearing when the engine and dashboard lights shut down and the truck comes to an abrupt, unbraked, halt. The engine is dead but the headlights keep burning, and 30 feet ahead Brian sees a huge, hairy, two-legged figure moving onto the road. This is less unusual in Washington State than most other places, but even here these figures are expected to move horizontally. The one Brian sees is descending vertically on huge membranous wings.

It comes down so hard that its clawed feet raise a cloud of dust when they hit the road. The creature doesn't approach the truck or even move, and Brian has time to take a good look. The creature looks like

97

it would be more at home on the roof of a medieval church. Folding wings frame its bulky, manlike body, which is nine feet tall and covered with bluish hair. Its hands are clawed and on the top of the head are two tufted, lynx-like ears. Its eyes are yellow and shaped like a piece of pie with pupils like a halfmoon. Its large mouth is filled with white teeth, but no fangs.

The monster stands motionless, staring straight at Brian for what seems like a long time. He is scared but gets the impression that the thing is more baffled than menacing; that it appreciates how much it does not belong here.

Eventually, its huge wings unfurl and begin beating with a force that bounces Brian's pickup on its springs. The creature rises off the road, out of the glow of the headlights, and into the sky. It flies off slowly in the direction of Mt. Rainier and disappears.

The only sound inside the darkened cab is breathing. Outside, the wind is dying away. All is quiet until the engine snaps back to life followed by the driver, who hell-for-leathers it home. He returns to the spot with his parents, a neighbor, a camera, and a gun. The creature is gone.

C. R. Roberts, the (Tacoma) *News Tribune* columnist who broke this story, doesn't know who dubbed the winged biped "Batsquatch," but it is the latest addition to the pseudo-sasquatches, a tribe of strange beings that prowl in Bigfoot's shadow.

A perfectly normal animal

Former FATE editor Jerome Clark once wrote, "The phrase *hairy biped* is in some ways generic. It does not always denote a paranormal version of Bigfoot." The descriptions on these pages are an attempt to expand the vocabulary available for describing and organizing things that look like Bigfoot but aren't.

Bigfoot is a familiar subject, but a basic sketch is necessary for comparison with the pseudo sasquatches:

Bigfoot/Sasquatch. Bigfoot is the only non-human, terrestrial, omnivorous primate indigenous to North America. Bipedal, it walks upright, standing between six and eight feet tall, with a broad, massive physique, crested head, short neck, heavy-browed face, and eyes that reflect light. It is covered in thick hair that is usually black, brown, reddish, or white. Feet are 15 to 16 inches long, wide for their length, and designed to carry great weight. Flat-footed and five-toed, with a double ball, rounded heel, and non-opposable big toe. Toes end in nails, not claws.

Bigfoot has a wide range of vocalizations. Most common are high-pitched, whistling screams. It can have a noxious smell. Nocturnal, shy, and wary, it avoids humans and is harmless. It swims, and the use of waterways could explain its baffling tendency to appear and disappear. Pre-Columbian distribution is unknown; now it is most often seen in the evergreen forests of the Pacific Northwest. Pocket populations may exist elsewhere.

Anthropologist Dr. Grover Krantz describes them as "perfectly normal animals" that eat, sleep, reproduce, die, and may have evolved from ancestors already known to paleontologists.

When is a Sasquatch not a Sasquatch?

Witnesses have reported seeing a wide variety of creatures that look like Bigfoot (*sasquatchiforms*) but are essentially different from the hypothetical animal described above. *Pseudo-sasquatch* is a useful term for describing these. The prefix "pseudo" in this case suggests a close or deceptive resemblance to sasquatches, an abnormality or aberrance, or a profound singularity which corresponds to nothing known. The examination of pseudo-sasquatches will be confined to North America.

Pseudo-sasquatches are outstanding examples of the cryptids, para-cryptids, and phantasms that make up the modern bestiary. They are reported in wild, rural, and suburban settings, working in underground mines, climbing trees, swimming in lakes and oceans, flying through the sky, and descending from hovering saucers. They are joined to other monsters by various transitional forms that mix and blur features, creating a series of intermediate animals that link paranormals together the way secondary colors link primary ones.

This article is the first step in an attempt to more accurately describe mysterious entities that mimic the habits and appearance of Bigfoot. It is done in the hope of giving witnesses and researchers a broader, more precise vocabulary for describing their experiences and organizing their findings.

Jerome Clark was right. "*Hairy biped*" isn't enough.

APEs (Anthropoid Pseudo-Sasquatch Entities)

APEs are the most Bigfoot-like pseudo-sasquatches. They appear to have solid, physical bodies that perform actions and activities that fit within the bounds of normal experience, despite occasional anomalies. APEs are consistently sasquatchiform in appearance.

Swamp APEs. Most common of the pseudos, Swamp APEs can appear almost any place where there is enough water and cover, even up to the edges of cities, but especially in the bottomlands of rivers connected to the Mississippi and Florida swamps. Their territories may overlap with those of bona fide Sasquatches. They stand three to 10 feet tall, averaging seven feet. Swampies are fully bipedal, stand erect, and move with surprising speed and agility. They're often tridactyl (three-toed; the largest known living three-toed biped is the emu) with a wide variety of forms. Their toes can number from two to five or more. The feet are the main difference between swampies and Sasquatches.

Swamp APEs are nocturnal. Their eyes reflect light or glow Jack-o'-lantern style, red, green, or yellow. They're fully covered in hair that can be reddish, gray, or white, but more often dark brown or black. It may look darker because it's wet. Swampies are thoroughly adapted to, and almost always in or near water, and are seen in many areas subject to flooding. Immersion in dirty water may explain why their coat is frequently matted, soiled, or slimy. They can have a nauseating smell, perhaps from eating carrion. Most dogs will run off or crawl under the porch before trailing a swampy. APEs kill or ignore pursuing dogs.

Swampies are omnivorous eaters. Food is probably the main reason they approach homes and roads. They will eat road kill and are known to raid farms for fruit, vegetables, garbage, and small livestock. They seem to be partial to pork, stealing sows in Arkansas, and hunting wild pigs in Louisiana.

Swampy vocalizations are unnerving: growls, baby cries, and shrieks are common. They're less phlegmatic than Sasquatches, but mainly harmless. They do not like cars, and will chase, pound, and shake vehicles, terrifying motorists. People hurt by swampies are usually in cars. They will circle campsites, enter backyards, and look through windows. They may sometimes inhabit abandoned buildings.

Swamp APEs are essentially physical beings but may appear immune to gunfire and be associated with disembodied voices, mysterious written notes, and UFO activity.

Small, red-haired, tree-climbing APEs are also reported in swamps. These may be young swampies that climb trees until size keeps them on the ground, like gorillas. Some of America's best-known monsters are Swamp APEs, including the Fouke Monster, Momo, and the Honey Island Swamp Monster. Swamp APEs set the pattern for pseudos and share traits with other creatures. Their tridactyl feet and watery surroundings are similar to Lizardmen. They are sometimes seen with beards and mustaches or wearing ragged clothes, two traits that connect them to the Man-beast, a kind of humanoid phantom.

Gully APEs. Gullies appear in deep river valleys, lonely desert areas, and mountains of the American West, near sources of water. They're similar to swamp APEs in behavior and appearance. Lyle Vann, director of the Arizona Bigfoot Center, suggests their bad smell is from sulfurous fumes in the caves where APEs work extracting precious metals for extraterrestrials.

Footprints separate gullies from swamp APEs. Their "pedal extremities really are obnoxious"—they leave a wide variety of tracks, some so huge and grotesquely formed that the feet making them seem unsuitable for walking. The strangest prints are found in southern California.

Gullies may figure in Navajo witchcraft. Navajo sorcerers are believed to turn themselves into werewolves called "skinwalkers." Gully APEs and skinwalkers are both fur-covered humanoids that run incredibly fast, chase livestock, howl like coyotes, and smell bad. Sightings of the former may reinforce belief in the latter.

Knuckle APEs. Swamp and bottomland dwellers, these are the most apelike of pseudo-sasquatches. Their main traits include pongid feet, fully opposable big toes, and walking bipedally with occasional use of the arms and knuckles. Knuckle impressions have been found with footprints. Loren Coleman identified this group as North American apes (NAPEs), and described them as green-eyed, evil-smelling, broad jumping *sasquatchiforms*. Knuckle APEs may be the explanation for scattered gorilla sightings.

LycanthrAPEs. Portmanteau word for werewolf-like pseudos seen in southern Wisconsin. LycanthrAPEs are broad-shouldered, human-sized, and malodorous. They are nocturnal and tend to appear near bogs and swamps. They feed on road kill, attack cars, and chase livestock. They are distinguished from other APEs by a long muzzle, pointed ears, and clawed hands and feet.

LycanthrAPEs are mammalian but share some Lizardman characteristics such as protuberant mouths and claws. One report describes three-fingered hands. (Lizardmen are rare but persistently reported swamp bipeds. They have scaly or wrinkled skin, huge eyes, beak-like protruding mouths, and clawed tridactyl extremities. Frog-like and reptilian varieties are reported.)

Ectoplasmics

Psychical researcher and author of *Phenomena of Materialisation* Baron Avon Schrenck-Notzing defined ectoplasm as "a material at first semi-fluid, which possesses some of the properties of a living substance, notably that of the power of change, of movement, and of the assumption of definite forms." It is this characteristic which defines the group.

Ectoplasmics are the least normal of the pseudo-sasquatches. They are APEs that display supernormal abilities and/or extreme variations of basic sasquatch design. A meeting with an ectoplasmic can be anything from an odd encounter with a strange animal to a fully rigged, four-masted, Fortean event. Ectoplasmic phenomena include transparency, "strobing" (appearing in different places without moving), non-corporeality, sudden vanishing, immunity to gunfire, mysterious engine failure, and association with UFOs. Many sightings take place near radio transmitters, power lines, and other energy sources. Some ectoplasmics may "steal" energy.

UFOREAs (Unidentified Flying Object-Related APEs). Widespread, and thoroughly documented in western Pennsylvania by investigator Stan Gordon. Basic swamp APE presentation (lingering sulfurous smell, dark color, tridactyl footprints) but often modified with fangs, extra-long arms or other peculiarities. Seen at night. May be in pairs or groups. Relationship to UFOs is unknown, but UFOREAs are often seen in the vicinity of glowing spheres and metallic disks and have figured in abductions. It's been suggested that they are projections, robots, aliens, or sasquatches under alien control. Encounters can involve extensive paranormal phenomena.

Chimeras. Chimeras are bizarre ectoplasmics that test the limits of what can be considered a pseudo-sasquatch. They are grotesque creatures made up of parts of various normal animals. Here are some common examples:

Catsquatch. Catsquatches are human size or smaller. They are light grayish-brown, black, or tawny. They look like a mixture of human, ape, and cat. Flat face, big mobile ears, long bushy tail. Some catsquatches are APEs with feline faces. Nocturnal. They walk quadrupedally and bipedally, and are strong, powerful jumpers on the ground and in trees. They prey on livestock. Catsquatches link pseudos to bipedal wampus cats and phantom kangaroos.

Batsquatch. (See introduction.) Chimerical form between pseudos and many different paranormals: Jersey Devil, giant bats, Mothman, and Thunderbirds. One report described a possible transitional form, a Thunderbird with a gorilla-like face.

Seasquatch. Examples are seen off Big Sur, California, and Cape St. Martin, where it is called "Bobo." Seasquatches are huge, mermaid-like marine pseudo-sasquatches. They have very long white hair directed down their backs, gray skin, monkey- or ape-like face, saucer eyes, and an "evil grin." Their long arms end in hands, but they have fish-like tails. This specialized form recalls the aquatic habits of sasquatches that swim in the ocean between coastal islands and the mainland.

Seasquatches are related to pseudos and rare anthropoid sea monsters like the Old Man of Monterey. They are found in an area dominated by Cadborosaurus (Bernard Heuvelmans's Mer-Horse).

Folklorics

Folklorics are pseudo-sasquatches that have merged with lover's lane monsters and now play roles once filled by ghosts, maniacs, and bogeys. These tales are told mainly by and to adolescents, a group likely to be driving at night and parking in out-of-the-way places to exchange ideas. They are responsible for many sightings and, doubtless, some hoaxes.

Goatman. Prince George's County, Maryland, is home to America's most famous Goatman, an eight-foot, hairy bipedal sasquatchiform that grunts and leaves deer-like hoof prints. Kills dogs and attacks cars with an axe. Originally satyr-like, it has become mingled with local swamp APEs that leave tridactyl footprints (hoof-like footprints are sometimes left by two-toed pseudos). Texas's Lake Worth monster was a goatman before turning into a light-colored swamp APE. Santa Paula, California, has the Billiwack Monster, a huge, off-white, sheep- or ram-headed gully APE with horns, claws, and yellow-green eyes.

Fluorescent Freddy/Orange Eyes. Fluorescent Freddy is a descendant of the Green Man, a bright green lunatic who haunted lover's lanes. He has become a giant sasquatchiform with bright red eyes and a fluorescent green body. Orange Eyes was first said to be just a pair of glowing orange eyes that peeked into back seats. It's still nosy but has become a giant orange sasquatchiform with glowing eyes.

Robert Damon Schneck: Author and researcher of Sasquatch and other cryptid creatures, and topics related to the paranormal and supernatural.

FATE April 1999

ENCOUNTERS

LEGACY OF A LEGEND: THE FOUKE MONSTER OF BOGGY CREEK

Lyle Blackburn

When it comes to legendary cryptids in the Bigfoot category, few loom larger than the Fouke Monster. This alleged creature, which can be classified as a Southern breed of Sasquatch, is not unlike other bipedal beasts said to roam the backwoods of small-town America. Yet its story has become far more famous than its counterparts due to the success of a 1972 drive-in classic known as *The Legend of Boggy Creek*.

For those unfamiliar with the movie, *The Legend of Boggy Creek* was a docudrama horror film inspired by sightings of an apelike creature near the small town of Fouke in southwest Arkansas. Dubbed the "Fouke Monster," the creature first became publicly known in 1971 when reports by local residents made headlines in regional newspapers and later circulated across the country as the stories were picked up by the Associated Press and others. The Fouke Monster—or "Boggy Creek Monster," as it came to be known—became even more infamous when its story eventually went viral due to the movie, which ultimately reached an international audience.

The Legend of Boggy Creek

A TRUE STORY

A HOWCO INTERNATIONAL PICTURES RELEASE

A PIERCE-LEDWELL PRODUCTION

Produced and Directed by CHARLES PIERCE · Written by EARL E. SMITH · Music by JAMIE MENDOZA-NAVA · Executive Producers L. W. LEDWELL/CHARLES PIERCE
Color by TECHNICOLOR® · Filmed in TECHNISCOPE

Film poster. Courtesy Lyle Blackburn.

The Legend of Boggy Creek was directed by first-time Arkansas filmmaker Charles B. Pierce who, like others, was drawn to the sensational stories running in his hometown newspaper, the *Texarakana Gazette*. The reports ranged from dramatic incidents in which the creature allegedly attacked people, to brief sightings on rural roads, to accounts of it traversing up and down a small waterway near Fouke known as Boggy Creek. The 1971 publicity brought forth previous eyewitness accounts, which established the creature's long history in the area, having been seen for at least 50 years prior.

According to the numerous witnesses who claimed to have sighted the creature in and around Fouke (which is located about 20 minutes east of Texarkana), it stands approximately seven feet tall, weighs between 300 and 500 pounds, and is covered in thick, shaggy hair three-to-four inches in length. The coloration ranges from dark black to brown to a reddish tone. Its skin is typically described as being dark brown with a face that has a broad, flat nose and a strikingly human appearance, albeit apelike in most respects. It effectively walks and runs on two legs though it has been seen moving on all fours much like known primates. Alleged footprints found in 1971 suggested the creature (or

Boggy Creek. Credit: Lyle Blackburn.

creatures) had three toes, although subsequent track discoveries indicate a four- or five-toed anatomy.

As noted in several of the prominent reports (and likewise reflected in the movie), the Fouke creature is aggressive at times and has even been known to terrorize humans. In the most famous incident—which made headlines in the *Texarkana Gazette* on May 3, 1971—Bobby Ford tangled with the creature as he and his brother, Don, and friend, Charles Taylor, confronted it one night outside their rental home north of Fouke. The creature had apparently been stalking around the house for nearly a week, so the men finally decided to take action. After firing at it with a shotgun, the trio walked cautiously to the woodline to see if it had been hit. When they didn't find blood or a body, Bobby got spooked and promptly headed back towards the house. At that point, a large, hairy animal emerged from the shadows and attacked him. After a narrow escape, Bobby was rushed to the emergency room at a Texarkana Hospital where he was treated for injuries and shock.

The Fouke Monster confronts Bobby Ford. Credit: Dan Brereton.

Both before and after the seminal Ford attack, the creature had been seen around other rural homes in the vicinity and had startled several hunters, some of whom responded with firepower. In 1965, 14-year-old Lynn Crabtree was squirrel hunting one evening when he was approached by a hair-covered "wild man" walking on two legs. Crabtree said he fired several shots at it before bolting for home, frightened to the core. Another hunter claimed to have seen a dark, bipedal animal approach her deer stand that same year, but she was too frightened to shoot at it.

The Fouke Monster's unsettling nature and outward aggression has reverberated through Southern Sasquatch lore, although in many cases the sightings were non-confrontational as the creature was simply seen crossing a country road or traversing through the woodlands in and around the vast Sulphur River Bottoms southwest of Fouke.

The Sulphur River. Credit: Lyle Blackburn.

In the spring of 1967—several years prior to public knowledge of the phenomenon—musician Carl Finch and his cousin spotted what may have been the Fouke Monster along the desolate stretch of Highway 71 where it crosses the Sulphur River. (Finch is the founder of the popular polka/rock band, Brave Combo, which has earned a slew of honors including two Grammy awards and a cameo appearance on *The Simpsons* cartoon.) According to Finch, they were traveling back to Texarkana from a late-night gig in Shreveport, Louisiana, when they noticed an upright figure running parallel to the road. Finch's first impression was that it must be "a guy in a brown coat." That seemed rather odd, however, as this was a very dangerous and unlikely place for a man to be out jogging, especially at night. As they got closer, they could see it wasn't a man. "We noticed that it had really long arms and fur… not a coat," Finch told me in an interview. "It was well-defined and running very fast." The creature kept moving as they drove by. Once they had passed it, the headlights no longer provided illumination, so it was impossible to get a look at the face. "We were too scared to stop," Finch admitted. At the time he knew nothing about the sightings of the alleged creature. It wasn't until the mid-1970s, when he saw *The Legend of Boggy Creek*, that he realized the significance of his own encounter.

In 1969, a family of four was driving on Highway 71 north of Fouke at night when they spotted what they also took to be a man in a fur coat. The figure was walking towards them on the opposite side of the road. It was cold and close to Christmas so they decided to slow down and offer a ride. As they got closer, they realized it was not a man in a fur coat, but instead some kind of thing covered in hair. As they approached with their headlamps on bright, the thing stopped and raised its arm to shield the light from its eyes. They could see the creature was "thick, hairy and muscular" with a body covered in brown, shaggy hair with longer hair over its face. The legs appeared to be "caked in mud from the knees down." Frightened, the family quickly sped off, wondering what they had just seen. Ironically, the location was very close to the Ford house which would eventually become the focal point of the news sensation.

Once the creature reports became public in 1971, Charles Pierce used them as the basis for his movie plot, which essentially reenacts the actual encounters, sometimes using the actual witnesses on camera. The film's success inevitably lured waves of sightseers and monster hunters to Fouke. This became a serious problem for local law enforcement as the outsiders trespassed on private lands and sometimes damaged crops and other personal property; not to mention the potential danger to human lives with so many armed individuals roaming the woods.

The movie enjoyed a long stint in theaters and drive-ins, and a subsequent run on television, until it eventually played out and things got quiet again in Fouke. Even the news media became disinterested, only running the occasional recap around Halloween. Casual followers of the story tend to believe the creature sightings ceased around that time in the mid-to-late 1970s. However, that simply wasn't the case. In the shadows, the creature still roamed.

On February 20, 1982, a Fouke teenager, Terry Sutton, was fishing in his family's pond around dusk when he heard someone walking through the leaves. His family owned a large section of private land, so unless it was his dad, he couldn't imagine who would be out there. As the footfalls continued, he caught sight of a large, hair-covered, bipedal figure walking on a ridge just beyond the edge of the pond. Sutton was a mere 60 feet from the spot, so there was no mistake he was seeing something other than a human, bear, or any other common animal.

"I couldn't believe what I was seeing," Sutton told me in a personal interview. He described its fur as being scraggly, three-to-five inches long, and dark in color. It had notably long arms, which swung as it walked, giving it an apelike demeanor. It also gave off a strong, musky odor. The startled teenager sat motionless in the boat as he watched the creature walk by. During this time it never looked back, presumably because it never heard him floating quietly on the water. After what seemed like an eternity, the creature walked down a ravine and was out of sight. Terry quickly paddled to the bank and ran for the house.

Following Terry's encounter, the creature (or, more logically, *creatures*) continued to be seen in and around Fouke and the Sulphur River Bottoms throughout the 1980s, 1990s and 2000s. A number of these incidents were investigated by local resident J.E. "Smokey" Crabtree, who not only appeared in *The Legend of Boggy Creek*, but had been instrumental in helping Pierce film the swampy scenery. Smokey was initially pulled into the Fouke Monster saga when his son Lynn confronted the hairy creature in 1965. Smokey himself never had a sighting, but he continued to pursue the creature until his death in 2016, penning three books about his life experience in the process.

The Monster Mart in Fouke. Credit: Lyle Blackburn.

Today the town of Fouke is still small, but its legend remains large. People come from all over the United States, and occasionally from other countries, to visit the home of the infamous Boggy Creek Monster. A convenience store called the Monster Mart offers a striking visual on Fouke's main strip with a huge, fabricated "monster" mounted on the roof, along with murals on the building, and a gift shop and small museum inside. Coverage on a variety of documentaries and television shows—such as *Finding Bigfoot*, *Monsters and Mysteries in America*, and *Mysteries at the Museum*—have kept the legend alive and even brought it to a whole new generation of Bigfoot enthusiasts.

Meanwhile, the sightings continue, though the creature and its presumed kind remain elusive. Among the most compelling reports in recent years include one in which a woman claimed to have seen one of the creatures in broad daylight. On November 24, 2014, Bonnie Ashton was driving on a county road north of the Sulphur River at 10 AM when she realized she had forgotten something at home. After she completed a three-point turn on the narrow road and began to head back, she was startled to see a hairy, bipedal animal standing in the road. The creature had apparently come out of a thick patch of woods on her left and was crossing behind her vehicle. The creature stood fully upright with an estimated height of five feet. It was covered in reddish-brown hair, except for the face which had dark, leathery skin and particularly piercing eyes. She could see the wispy hair on its arms waving in the gentle morning breeze. It gazed at the woman for a few seconds before it turned and ran back into the woods.

In the early morning hours of May 15, 2016, Traci Sanders was delivering newspapers for the *Texarkana Gazette* when she saw a tall, bipedal figure run across Highway 71. She could see it well enough in the headlights to conclude it was some sort of animal rather than a human. Her car window was down and she could smell a strong, musky odor as the thing disappeared into the dark trees which surrounded the roadway.

Just recently, in the fall of 2018, two women were driving south of Fouke near Boggy Creek when they also saw a large, bipedal thing run across the road in front of their vehicle. It was near dusk, but there was enough light to give them a fairly clear view as they watched it run down a side road toward the woods. Whatever it was, it didn't appear to be a human—even one dressed in a costume. The women are longtime residents and had always been skeptical of the so-called monster reports. That night, however, their doubt was completely turned upside down. Something strange seems to be stalking the woods of Fouke, and its presence is no less tangible today than it was back in 1972 when *The Legend of Boggy Creek* first flickered to life on the big screen.

[Portions of this article are excerpted from the book The Beast of Boggy Creek: The True Story of the Fouke Monster *by Lyle Blackburn, published by Anomalist Books (2012).]*

Lyle Blackburn: Author of books on the Fouke Monster and Lizard Man; founder of the rock band Ghoultown; columnist for the horror magazine Rue Morgue; *and narrator/producer of documentary films such as* The Mothman of Point Pleasant *and* Boggy Creek Monster.

2019

IN SEARCH OF THE BRITISH BIGFOOT

Nick Redfern

There can be few people fascinated by the mysteries of this world and beyond who have not heard of the North American Bigfoot, the Yeti—or Abominable Snowman—of the snow-capped Himalayas, and Australia's very own man-beast, known as the Yowie.

What is perhaps less well known, however, is the rich body of data that exists on sightings of similar creatures in the British Isles. At first glance, the idea that jolly old England could be home to a hidden race of large, apelike animals seems manifestly absurd; the country is less than 1,000 miles in length, it has a bustling population of 60 million, and, although the British scenery is certainly beautiful, its forests and mountains are hardly of a size that would allow for a species of Sasquatch-sized beasts to flourish in stealth. And yet people have seen such animals with surprising regularity—and for centuries, too.

Captured!
Ralph of Coggershall, whose 800-year-old account concerning a wild

man captured on the east coast of England at a town called Orford, is a classic example. In *Chronicon Anglicanum,* he wrote:

> *In the time of King Henry II, when Bartholomew de Glanville was in charge of the castle at Orford, it happened that some fishermen fishing in the sea there caught in their nets a wild man.*
>
> *He was naked and was like a man in all his members, covered with hair and with a long shaggy beard. He eagerly ate whatever was brought to him, but if it was raw he pressed it between his hands until all the juice was expelled. He would not talk, even when tortured and hung up by his feet. Brought into church, he showed no signs of reverence or belief. He sought his bed at sunset and always remained there until sunrise. He was allowed to go into the sea, strongly guarded with three lines of nets, but he dived under the nets and came up again and again. Eventually he came back of his own free will. But later on he escaped and was never seen again.*

The man-monkey

On the cold and moonlit night of January 21, 1879, a man was riding home with his horse-and-cart from Woodcote in the county of Shropshire to Ranton, Staffordshire, England. Enveloped in darkness, he pulled his jacket tightly around him to keep out the biting wind. Approximately a mile from the village of Woodseaves and while crossing a bridge over the Birmingham and Liverpool Canal, the man got the shock of his life. Out of the trees leapt a horrific-looking creature. Jet-black in color and with a pair of huge, glowing eyes, it was described by the petrified witness as being half-man and half-monkey. The creature jumped onto the back of the man's horse (which bolted out of sheer fright) and a fierce battle for life and limb began atop the cart. Incredibly, according to the man, when he attempted to hit the beast with his whip, it simply passed straight through its body. Suddenly and without warning the spectral man-beast vanished into thin air, leaving an exhausted horse and its shell-shocked owner in a state of near collapse.

As with the events 600 years previously at Orford, the mystery of the "Man-Monkey of Ranton" (as the creature came to be known) was never resolved.

The big gray man

As the researcher Andy Roberts notes, Ben Macdhui, at 1,309 meters, is the second highest mountain in the British Isles and lies in the heart of the Scottish mountain range known as the Cairngorms. Atop the mountain is a high plateau with a sub-arctic climate, often covered in snow for months at a time. Weather conditions can be extreme and unpredictable. Sadly, the Cairngorms have been defaced by ski lifts and restaurants but until recently remained remote, and still require considerable physical effort and mountain craft to navigate successfully. The wild nature and relative inaccessibility of the area has contributed to its popularity, and the Cairngorms have been a playground for climbers, walkers, skiers, naturalists, and those who love the high and lonely places for hundreds of years. While on Ben Macdhui, various witnesses to a phenomenon known as the Big Gray Man have described encountering footsteps; a sensation of a "presence"; sightings of a large, hairy, man-like animal; and an overpowering sense of panic. Sightings span more than a century and the experience has been terrifying enough to compel witnesses to flee in blind terror, often for several miles. Whatever the nature of the beast, it seems content to remain hidden deep within the safety of the Cairngorms and far away from civilization.

Ape-man or cave man?

While working as a nurse at the Royal Western Counties Hospital, Devonshire, in 1982, Britain's leading cryptozoologist Jonathan Downes (of the Center for Fortean Zoology) was told a strange tale by one of the staff doctors who, at the time, was then approaching retirement. According to the doctor, he had been on duty one morning in the winter of 1948 when he received several unusual telephone calls—all from local officials, and all informing him in a distinctly cryptic manner that a highly dangerous patient, who had been captured on the wilds of Dartmoor, would be brought to the hospital within the hour, requiring specialist care and an isolated room.

Within 45 minutes a police van arrived at the hospital and backed up to a side door. Seven policemen jumped out of the vehicle while simultaneously trying to hang on to what the doctor said resembled a hair-covered caveman. The policemen dragged the creature along the hospital's corridors and into the already-prepared isolation room. The door was quickly slammed shut behind it.

The beast stood slightly over six feet in height and was completely naked, with a heavy brow, a wide nose, and very muscular arms and legs. It was covered with an excessive amount of body hair that enveloped its whole body apart from the palms of its hands, the soles of its feet, and its face, and had a head of long, matted hair.

Over the course of the next three days, telephone calls bombarded the hospital from the police, the Lord Lieutenant of the County, and the Home Office in London. Then came the news that the man-beast was being transferred to a secure location in London for examination.

Again late at night, the creature was removed from the hospital by the same group of policemen. This time, however, they succeeded in holding the thing down long enough for it to be heavily sedated by the doctor, whereupon it was tied with powerful straps to a stretcher and loaded again into a police wagon with an unidentified doctor in attendance for the journey that lay ahead. Less than 20 minutes after they had arrived, the police departed into the night and the creature was gone forever.

Interestingly, the renowned folklorist Theo Brown collected a number of similar, decades-old stories of unusual encounters in Devonshire, and specifically near the village of Lustleigh. A friend of Brown's confided that she had been walking alone at dusk one night near the Neolithic earthworks at the top of Lustleigh Cleave on the extreme eastern side of Dartmoor when she had seen a family of "cave men," either naked and covered in hair or wrapped in the shaggy pelts of some wild animal, shambling around the stone circle at the top of the Cleave.

Sightings abound

Bringing matters more up to date, a British family had an awe-inspiring daylight encounter with one of these beast-men in 1991 in an area known as the Peak District. The specific location—identified thanks to the research of the prime investigator of the case, Martin Jeffrey—was the Ladybower Reservoir on the Manchester-to-Sheffield road. On a nearby hillside, one of the family members spotted a large figure walking down toward the road. But this was no normal man.

The car was brought to a sudden halt as an enormous creature—approximately eight feet tall and covered in long, brown hair—came into full view. It was described by the startled family as walking in a "crouching" style and proceeded to cross the road directly in front of them. Then it jumped over a wall that had a 10-foot drop on the other side and ran off, disappearing into the safety and seclusion of nearby woods.

Hangley Cleave and Smitham Hill in Somerset have played host to a number of similar encounters. Many years ago the area around what is now an abandoned mineshaft was linked to tales of strange beasts seen watching the miners. Sometimes on returning to work in the morning, the men would find that carts and equipment had been pushed over and thrown around during the night by a creature that one witness would describe as a "large, crouching man-like form, covered in dark, matted hair and with pale, flat eyes."

And as late as 1993, reports continued to surface from this part of Somerset that eerily paralleled the reports of yesteryear. From the files of Jonathan Downes comes the following witness testimony:

> *I was on a walk through the woods when I heard a twig snap. I thought nothing of it and continued on. Suddenly the dogs became very agitated and ran off home. At this point I became aware of a foul smell, like a wet dog, and a soft breathing sound. I started to run, but after only a few feet, I tripped and fell. I decided to turn and meet my pursuer only to see a large, about seven feet tall, dark brown, hairy, ape-like man. It just stood, about ten feet away, staring at me. It had intelligent looking eyes and occasionally tilted its head as if to find out what I was. After about 20 seconds it moved off into the forest.*

The Scottish Bigfoot

Mark Fraser is one of Scotland's most respected researchers of unknown animals and mysterious beasts and has uncovered details of a fascinating encounter from Dundonald Castle, Scotland. Set on top of a hill that overlooks north Kilmarnock, the castle is visible for miles around. The hill was occupied as far back as 2000 BC. In the 12th century a timber fort was built by Walter, the High-Steward of King David I, and a more substantial Dundonald Castle was constructed by the Stewart Family in the 13th century. Although much of the castle was destroyed during the Wars of Independence with England early in the 14th century, it was rebuilt in the middle of that same century by King Robert II and remains standing to this day. In 1482 the castle was sold by King James III to the Cathcart family and was subsequently purchased by Sir William Cochrane in 1636. In recent years, however, the castle has been looked after by the Friends of Dundonald Castle and by Historic Scotland, the latter having a small visitor center on the site.

According to Mark Fraser: "Josephine Aldridge from England says she will never go up the hill again as long as she lives." It was the summer of 1994; and while walking on Dundonald Hill, her two Labrador dogs suddenly "went berserk," as a truly immense, gorilla-like creature—estimated to be around 10 feet in height—appeared some distance to the side of her.

The terrified woman began to pray, at which point the beast vanished—quite literally—into thin air. As Mark Fraser astutely notes: "Josephine left Dundonald Hill in a hurry, not too far behind her whimpering dogs."

Also from the files of Mark Fraser comes the July 1994 encounter of Pete and George, who were walking through a forestry track in woods near their home of Torphins 20 miles from the Scottish city of Aberdeen. When nearing the end of the track, Pete saw a dark figure run from the trees on the left, head across the track, and disappear into the trees on the right.

A few weeks later the two friends, along with a third, were driving along the road into Torphins when: "Suddenly from the side of the road there came this great, muscular, hairy figure bounding out, which started to run behind the car. At one point it caught up and ran alongside the vehicle, not seemingly out of breath as it approached speeds of up to 35 to 40 miles per hour." The creature would be described as strong and muscular, with a hair-covered body and possessed of a pair of "red, glowing eyes."

IN SEARCH OF THE BRITISH BIGFOOT

A near-collision with Sasquatch

A high plateau bordered by the Trent Valley to the north and the West Midlands to the south, the sprawling mass of forest known as the Cannock Chase has been an integral feature of the Staffordshire landscape for centuries. Following an initial invasion of Britain in AD 43, Roman forces advanced to the south of what is now the town of Cannock and along a route that would later become known as Watling Street, a major Roman road. The surrounding countryside was heavily wooded even then, as can be demonstrated by the Romans' name for the area: Letocetum, or the Gray Woods.

Jackie Houghton, who lived in Cannock for a number of years in the 1990s and worked in nearby Stafford, had a truly remarkable encounter on February 18, 1995, when she was driving across the Cannock Chase and along the main road that links the towns of Rugeley and Cannock. It was 1 AM and her shift at the restaurant was over. As she approached the village of Slittingmill, however, she was suddenly forced to swerve the car and narrowly avoided collision with a large, shambling creature that stepped out into the road at a distance of about 200 feet from her. Considering that she was traveling at high speed, said Jackie, it was a miracle that she didn't hit the thing.

The encounter lasted barely a few seconds, but she had caught sight of the animal and was certain that it was man-like and tall, very hairy, with two self-illuminating, glowing red eyes. It quickly vanished into the trees.

The green-faced monkey

Over a six-week period in the summer of 1996, a strange animal was seen on repeated occasions at Churston Woods, close to the British holiday resort of Torbay. No fewer than 15 separate witnesses reported seeing what they could only describe as a "green faced monkey" running through the woods. And while some of the descriptions were somewhat vague, most of the witnesses told of seeing a tailless animal, around four to five feet tall with a flat, olive-green face, that was occasionally seen swinging through the trees.

There are no creatures fitting this extraordinary description that are indigenous to the British Isles.

A letter to the editor

The Beckermet area of Cumbria was apparently the location of an equally intriguing incident in January 1998. According to a letter to the editor published in the *Whitehaven News* of March of that year:

> It was about 5.00 PM and starting to get dark so my visibility was not that good, but as I walked past the woods I heard the snapping of branches. Thinking it was an animal, I stopped to try and see it. Looking through the trees I noticed a large creature covered in a sort of ginger brown hair that seemed to be drinking from a pond about 150 meters into the woods. As the lighting was getting bad I was straining to make out what it was, but as I stopped and stared, it appeared to notice me. At this point it reared up onto its hind legs and made off slowly further into the woods. I would estimate its height when upright to be around six feet six inches.

The beast goes back to Cannock

Eight months later, the Cannock Chase was once again the site of an encounter with one of our mysterious beast-men. It was just after midnight in September 1998 when a group of four was driving along the A34 road from Stafford to Cannock. As one of the witnesses stated: "It was a star-filled night, clear, but dark, and we were all in the car driving home, happily chatting and joking. Suddenly we all fell dead serious, the people in the back sat forward, and we all pointed to the same shape. It was a tall, man-like figure, sort of crouching forward. As we passed, it turned and looked straight at us. In my own words I would describe it as around six feet eight inches tall, legs thicker than two of mine, very strong looking and with a darkish, blacky [sic] brown coat. I just could not explain it and I still get goose bumps thinking of it."

Recent encounters of the hairy kind

"Some Thing in the Woods" was the headline that appeared in the November 28, 2002, issue of the *Nottingham Evening Post*. Chris Mullins, a well-respected British-based mystery animal researcher, had been given the details of an "eight-foot, hairy man-beast with red glowing eyes" seen within the legendary Sherwood Forest of Robin Hood fame. And it was this specific newspaper article that would prompt an elderly man to contact Chris several days later with details of his own sighting of a seven-to-eight-foot-tall apelike creature in the vicinity of Sherwood Forest late at night two decades previously.

On December 11, 2003, the *British Express & Star* newspaper published a report from a somewhat reluctant witness who nevertheless related that he and a friend had seen, only eight weeks previously, a huge, apelike creature at the side of the road on Levedale Lane between Stafford and Penkridge—which, once again, was in the direct vicinity of the heavily forested Cannock Chase.

"I saw something in the corner of my eye," said the witness. "It was coming towards the car, running very fast. It wasn't a dog or a deer. It was running like a human would run, but it was really hairy and dark. It came level and jumped at the car but just missed."

And as 2002 came to a close and a new year began, the sightings continued unabated. In an article published in the *North of England Evening Chronicle* of January 6, 2003, it was stated: "A yeti with glowing eyes is living in a North East park, according to a fisherman's tale. A report on a website dedicated to hunters of the Yeti and his Big Foot buddy carries details of three encounters between the half-ape creature and three pals.

"They tell how they spend hours in Bolam Lake near Belsay, Northumberland, pike fishing late at night. But their tranquility was disturbed on one fishing trip by a catch they did not expect to make. The anonymous writer tells how he was between his friends Neil and Nathan walking on a wooden path back to the car park, just after midnight. 'About halfway along the path I turned around to talk to Nathan. He was further back along the path, picking his bag up off the track. Behind him, standing in the middle of the track, was a dark figure. The light was moonlight and shining through the trees.'

"The others did not see it at first until he pointed it out to them. He said it was 'a dark figure, looked about eight feet tall, heavy built, its eyes, or what seemed to be its eyes, glowed in the darkness. We ran, top speed, all the way back to the car.'"

Interestingly, the newspaper revealed that during the previous March, a similar creature had been seen on a hill close to the remains of an Iron Age settlement near the park's boundary. On January 15, 2003, Jon Downes headed to Bolam to conduct a firsthand investigation of the sightings. Four days later, he telephoned me: "I have seen the beast," he said quietly and with a degree of fear and trepidation in his voice. It transpired that Jon and five members of a local research group, the Twilight Worlds Paranormal Research Group, were on watch at Bolam Park the previous evening as darkness began to fall. Suddenly "something" appeared that defied all explanation, said Jon. He and three of the group only caught a glimpse of it for the briefest of moments, but the fast-moving creature was around eight feet tall, three feet wide, and dark in color.

Although lost in the failing light and the trees, Jon was able to determine that the "creature" seemed to be without real form and, incredibly, one-dimensional in appearance.

The British Bigfoot and historic sites

In late April 2004, Alec Williams was driving across the aforementioned Cannock Chase, close to a landmark known as Castle Ring, when he had a close encounter of the distinctly hairy kind. Constructed between 500 BC and AD 40, Castle Ring is an Iron Age structure of the type commonly known as a Hill Fort. The highest point on the Chase, it is 801 feet above sea level. Its main ditch and bank enclosure is 14 feet high and, at its widest point, 853 feet across. Little is known about the people that built Castle Ring, except that the creators were already in residence at the time of the Roman invasion and remained there until around AD 50.

Williams's encounter lasted for barely seven or eight seconds; however, he was adamant about the details: "It was about seven feet tall, with short, shiny, dark brown hair, large head, and eyes that glowed bright red." Interestingly, Williams stated that he witnessed "what looked like a camera flash" coming from the depths of the woods, and heard a cry that was somewhat similar to that of an owl.

The UK man-beast: physical or paranormal?

It will have become apparent to the reader that the British Bigfoot exhibits evidence of truly high strangeness as well as curious character traits, such as having the ability to appear and disappear at will and possessing a pair of self-illuminating red eyes. Nor should it be forgotten that many encounters are reported in the direct vicinity of stone circles; ancient burial mounds; and areas of historic, archaeological, and folkloric interest.

This has led a number of researchers to suspect that the British man-beast has paranormal origins rather than being a wholly flesh-and-blood entity. As Jonathan Downes astutely notes: "Unlike the phenomena in other parts of the world, each of the historic British cases have a convenient little folk story, or ghost story, attached to them to explain the presence of these apparitional creatures in the relevant region. The Ghost Ape of Marwood, for example, was, when alive, said to be a pet of a local landowner who one day grabbed the landowner's young son and climbed a tree with him, refusing to come down. And after being killed, the monkey's ghost supposedly haunted the surrounding area.

"Whereas the well-known specter of Martyn's Ape at Athelhampton House in Dorset is supposed to have been the pet of a member of the Martyn family that was either accidentally bricked up alive during building work, or was entombed when the daughter either committed suicide in a locked, secret room or was walled up by an unforgiving parent—depending on which account you read and accept.

> The Martyn family built the earliest part of this house in the 15th century; and, interestingly enough, their family crest was of an ape sitting on a tree stump and the family motto was "He who looks at Martyn's ape, Martyn's ape will look at him."

Downes is firmly of the belief that these accounts were nothing but folk tales created by superstitious villagers in centuries past in an attempt to explain sightings of apelike entities that were more phantom-like than physical in nature. He also offers the intriguing opinion that the British beasts, at least, may be Tulpa-like thought-forms created out of the collective unconscious of the human race. Moreover, he suggests that those same thought-forms may have now achieved a degree of independent, quasi-existence in our world.

According to Scottish legend, the Kelpie—or water-horse—is a supernatural entity that haunts the rivers and lochs of Scotland and that has the ability to shape-shift. The most common form that the Kelpie takes is that of a horse. It stands by the water's edge, tempting any passing and weary traveler that might consider continuing his or her journey on four legs rather than two, to mount it. That, however, is the downfall of the traveler, as invariably the beast is then said to rear violently and charge headlong into the depths of the river or loch, drowning its terrified rider.

Ancient folklore states that the male Kelpie could transform itself into a large and hair-covered man that would hide in the vegetation of waterways and leap out to attack the unwary—not unlike the infamous Man-Monkey of Ranton.

While the theory that the many and varied cryptozoological mysteries of our world are merely Tulpas and shape-shifting thought-forms will certainly not please the more down-to-earth cryptozoological community, in the British Isles it is a theory that many researchers view favorably.

Whatever the origin of the British Bigfoot, however, of one thing we can be certain: the phenomenon shows no signs of stopping.

Nick Redfern: Investigator of cryptids, mysterious phenomena and UFOs; author of numerous books.

FATE July 2005

THE RISE OF THE PLANET OF THE BIGFOOT

Brad Steiger

Cryptozoologist and author Paul Bartholomew shared with me an account of a terrible midnight attack suffered by a National Guardsman near Whitehall, New York. Although the horrific incident had occurred over 20 years ago, the guardsman had kept his nightmarish encounter to himself for fear of ridicule.

According to Bartholomew's experiencer, he had been awakened late one night by the sound of his kitchen door being slammed open and the sounds of furniture being tossed around his kitchen and living room.

Picking up a baseball bat to defend himself and his home, the guardsman started down the stairs to confront the violent intruder, but he found himself paralyzed with fear when his descent on the steps was blocked by a dark, shaggy figure with red-glowing eyes. He told Bartholomew that he estimated the monster to be well over six-feet-five inches and to weigh more than 300 pounds. The beast exuded a terrible smell, like rotten eggs.

The terrified guardsman shouted out a prayer of protection. Whether driven away by divine intervention or the man's scream of terror, the monster appeared almost to vanish and to leave the frightened homeowner alone to stagger back into his bedroom. It was there, he admitted to Bartholomew, that he stayed until morning.

When he summoned the courage to investigate the state of the downstairs, he found the kitchen door wide open and furniture either broken or thrown about in every room.

Was it Bigfoot or a demon?

What, he asked Bartholomew, the area expert on such matters as monster sightings, had he seen rampaging through his house? Was it a Bigfoot or was it a demon?

We will assume for purposes of this article that it was not a demon raising indiscriminate hell. Rather, we will speculate that it was one of the forest creatures popularly and collectively known as Bigfoot, Sasquatch, Yeti, Oh-Mah, Boqwish, and Skunk Ape, that had simply had enough of "Bigfoot Hunters" tracking it through its leafy realms, making casts of its feet and buttocks, making records of its grunts and growls, and, in general, behaving rather badly during safaris into the backyard of the Bigfoot. And adding to the disgust and growing impatience of Bigfoot, what if among the mysterious forest tribes there exists a bright and belligerent "Caesar" or two, very much akin to the intelligent apes in the *Planet of the Apes* cinematic series? What if Bigfoot is collectively shouting, "We are mad as hell, and we are not going to take it anymore!"

Researchers discouraged from taking evidence

Dave Oester and his late wife Sharon were well known for their investigations of the paranormal, but even before they involved themselves in ghost research, one afternoon in 1990 they were in a remote canyon where they found themselves under attack by rock-throwing Bigfoot.

At the time they were living in Utah, and they had discovered that not far from where they resided there was a site where many stagecoaches had fallen into a steep canyon during frontier times. Rumor had it that gold coins and valuable items had never been recovered.

The Oesters asked two of their friends to join them in a day of hiking to investigate what the canyon was all about. It was a blustery day with the wind howling, and remnants of past snowstorms remained in nooks and crannies in the mountains.

The four friends walked side by side for a short time, but soon found that they had to walk single file as the trail angled around rock outcroppings, rising and falling, narrow enough for only one person at a time. It was cold, yet beautiful, and they felt as if they were a world away from civilization.

As they went deeper and deeper into the canyon, Sharon told me later that, "We all agreed it was getting very eerie, and we felt as though we were being watched even though we knew we were totally alone. We reasoned that maybe because all outside sound was blocked out and because we felt isolated from other people, we felt the discomfort. No one really knew where we were if something were to happen."

Then Dave found a solid footprint in the partially melted snow, about 18 inches long. There were signs of what could have been more prints, but little was left and only one print remained clear enough to identify. It was not the print of a bear, but something close to human with huge feet.

Next Dave discovered a bone lying on the ground. He held it up, and they all looked closely at it. It was fairly long and very unusual, Dave and Sharon recalled, "...unlike a human bone or that of any animals we had seen before. We felt very uncomfortable, as though we were trespassing on private property."

Dave turned and pointed down to the canyon floor below them, and there among the trees and snowy ground was what appeared to be a makeshift type of shelter. It was roughly put together with tree branches and leaves.

"We immediately thought that someone had built a shelter because they had gotten caught in a snowstorm," Sharon said. 'We looked closer and found no sign of life, not fire residue, or evidence of human presence. It was then we realized we might have found a Bigfoot lair in the middle of nowhere.

"Dave had slipped the bone into his pocket as we had decided to take it with us to see if someone could identify it. As the decision was made, the first rocks started to fall. "We started to turn to leave when the rocks started falling closer to us. They were also more numerous and larger than before. It seemed that as we started to walk, the rocks started coming down harder and faster, and they were getting bigger all the time."

The friends felt that there was little else they could do other than run. They all felt they were in danger. They also felt there was more than one "creature" and that their actions were closely scrutinized and had been for a while.

"We still could not tell which direction the rocks were coming from, only that it seemed they were coming down all around us now," Sharon recalled. "It seemed that someone or something was not only warning us but was preventing us from leaving. We had to have hiked two miles up into the canyon and there was one way out. It was slow going at best along a narrow, slippery trail. We hoped that we didn't have to run from whatever was out there that remained unseen.

"The rocks had turned into boulders coming down from above us and we didn't know what to do about the situation."

And then it occurred to Sharon: "Dave, the bone, they want us to leave the bone."

Dave took the bone out of his coat pocket and placed it back where they had found it.

When the bone was returned, and they stepped away, the rocks and boulders stopped completely. The canyon was silent once again, and the four friends made their way out of the canyon without further incident.

"We discussed what happened many times," Sharon said, "but always came to the same conclusion. It had to be that we stumbled into a lair, and the encounter was with Bigfoot. It could have ended badly, but rather ended up as an experience to share. We'll never forget it."

Case of the mutilated deer

Eric Altman's journey into researching the paranormal began at the young age of 10 when he watched the 1970s docudramas *Legend of Boggy Creek* and *Creature from Black Lake*, allegedly based on events that took place in the deep south of Arkansas and Texas. The two films inspired Eric to begin 27 years of research into the paranormal; however, his main interest is studying hominid creatures such as Bigfoot. Eric currently heads the Pennsylvania Bigfoot Society, a group of dedicated researchers who investigate encounters and sightings of Bigfoot in the "Keystone State."

When I asked Eric for a case currently under investigation, he told an interesting story involving a family and the discovery of a dead deer that appeared to be the victim of a Bigfoot.

According to Eric:

In the small town of Wysox, Pennsylvania, a family was visited by some unusual but violent being(s) on the night of July 4, 2006. The family had returned from a family outing, and as they were walking from the car to the house, they began to hear loud screams coming from the wooded area behind their home. What they heard not only puzzled them but frightened them as well.

They own several hundred acres of forest behind their home, and somewhere, around 11 PM, there were three "things" in the forest screaming.

One animal or being would scream. A few moments later, something would respond in kind with a loud scream. Within what seemed another few moments, another shrill answer would respond in kind with yet another scream corning from another location in the wooded acreage. This calling and answering occurred for over 15 minutes before the family went into their home.

The next day, the children of the family decided to explore the woods. What they found would not only shock the family, but also the researchers involved in the investigation.

The family discovered a dead deer. The animal was found with its right front leg wedged tightly in the "Y" of a small tree. How it got there in that position was a mystery.

But the bizarre occurrence didn't end there. The deer appeared to have bloody welts on the top of its head as if it were beaten by a blunt object. The deer also was ripped apart from the midsection back. A large hole was ripped in the side and underbelly of the deer, and its right rear leg was missing.

The method of the deer's brutal death was accompanied by the discovery of a large bloody rock found not far from the animal, along with several large human shaped impressions in the ground which led the family to speculate that a "Bigfoot" or similar type creature was responsible for the death of the deer.

The family found several broken trees and branches in the area. They also found several trees ripped out of the ground with the roots still intact.

Upon contacting our group, our researchers visited the location about eight days afterwards to look at the deer. It was still there; no other predators had touched it, and the evidence of the tracks and so forth were still there.

During our investigators' visit with the family, our researchers heard the screams the family had heard on that first night, July 4th. Although the person/creature responsible for the screams and the brutal death of the deer was never seen or discovered, some of the circumstantial evidence leads to the possibility of a Bigfoot being the culprit. Unfortunately, by the time our researchers arrived, there was no fresh evidence to collect to be tested. The weather and elements had contaminated the tracks, deer, the tree, and the rock.

While the thought of screaming Bigfoot using primitive weapons and tools to brutally slaughter a deer and to leave the bloody body near the home of humans as a kind of sign of what might happen to them if they interfered with the Bigfoot lifestyle in any way, the strange account of how the Nantiinaq drove away the community of Port Chatham may truly demonstrate the hostile actions of which the Bigfoot may be capable.

Entire villages in Alaska flee from Bigfoot

On the southernmost tip of Alaska's Kenai Peninsula there once was a thriving little community named Port Chatham. Through the centuries, the village had offered friendly hospitality to strangers. When Captain Nathaniel Portlock visited the place on his 1786 Alaska expedition, he and his men were made to feel welcome.

In the mid-1930s, strange and terrible things began to happen to the people of Port Chatham. The Nantiinaq ("big hairy creature" in the native Sugt'sun) had become bolder and had begun to terrorize the villagers. Sometimes they could even come into the village and hurt people. Some witnesses swore that the Nantiinaq were led by the spirit of a woman dressed in flowing black clothes who would materialize out of the cliffs and summon the Nantiinaq.

A logger was killed instantly when he was struck from behind with a piece of log-moving equipment.

A gold prospector who was working his claim disappeared one day and was never seen again.

A sawmill owner saw a Nantiinaq on the beach, tearing up the fish traps that had been set.

By about 1936, the people of Chatham left the village en masse. They abandoned their houses, the school, everything, and vacated their once peaceful town to move to Nanwalek.

In the early 1900s, the town of Portlock, named for Captain Nathaniel Portlock, was established as a small cannery town. In 1921, a US post office was opened, and the town appeared to be prospering. The population was made up largely of natives of the region who were mostly of Russian-Aleut heritage and who had lived in peaceful interaction for decades.

Sometime in the early 1940s, the same kind of strange occurrences that drove the people out of their village of Chatman began to happen in Portlock. Men who worked at the cannery began to disappear. Some would go hunting for Dall sheep and bear and never be seen again.

Reports of sighting the Nantiinaq became common. So did the reports of mutilated and dismembered human bodies floating in the lagoon.

Hunters tracking signs of moose would suddenly find the tracks of the great animal overlaid with giant human-like tracks over those left by the moose. Signs of a struggle in the snow were mute testimony that the giant human had slain the huge moose. Then the only tracks remaining were the monster manlike tracks heading back toward the fog-shrouded mountains.

As with the people of Port Chatham before them, the residents of Portlock moved en masse, leaving their homes, the school, and the cannery. In 1950, the post office closed.

Naomi Klouda of the *Homer Tribune* (October 26, 2009) interviewed Malania Kehl, the eldest resident in Nanwalek, who was born in Port Chatham in 1934 and who remembers how the entire village left everything behind to escape the Nantiinaq. It was her uncle who had been killed with the piece of logging equipment. Once the people of Port Chatham left their community, Malania said, the Nantiinaq stayed far away from them and left them in peace.

According to Sugt'stun culture, the Natiinaq may once have been fully human, but now, through some events not understood, this is a different kind of creature, half-man, half-beast.

Their definition of the creature may be as good as any thus far as we ponder the possibility of a rise of a planet of the Bigfoot.

Brad Steiger (1936 -2018): Author of more than 100 books on the strange and unknown; frequent contributor to FATE.

FATE 726

REPORTER VANISHES

Charles W. Sasser

The disappearance of a reporter for *The Mena* (Arkansas) *Star* has baffled local, state, and federal investigators and fueled wild speculation as to what may have happened to her.

"Bigfoot walked off with her," declared Don Thomas, a member of the search party that scoured the rugged Talihina Mountains of western Arkansas for 68-year-old Gloria McDonald.

According to the Polk County Sheriff's Department, the slender, five feet-six-inch woman arrived at Queen Wilhelmina State Park on January 26, 2001, with her husband Dan, her stepson Sean, and Sean's fiancée Erin. They parked their car at the lodge and set out to walk a short, well-marked trail to "Lover's Leap," a popular sightseeing point.

About 150 yards down the trail, Gloria decided to return to the warmth of the lodge. It was a cold winter day, with snow and ice still on the ground. Her husband, stepson, and future daughter-in-law continued their hike. Gloria was never seen nor heard from again.

No ordinary case

"It's hard to get lost in that short a distance," said Polk County Sheriff Mike Oglesby. "The state park initiated a search immediately, then contacted the sheriff's office about 3 PM. We searched with volunteers, then called in state police, who brought in a helicopter from Little Rock. We continued to search that night, and the next morning we brought in a fixed-winged aircraft for two hours. Visibility was perfect, but there was still no sign of McDonald. That afternoon, we called in the bloodhound teams, but they came up empty-handed as well."

Don Thomas recalls how the bloodhounds trailed the missing woman's scent for only a short distance before they refused to continue. They bolted back, whimpering, hackles raised, further arousing concern that McDonald's was no ordinary missing person case.

Authorities soon learned that an apelike creature had been spotted in the area on three separate occasions less than two weeks previously.

More than 500 Bigfoot sightings are recorded each year in the United States. According to North American folklore and Native American legends, Bigfoot inhabits remote wildlands from the swamps of Louisiana to the temperate rainforests of the Pacific Northwest and Canada. He is commonly described as a bipedal, manlike creature coated in dark, coarse hair and standing upwards of seven feet tall.

An elderly farm couple at the foot of the Queen Wilhelmina Lodge mountain observed a Bigfoot running from north to south across a fallow field. The next day, an over-the-road truck driver traveling through Arkansas between Acorn and Mena spotted a hairy form of surprising dimensions darting across the road in front of him.

Don Thomas encountered the creature late the same afternoon. Thomas is an experienced outdoorsman and wildlife expert who volunteers at the wild animal rehabilitation center at Queen Wilhelmina State Park, caring for injured or abandoned raccoons, eagles, bears, and other creatures. It is highly unlikely that he would make a mistake in identifying any animal.

Thomas and a friend were exploring a logging road near the park, checking out hunting territory, when several deer bolted across the road in front of his truck. Then, even more spooked, they returned the same way they had come. Looking to see what had frightened them, Thomas espied a beast like none he had ever encountered.

138

It stood leaning with one hand against a tree with the late afternoon sun behind it. It was big, but not exceptionally bulky, standing at least six and a half feet tall and covered in dark brown or black hair.

Shocked, the two men watched as the creature turned and walked upright like a man down the other side of the mountain and vanished in the forest.

"I got the impression from its appearance and behavior that it was an adolescent male," Thomas said. "I keep thinking it may have been looking for a mate. Maybe Mrs. McDonald's perfume attracted him to her."

Whatever happened that winter day in Wilhelmina Park, Gloria McDonald's disappearance remains one of the mysteries of the century. No one has heard from her since that day, not her children, not her friends, and not her husband. Polygraph tests were administered to everyone concerned, and all passed. And while authorities from all levels of government have continued their search for the missing reporter over the past seven years, they have uncovered not one scrap of evidence, not a single clue as to what might have happened to her. For all practical purposes, she vanished into the thin January air.

Could she indeed have been carried off by a Bigfoot?

Attacked by ape-men

Although Bigfoot is assumed to be a gentle, reclusive vegetarian, numerous reports over the years list the forest giant as a suspect in human attacks, kidnappings, and even murders.

In 1908, gold prospectors Willie and Frank McLeod were discovered beheaded at their Gold Creek claim in Canada's Northwest Territories. Rumors circulated that the brothers had intruded upon the domain of the "hairy men of the forest" and were slain for their trespass.

In 1924, Fred Beck and four partners were attacked in their miners' cabin at the foot of Mount St. Helens in Washington. Hairy giants stormed the cabin and its terrified occupants again and again throughout the night, leaping onto the cedar-shingled roof in an effort to break through. The men fought off their attackers, killing one, and fled the scene at dawn, never to return.

Albert Ostman of British Columbia claimed that a group of four Sasquatches, two adults and two juveniles, kidnapped him from his camp in 1924 and carried him for four hours, sleeping bag and all, before he managed to escape.

A Nootka Indian called Muchalat Harry suffered a similar fate in 1928 on Vancouver Island when a party of at least 20 Sasquatches of various genders, ages, and sizes abducted him and kept him prisoner for several days before he escaped.

During World War II, O. R. Edwards watched in horror while a Bigfoot made off with his friend Bill Cole. The two men were on a hunting trip in California's Siskiyou Mountains when, as Edwards described it, "I heard the pad-pad-pad of running feet and the whump and grunt as their bodies [Bigfoot's and Cole's] came together. Dashing back to the end of the bush I saw a large manlike creature covered with brown hair. It was about seven feet tall and it was carrying in its arms what seemed like a man."

The beast carried Cole for about half a mile before it released him, unharmed.

Charles Buchanan was camping out on the shores of Lake Worth, Texas, in 1969, sleeping in the bed of his pickup truck when something startled him awake about 2 AM. His eyes shot open to observe "a cross between a human being and a gorilla or ape" towering over him. The thing jerked him to the ground, sleeping bag and all. The quick-thinking Buchanan reacted by shoving a bag of leftover chicken into the monster's face. That apparently saved him. The Sasquatch snatched the sack in its jaws, made some guttural sounds, then loped off through the trees.

Boggy Creek monster returns

So far, Gloria McDonald appears to be the only female to have been kidnapped by the hairy man of the mountains, if, in fact, that is what happened to her. Such conjecture may not be that far-fetched, considering that Mena lies less than 100 miles north of Fouke, Arkansas.

In the 1960s and 1970s, rural residents around Fouke were terrorized by a rampaging Bigfoot who killed pigs, chickens and dogs, stampeded cattle, scared off visitors, and attempted to break into occupied houses. The monster was made famous by the 1972 cult movie entitled *The Legend of Boggy Creek.*

Karen Crabtree was nine years old at the time and still lives in Fouke. She recalls seeing the "Boggy Creek Monster" leap out in front of the car in which she was a passenger on a rural road near her home. A few nights later, she and her family heard it scream in rage right outside their door. Terrified, they barricaded themselves inside and maintained a wary, armed vigil until daybreak.

Karen believes it absolutely possible that Gloria McDonald could have been kidnapped by such a beast.

"I saw it," she says, shuddering at the memory. "I saw it."

Charles W. Sasser: Freelance writer and author.

FATE March 2008

LAKE WORTH MONSTER: A TRUE TEXAS MYSTERY

Lyle Blackburn

On July 10, 1969, just after midnight, Bill Morris was sitting in a café near Lake Worth, northwest of Fort Worth, Texas. He was quietly enjoying a meal when a young couple burst into the restaurant looking for a phone. They were visibly upset and in a state of panic as the male dialed 0 and asked for the police. Morris couldn't help but overhear the conversation as the young man recounted a frightening incident that had occurred just moments before in a heavily wooded area on the north end of the lake.

The young man told the dispatcher that he and his wife had been out parking near Greer Island (a popular "Lover's Lane" hangout at the time) with two other couples when something leaped from a nearby tree and landed on their car. The thing, which he described as "half-man, half-goat with fur and scales," tried to grab his wife, but he managed to drive off before it got a hold of her.

The man hung up the phone and comforted his wife until four police units arrived. After a short conversation, they were escorted away by the officers. It was the beginning of a Texas-sized legend that endures to this day.

The following day, an article titled "Fishy Man-Goat Terrifies Couples Parked at Lake Worth" appeared in the *Fort Worth Star Telegram*. In the article, journalist Jim Marrs explained that the police accompanied John Reichart and his wife back to the location of the incident. They found no evidence of the attacker there, but Reichart was able to show the officers an 18-inch scratch down the side of his car allegedly made by the attacker.

Author and investigator Lyle Blackburn. Credit: Lyle Blackburn.

"We did make a serious investigation because those people were really scared," the patrolman told Marrs. The police had been receiving calls of a similar nature since June, but until that morning, they had simply been disregarded. After investigating the claim by Reichart and his friends, the police concluded it must have been the work of a "prankster."

However, that didn't stop the public from becoming enthralled. The article, along with radio and television reports, created such a stir that people began to assemble at Greer Island, hoping to confront the "goat-man" themselves. By the evening of July 11, there were as many as 30-40 people—including members of the Tarrant County Sheriff's Department—gathered near a landmark known as "The Pit" when the creature appeared on a high ridge above. In a second news article by Marrs, the creature was said to have "uttered a pitiful cry" before it threw a heavy tire (with the rim) nearly 500 feet above the heads of the awestruck assembly!

Lake Worth terrain. Credit: Lyle Blackburn.

The crowd was so alarmed by the display of power, they began to flee. One young man reportedly backed his car into a tree as he tried to get away. What started as a rather innocent "monster hunt" ended in a frightening experience that left the locals questioning whether it was a real creature or a crazy, costumed prankster with a death wish. Bill Morris confirmed that some of the would-be monster hunters were armed.

The general description of the thing was that it was big with gray or white hair like a goat on its body. Some, such as the original witnesses, said it was partially covered with scales, while some believed they also saw horns. Jack Harris, one of the eyewitnesses, told reporters that "the creature walked like a man but didn't look like one. He looked like he was seven feet tall and must have weighed about 300 pounds." These bizarre descriptions create a cryptozoological conundrum since some of the traits would place it into the "Goatman" category, while others would lump it into the "Bigfoot" category, if of course, it wasn't human.

In a *Star Telegram* article dated July 14, a representative of the Fort Worth Museum of Science and History stated that he believed the "monster" to be a bobcat. A naturalist at the Greer Island Refuge and Nature Center backed him up, saying that a pet bobcat had been turned loose in the area at one time. A bobcat might account for the "pitiful cries," but by no means can a cat of any size throw a tire 500 feet over the heads of 30 plus witnesses. Another theory was offered by a local kennel owner who said he was "tracking a 40-pound runaway macaque monkey

Lake Worth terrain. Credit: Lyle Blackburn.

146

near the lake," but this too ignores the fact that witnesses had seen a much larger, bipedal type creature.

In the weeks that followed, more incidents involving the monster were said to have occurred. On one occasion the creature was reportedly seen running across an open grass field. In another, five people claimed they witnessed it breaking the limbs of a huge oak tree. These accounts were either ignored or unknown to the press, but luckily a writer by the name of Sallie Ann Clarke saw the value of following up on the story, which she documented in her book, *The Lake Worth Monster*, published in 1969. The book includes interviews with numerous witnesses, including Ronnie Armstrong, who claimed the creature had been wounded by a gunshot that produced a trail of blood leading down to the water's edge. A set of tracks was also discovered by three individuals who showed them to Clarke and Armstrong. "We measured the ape like tracks," Clarke explained in her book. "[T]hey were sixteen (16) inches long with a toe spread of eight (8) inches. The tracks appeared to have been made by a real heavy animal or a being of some kind."

Armstrong, who helped Clarke investigate the incidents, felt that it might be a "big white ape," based on his own sightings and interviews with others. Vic Franklin of Fort Worth also claimed to have seen the creature a number of times. He told Clarke it was at least seven feet tall and looked like a "real hairy" human. Another eyewitness, Jim Stephens, told Clarke the thing jumped on the hood of his car one night as he and two other men were driving around the lake. They had heard about the creature while fishing that day and decided to look for themselves. Stephens said the creature remained on the car's hood until he swerved and ran into a tree. At that point, the thing "jumped off and ran into the woods." He described the creature as "real big and human-like with burnt scars all over its face, arms and chest."

Clarke's book is ultimately a semi-fictional treatment of the subject that includes both facts and interviews with witnesses, along with fanciful passages in which she imagines what it would be like to see the creature herself. This approach tends to muddy the waters in terms of accurate, cryptozoological research, but Clarke's intention at the time was to document the events while at the same time writing an entertaining book. Ironically, she would later have the opportunity to see the creature for herself as she continued her research after the book's publication.

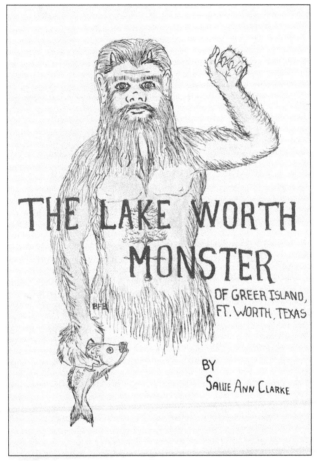

The cover of Sallie Ann Clark's book. Credit: Lyle Blackburn.

In an interview with Sean Whitley, producer of the documentary film *Southern Fried Bigfoot*, Clarke stated that she ended up seeing the monster a total of "five times." On the first occasion, Clarke said she was at the lake when she found a "big track." Later she was sitting in the back of a friend's camper when she saw the creature through the screen door. "I put a metal plate with some shrimp in it on the back of the camper, and that thing come up and stood there, and carried off the plate," she recalled. "I watched it. Boy, I mean, that thing scared the devil out of me. It was just a big, tall white thing."

Clarke lamented that she didn't have a camera with her at the time, but fortunately someone did capture an image of the alleged beast. On November 19, Fort Worth resident Allen Plaster told a reporter from the *Star Telegram* he was driving west on Shoreline Drive with another couple at 1:35 AM when one of them saw a large, white figure stand up near the road. Plaster managed to snap a Polaroid picture as it ran away. The resulting photo shows a blurry white figure that resembles a cloud with a head.

Plaster later downplayed the photo, saying that he believed whatever it was "wanted" to be seen. But regardless, it did show something big and white, which was not a fabrication by the photographer.

Just weeks before the photo event another man claimed to have been attacked while he slept in the back of his truck near Greer Island. On November 7, Charles Buchanan said he was in his sleeping bag around 3 AM when something began dragging him out of the truck's bed. Thinking fast, Buchanan reached for a sack of barbeque chicken he had left over from dinner and shoved it towards the beast. The thing promptly let go of the sleeping bag and shoved the chicken in its mouth before running off towards the lake. It then plunged into the water and swam in the direction of Greer Island.

As 1969 came to a close, monster fever around Lake Worth began to dwindle as the sightings diminished. Some folks, such as Sallie Clarke and my friend Bill Morris, continued their research, but for the most part the newspapers moved on and so, perhaps, did the monster.

In the years that followed many speculated as to what had really happened at Greer Island that summer. A number of people claimed credit for a grand hoax, as often occurs in these cases. According to a 2009 article from the *Victoria Advocate*, back in 1969 police questioned several students from a high school in Fort Worth who were found with a "faceless gorilla outfit and a mask." In 2005, the *Star Telegram* received a letter from an unnamed person who claimed he and two friends "decided to go out to Lake Worth and scare people on the roads where there were always stories of monsters." The writer said they used "tinfoil" to make a homemade mask.

The tinfoil and faceless gorilla costume (which would have most likely been black or brown) don't match the white creature the majority of eyewitnesses reported, but other claims accounted for this by saying the creature frenzy was inspired by a goatskin or carcass that was being displayed on the hood of a car or, more dramatically, cast down from trees onto the parked vehicles of couples making out below.

To evaluate yet another rumor, a reporter from *Fort Worth Magazine* tracked down a man by the name of "Vinzens" who claimed credit for the tire-throwing incident. According to his article, Vinzens affirmed that he and two other guys had gone to Greer Island to party on July 11 where they ended up on the bluff overlooking The Pit and the throng of monster seekers below. In an innocent attempt to "fire up the festivities" and impress some girls, he and his buddies rolled a tire down the bluff. He said it looked more like a "toss" because there was a "bump" toward the bottom of the bluff that launched the tire into the air. Vinzens said that "when the incident made the papers the following day, he and his friend decided to lay low" to avoid any repercussions from police or the armed monster hunters who were stalking the area day and night.

Interesting, but Vinzens is not the only person to take credit for the tire toss. A woman named Jan Galloway told a blogger at the *Domain of Horror* her brothers were responsible for all the "goatman" incidents. "They tied ropes and grapevines off in the daytime and at night my younger brother Jack Shelby [11 years old] wore my rabbit coat and they would fly across the hoods of the cars and barely touch the hoods," Galloway explained. "One night my brother Billy Shelby [15 years old] decided to come across the ground on all fours like a monkey... he jumped on top of a car and scratched the windshield and made a Tarzan sound and jumped off."

Billy's prank supposedly sent the first couple to call police. Later, she said, Billy put on cut-off shorts and a white t-shirt, then smeared a "black eye pencil" on his face, arms, and legs. After ascending the ridge at Greer Island, he and several boys used a giant slingshot to launch the tire across the pit while Billy beat his chest and made more "Tarzan sounds."

With so many ridiculous claims, it's hard to sift out the truth in the matter, be it man *or* monster. The only certainty is that strange things were going on at Lake Worth and there were witnesses who believed they had seen something not of human origin. To add to the mystery, sightings in the area didn't start in 1969, nor did they end there. For years people had talked of a creature that haunted the lake. Some called it the "Mud Man" or "Mud Monster," while others simply referred to it as a ghost. A resident who had lived there for 40 years told Sallie Clarke he saw something fitting the description at least 20 years earlier.

Could the Lake Worth Monster have been a rogue Bigfoot with white hair? There have been reports of Bigfoot creatures in North Texas over the years. In 1963, the *Denton Record-Chronicle* reported someone near the town of Denton, Texas claimed to have seen a "hairy, eight-foot thing" which the locals referred to as a "monster." The details are sketchy, but Denton is a mere 30 miles north of Lake Worth.

An earlier incident was said to have taken place in 1938 near the town of Red Oak, 40 miles southeast of Lake Worth. And this time the creature was described as having *white hair*. According to a report submitted to the Western Bigfoot Society, four men were coon hunting one night in the heavy woods surrounding Red Oak Creek. As they sat in camp waiting for their dogs to sniff out a raccoon, they noticed the dogs weren't barking as they usually did on the hunts and were instead sitting close to the fire acting scared. "About that time they noticed a huge, white haired figure standing about 30 or so yards from the fire," one of the witness' sons stated. "It was just standing there watching them." The frightened hunters quickly grabbed their guns and dogs and fled from the bottoms. The next day they told others of the encounter, but no one believed their story. "My father was a very honest man… and I know his story to be true," the son affirmed.

During my own research I spoke to a woman by the name of Cynthia Dunston, who told me of a possible Bigfoot encounter she had on the north side of Lake Worth in 1982. She was young at the time and was visiting her grandparents, whose house was located near the lake. She spent many afternoons exploring the woods surrounding the home, and on this occasion she had followed an old cow path from their barn to nearby Ash Creek. "I got about halfway down the path when I saw something," she told me. "There was a dark shape in front of the fence at the end of the path."

Cynthia, a rather experienced outdoorswoman for her age, felt there was no reason to be alarmed so she kept walking. As she got closer, however, the shape moved and she could see it more clearly. "Then I froze," she recalled. "I knew exactly what it was."

Standing before her was a hairy, man-like creature. "I remember that its hair was longish and a dark auburn color," she told me. "It looked as tall as an average man but not freakishly tall."

The young girl was startled, but not terrified. To her understanding, Bigfoot did not eat people. "This was more like extreme apprehension and caution of a large animal when you don't know what it is going to do," she recalled. "This appeared to be a natural animal."

Despite her faith in the creature's benign eating habits, Cynthia promptly turned and started back towards the barn. She didn't want to run, thinking it might give chase, but hurried at a good pace nonetheless. "When I was almost to the barn, I looked back," she continued. "It had followed me but had stopped past the halfway point where I had been standing before. As soon as I had the house in sight, I made a wild dash for the gate to the backyard. Safely inside the gate, I looked back toward the barn. There was nothing there."

While the creature Cynthia saw did not have white hair, it does suggest that perhaps Bigfoot creatures could have been present in the area. And where there's one creature, there could be others.

In recent times, the wilderness surrounding Lake Worth has given way to considerable development (save for a 300-acre nature preserve around Greer Island), but at the time of the main incidents it was a truly wild place. The lake itself is a reservoir created by the west fork of the Trinity River, a lengthy waterway that feeds it from the north and extends well beyond to the south. The area was sufficiently wooded, and all along the river's corridor we find a host of strange incidents not unlike those that became famous in 1969. The Lake Worth Monster of Greer Island, it seems, is just one piece of a larger, hairier puzzle.

[Portions of this article are excerpted from the book The Beast of Boggy Creek: The True Story of the Fouke Monster *by Lyle Blackburn, published by Anomalist Books (2012).]*

Lyle Blackburn: Author of books on the Fouke Monster and Lizard Man; founder of the rock band Ghoultown; columnist for the horror magazine Rue Morgue; *and narrator/producer of documentary films such as* The Mothman of Point Pleasant *and* Boggy Creek Monster.

2019

PARAPHYSICAL BIGFOOT
AND
THE UFO CONNECTION

BIGFOOT, STENCHES AND UFOS

John Keel

For centuries, nearly every country on Earth has had reports of evil-smelling creatures with bright, self-luminous eyes.

That could be why the Abominable Snowman of the Himalayas is considered abominable and the frequently sighted Skunk Ape of Florida is often compared to odoriferous road kill. From Europe to China, these creatures were once thought to be dragons that followed a regular "dragon route" which circled half the world.

A rose by any other name

In Australia, the natives called them "Yowies," while American Indians had 100 different terms for them.

A famous British linguist, retired diplomat Gordon Creighton, sat down in the 1960s and systematically tried to research the various names given such creatures. He compiled a list of 131 before he gave up.

The former Soviet Union has 127 different languages and probably more smelly hairy creature reports than any other country, with scores of terms for them. Central and South America also appear to be riddled with monsters hiding behind more names. In recent years, both Russia and China have launched expeditions into areas where the Snowman has been most frequently reported, without finding substantial evidence. Controversies over these elusive creatures continues to rage in both countries.

In the United States, millions of dollars have been spent chasing our overfragrant Bigfoot in the past 30 years. Television shows, movie companies, magazines, newspapers, and a number of wealthy individuals have searched the Northwest with airplanes and helicopters, to no avail. Rugged outdoor types have devoted years of their lives to this ultimately futile quest. Even I, your cynical, savvy FATE columnist, have wasted considerable time, money, and physical effort trying track these bathless bogeymen.

If a 10-foot-tall hairy monster really exists out there, it would require a considerable amount of food and leave behind some enormous piles of dung. It would need a place to sleep and a place to die. Yet all we have ever found are some footprints in the mud or snow, a few strands of hair, and that awful, awful stench.

Since no one has managed to catch one, or even to get a really decent photograph of one, maybe we should rethink the whole problem. Perhaps we should stop trying to follow those footprints that never lead anywhere and concentrate on that abominable body odor.

Fumigating the planet

Some leading Russian scientists, baffled by innumerable folk tales about *Almas* or *Snezhnyy Chelovek,* tried to organize the reports on a map. They came up with a chart almost identical to the old dragon routes. To compound the confusion, these were also the routes most frequently used by UFOs.

Could all of our mysterious phenomena be interrelated? Many UFOs are accompanied by the stench of rotten eggs. In fact, some people have complained of being deliberately gassed by UFOs. Several years ago, a night watchman in New Jersey received worker's compensation after claiming to have been incapacitated by a low-flying saucer that emitted some sort of fumes. The strange light that landed on a hilltop in West Virginia in 1952 (sometimes called "the Flatwoods Monster") was so acrid that a group of witnesses fled for their lives. One fainted. The dog with them became violently ill and vomited.

The whole world of the supernatural includes a range of disquieting smells. Poltergeists, those invisible mischief makers, are also noted for some ugly odors. While the good ones traditionally smell like flowers, the others smell like Bigfoot. The invisible Bell Witch was so putrid that the Bell family had to leave their house. In ancient times, when early writers were describing the *Wodwos*, "wild men of the woods," the rotten-egg smell of brimstone was believed to mark the presence of the devil.

The natives of Tibet, Nepal, and Bhutan always believed, probably for good reason, that the *Kang-mi* (man of the snows) was a demon and bad luck for anyone who saw—or smelled—it. Sadly, few Yetis have been seen in recent times because too many tourists are stinking up the Himalayas. (Western tourists are said to smell like wet chicken.)

Brimstone and stink bombs

In high school chemistry you may have whipped up a few stink bombs. They were simply made with hydrogen sulfide, which smells like rotten eggs. A few drops will clear out a classroom, sometimes a whole school.

The Abominable Snowman smell is reportedly much more intense. Some witnesses end up choking and gagging. And if you have ever been in a war or a morgue, you can recognize the odor immediately. Here's how journalist Pierre Jovanovic describes it: "The skin emits gases like methane and hydrogen sulfide, which mix and give off a terrible odor. You would never guess that such a stench could exist."

Could our big hairy monsters be rotting corpses? Or could they be composed of dead animal matter that is somehow formed temporarily into animated beings, sort of like zombies with hair? This notion has been circulating in occult circles for hundreds of years.

Fiery red eyes are another sign of supernatural beings who mutilate or feast on the dead. The ancient Greeks called them chimeras.

Did they know the answers? Have our scientists, explorers, zoologists, ufologists, and exobiologists been running around in a circle that leads nowhere? Could UFOs be a part of this? If we should ever recover an alien body would it smell of hydrogen sulfide and disintegrate into thin air?

The pre-1900 folklore of monsters and wild men is much more impressive than the contemporary accounts of hairy stinkers. There are even stories of the capture and the domestication of these beings in Russia and China. Humans supposedly mated with snowwomen in China and produced offspring which lived full lives. Maybe there were real snowmen once, but our modern pollution has gassed them out of existence, leaving nothing but a few random chimeras frolicking in the mountains of Russia and the swamps of the Florida Everglades.

John Keel (1930-2009): FATE *columnist and contributor; researcher and author of groundbreaking books on UFO phenomena.*

FATE January 1998

NEW YORK COLLEGE PROFESSOR LINKS BIGFOOT TO UFOS

Joseph Flammer

What are Bigfoot? Well, if they're not extraterrestrials, then they're possessors of alien-like "interdimensional" abilities, claims a trailblazing professor at one of New York's biggest colleges.

As further evidence of their out-of-this-world connection, the professor says Bigfoot have been linked to UFOs, sometimes appearing simultaneously to people.

Professor Ted Benitt of the Physical Sciences Department at Nassau Community College in Garden City, Long Island, says Bigfoot share abilities possessed by extraterrestrials such as grays.

For example, they can dematerialize at will, communicate telepathically, read minds, and produce "mind screens" that result in episodes of missing time.

"The extraterrestrial connection does a wonderful job of explaining questions regarding variations in appearance and why—or how—they are so clever, telepathic, and capable of teleportation," explained Professor Benitt.

Speaking to a packed audience of UFO enthusiasts from across Long Island at a Mutual UFO Network (MUFON) meeting at the Commack Public Library, Benitt said the hairy giants appear to people in areas where spaceships are also seen in the skies; and when the spaceships vanish, so too do the Bigfoot, he said.

Further elaborating on the incomprehensible alien-like qualities of Bigfoot, the professor added they are known to deflect powerful rifle bullets to their chests.

"They are invulnerable to bullets," he said.

Bigfoot, he went on, are known to throw 200-pound boulders hundreds of feet with near-pinpoint accuracy—often to scare humans away.

Moreover, the secretive cryptids are capable of producing a nauseating stench that repels human invaders, and this is the reason they are known as "skunk apes" in some parts of the United States, he added.

"The big question which still remains is, what are they?" Professor Benitt said to audience members. He handed out copies of a life-size photo of a Bigfoot footprint taken from a casting, which shows a five-toed foot 18 inches long and eight inches wide.

"DNA of hair and blood indicate they are primate—almost human—but not human," Benitt said. "Are we looking at an indigenous Earth creature from the past, perhaps *Gigantopithecus blackii*, which was altered genetically by the aliens who are now showing us our precursors—a sort of mind game to see if we can make the recognition?"

One of the strangest interdimensional abilities Bigfoot possess is disappearing and reappearing at will, said the professor.

"Always look a Bigfoot right in the eyes," Benitt warned. "The one thing you don't ever want to do—if you should come face to face with one—is take your eyes off of its eyes because it can vanish and get behind you if you do."

The professor described a case in which a man came upon two Bigfoot in the woods, met eyes with one, and just for an instant switched his gaze to look at the other. When he looked back to the first Bigfoot, he found it had disappeared in a flash. Then he discovered a Bigfoot was standing behind him, breathing heavily. Luckily, the man was able to escape without harm.

The professor said in addition to disappearing and reappearing at will, Bigfoot can also cause episodes of missing time in people's minds, possibly through the use of infrasound. In this case, the sound would not be detectable by human ears because it's too low of a wavelength, but it might nonetheless temporarily stun people with its low vibrations, confusing them. Stunning humans might allow Bigfoot to escape a possibly dangerous chance encounter with a human before any harm is done to either party.

Benitt said Bigfoot tend not to hurt or bother humans. But they are known to visit human habitats to invade garbage cans for food. He added that during chance meetings in the woods, Bigfoot have telepathically communicated to their would-be human hunters that they would be killed if they should in any way challenge the Bigfoot or pursue it.

"Bigfoot are found in every one of the contiguous states," said Benitt. "They are found around the world. They're all over...They go by different names."

He said the mysterious creatures can stand nine feet tall and weigh up to 1100 pounds. Depending on the region, Bigfoot has either three or five toes. Their ape-like strides are between four-and-a-half and five feet long, he added.

No skeletal remains of a deceased Bigfoot has ever been found for study, though a jawbone of one was unearthed in China, said Benitt.

"Bigfoot display preternatural aspects and interdimensional aspects," said Benitt. "Their preternatural aspects cause anthropologists much consternation because they defy explanation in the paradigm of zoology..."

Benitt said he has been teaching a popular science elective called "Meta Sciences 141" at Nassau College for 40 years. Nassau is the largest single site college campus in New York State, with nearly 40,000 full-time and part-time students. During the semester Benitt teaches his students not only about Bigfoot, but also about UFOs, ghosts and other paranormal phenomena. He said his collogues sometimes scoff at the non-academic syllabus, but students consistently rush to register for the popular trailblazing course, filling up the registry within a few hours of its offering.

Joseph Flammer: Researcher and author of books on paranormal phenomena.

FATE September-October 2013

Sasquatch: A Terrestrial-Extraterrestrial?

Kewaunee Lapseritis

"Wake up! Come outside! Come outside," a friendly female Sasquatch voice telepathed to my wife, Kelly. We were camping in a wilderness area in Washington State where a tribe of forest giants live. On the night of July 7, 2014, the beings woke us up so we would have the opportunity to see a spaceship landing near our tent. However, we lingered while gathering our thoughts and missed what could have been a rare view of a spacecraft. We were fortunate enough to hear the craft and see the lights from the ship departing as we stepped out of the tent. The Sasquatch said that three of their people had been dropped off.

After 57 years of research in crypto-anthropology, I have discovered the forest giants are really an evolved, nature people who migrated to earth with the help of friendly Star People millions of years ago, long before hairless humans were "seeded" here (their words). That was in September 1979 when both an ET and Sasquatch spoke to me telepathically. It was the shock of my life! The Sasquatch are actually terrestrial-extraterrestrials. They gave me, my wife, and several other experiencers precisely the same information about where they are from.

To date, I have documented 277 percipients who have had ET/ Bigfoot/ psychic (psi) encounters. Most experiences are with mental telepathy and 17 percent of encounters involved witnessing ETs, spaceships, or interdimensionalism in conjunction with the Sasquatch contact. Plus, Kelly and I have had astral visits from the Sasquatch, and on occasion, different races of Star People over the years. Our goal has always been to unveil the truth behind this phenomenon, not to exploit or acquire empirical proof which pushes the beings away from a researcher, reducing one's percentages of having a meaningful encounter.

I have discovered that the Sasquatch are more human than we are. They do not start wars; they do not pollute the planet; nor do they kill friends or members of their family. We, as a society, have a lot to learn from them. The only monsters I know are those people who are trying to hunt and harass them. Some people would murder a Sasquatch even though they do not know who or what they are killing. The forest giants are interdimensional hairy people and do not have fur like animals. The Sasquatch can dematerialize to elude hunters, plus can walk through a portal, an invisible door that leads to another world layered on top of our limited three-dimensional one.

The precise reason all the "experts" have been stymied after nearly 60 years of intense searching is because researchers are looking for an animal that doesn't exist. The Sasquatch People are a hundred times more intelligent than so-called modern man. The prejudice toward these hairy people is appalling and disgraceful. If one doesn't understand it, don't kill it—befriend it instead without the negative monster label. That is what Kelly and I did. This peaceful, non-threatening field methodology has been working successfully for 35 years now. Like attracts like. This is a truism with sensitive Sasquatch research.

Camera and gun-free Sasquatch research

My wife and I have observed both ETs and Sasquatch together. Contactees Andrew Robson and Todd Michael have also experienced the psychic Sasquatch with an ET/UFO connection. There are hundreds of more experiencers from around the world that contact me to tell of their encounters as well. The Sasquatch People continue to clandestinely help contactees in a friendly manner. In turn, the four of us and many others publicly speak the truth concerning who and what the forest beings really are. Psychic communication is the KEY. No guns or hidden cameras or negative emotions allowed. Unwittingly, on an unconscious level, a person telepaths to a Sasquatch while planning an expedition forewarning the man-creature that the hunter is coming. Harboring fear is also detrimental. So why not wittingly telepath friendly emotions without being conditional or having a selfish motive? Anyone who tries to trick them will not have another chance. The forest giants command respect with their profound psychic ability. They are the ones in control, not us. These profoundly evolved nature people can master several facets in the application of quantum physics. Some can even shapeshift. The manipulation of psi in relation to the physical world is the forest people's greatest survival skill used to evade hostile, not-so-modern man.

In June 1983, while on an expedition in central Wisconsin, a Sasquatch told me telepathically that a spaceship would be letting off some of his people in two days between 11 PM and 1 AM. Since I had to be back to work in Milwaukee, I asked the family I was staying with not to tell anyone else about the Sasquatch's message. However, they told all their friends and neighbors! Several people in two cars drove the back roads looking for anything unusual. Shortly after midnight, while rounding a bend in the road, a glowing spaceship was observed in a field by 11 witnesses. The craft suddenly shot vertically into the night-time sky and disappeared. As the beam of lights from the second car pulled up behind the first one, an eight to 10-foot-tall Sasquatch was seen ambling into the woods from where the ship had initially landed. Later, I interviewed every witness separately and received exactly the same detailed information with a lot of charged emotions while describing the event.

Sasquatch healers

The Bigfoot/UFO connection is not a theory or concept but is based on three and a half decades of documentation, plus my ongoing, personal encounters. Most experiences are psychic in nature and involve telepathic communication about healings, the importance of resolving karma, instructions for writing books for them, instructions for a more effective approach to meditation used by ETs, sharing of certain healing practices, and patiently giving wise spiritual counseling.

In early 2012, I was diagnosed with a brain tumor. When I told my Sasquatch guide about my malady, he prescribed a specific herbal formula. Then he told our friends, the Star People, so they could speed up the healing process. The Star Beings took me six times, and after a few months, I was completely healed. My relationship with these interdimensional people has always been positive and symbiotic.

In May 1989, a man called me at 2:50 AM to say that his wife was dying of an asthmatic attack. For four days, the exhausted woman could barely breathe, and could not eat, sleep, or talk since the episode greatly weakened and debilitated her. The distressed woman had been to a medical doctor, a naturopathic physician, an acupuncturist, even took medicinal herbs with still no results. While I was driving through the wilderness to visit this woman, a Sasquatch telepathed to me that he heard the phone conversation from the husband in despair. I asked him for help in saving the woman's life. He told me that he was above me in a ship with some of his people and with ETs, that I was not to worry and they would assist me in a shamanic ritual.

After arriving at the ailing woman's home, I asked her husband to shut the door and not disturb us. The sight of the young, dying woman scared me. As I prayed and spiritually prepared for the ritual, two ETs and three Sasquatch appeared behind me in a semi-circle. When I reached out to touch the woman, an intense electrical energy shot through my system as if it was sent from a powerful vibrator. To my amazement, the woman let out a gentle sigh and instantly began to breathe normally.

She still appeared exhausted and her eyes were sunken into her head after days of laborious breathing and not eating, but she was able to take a normal, life-giving breath. She was healed! Her husband was elated. I never told him what actually occurred in the room. His wife was in a semi-conscious state and had no knowledge that I was a mere conduit, and that my interdimensional friends were the source of her healing with God's help.

A year later, I met the same woman while grocery shopping. She looked healthy and happy. Previously, she had two to three asthmatic attacks a month. Surprisingly, she reported that she no longer has asthma or any respiratory problems whatsoever. My kindly ET friends used me to save another person's life. They are hardly anyone to fear, and they don't deserve to be hunted. All my encounters with them have always been loving, insightful, and profound.

Portal travelers

The day after my wife and I received communication from the forest people while camping, we investigated a portal deep in the forest. I have discovered that they use these portals for safety as they are doorways to a parallel world. In the past, I have camped beside four different portals, and at night, I would hear both heavy footfalls from the Sasquatch People as well as a strange unintelligible language.

When Kelly and I approached the portal on July 8, 2014, we discovered a 13-inch Sasquatch track. Within minutes, a female forest being named Tamala appeared and began a conversation with my wife. She explained that she was the mate of Chief Sissesqua. Their tribe (as they describe themselves) inhabited the area. Then two small hairy children peeked from behind a tree. They looked at us apprehensively. Suddenly, there was the loud sound of four-wheelers somewhere on the rugged dirt road echoing behind us. The youngsters quickly withdrew in fear. But the mother nonchalantly told them, "It's okay, it's just a couple of rednecks making noise." This remark humored us both. When Kelly inquired about Tamala's use of the work "redneck," she was told that they have heard this word from humans. The forest giants use it as a descriptive word to explain human behavior and characteristics rather than as an insult. They liken the word "redneck" to our use of the word "bigfoot" to describe their race. Of course, to them, their feet are normal just as exhibiting destructive behavior is normal to humans.

I was taken twice through a portal but cannot remember what I experienced. The giants said they took me through to their world but brought me back at the exact same time as if the experience never happened. The beings said that I was given knowledge that will be revealed at another time. This somewhat frustrated me as I was unable to report on my visit. This event took place in Oklahoma in March 2006. Just before they took me, I counted 12 spaceships over a two-hour period. One of them was at treetop level, about 60 or 70 yards behind my camp.

Unbeknownst to me, on that very same night, two turkey hunters were camped in the forest approximately 100 yards behind me. At 4:45 in the morning, while making coffee, the two woodsmen became scared out of their wits when a spaceship was seen slowly gliding over the tree tops heading straight for them. When it stopped directly above them, sending down an intense beam of light, the two men scrambled for their camper and went speeding down the road. As they came around a curve, they were shocked to view a 10-foot-tall Sasquatch standing right in front of them! They were driving too fast to stop. Just as they were about to collide, the man-creature turned and faced them... then faded, disappearing into another dimension.

In essence, their vehicle drove right through the hairy man. There are many more psychic and paranormal encounters with a UFO connection occurring all over North America, but the majority of experiencers are not talking publicly for fear of ridicule. William James said, "It takes only one white crow to prove that not all crows are black." I have documented 277 white crows! That's not empirical proof, but it is strong evidence not to be ignored.

In 1989, in Northwest coastal Oregon, I interviewed a woman who lived with her family on an isolated ranch. The witness stated that during the daytime hours, a spaceship landed in her driveway. Previously, the Sasquatch People had talked to her several times, but she was afraid of ETs. The woman built up her courage and stepped outside. The witness said there were no visible windows or doors on the craft. Then, like magic, she was standing in front of an open door on the ship. A pleasant-looking, human-like figure stepped forward. He told her not to be afraid. The witness was startled to see a Sasquatch standing several feet behind the ET, inside the craft. The incident was reported to the Mutual UFO Network (MUFON) for documentation. How many more percipients have had these profound encounters but are not sharing their stories?

Seeking the wrong creature

Conservative Bigfoot researchers are still in denial of a psychic Sasquatch with a connection to UFOs. They remain busy looking for a monster that does not exist, which is precisely why all the experts have not progressed in their research for more than a half century. Aggression pushes the forest people away. A kind and loving heart attracts them. I have seen fear and hostile intent in people which received a negative response from the forest giants. Because I have been personally contacted by the hairy people well over a thousand times in 35 years, and intermittently have visitations from seven different races of Star People, I can emphatically state that the Sasquatch People are indeed terrestrial-extraterrestrials! Yet, my primary concern is the importance of the message behind the phenomenon. These beings advocate forgiving others, walking in unconditional love and stop destroying the planet, going to war, and harming each other.

Sasquatch researchers should become more creative by revamping their field methodology to something more viable, friendly, and realistic without guns and cameras. Whatever a person is holding onto in their heart, whether it be positive or negative thoughts, that is precisely what they are unconsciously projecting to these sentient beings. Everything must be done with integrity if there is to be success. This research is heartfelt and highly sensitive. When I became too analytical and intellectual, my woodsy friends would say, "Little brother, get out of your head and back into your heart." Both the Sasquatch People and Star People operate strictly from a heart space. From this perspective, the crypto-anthropologists, ufologists, paranormalists, cryptozoologists, and all aficionados would benefit from synthesizing and revising their concepts to a more evolved, non-violent approach if we are to progress into the next stage of an altruistic and compassionate society worthy of being called "human."

Kewaunee Lapseritis, AS, BA, MS: Holistic health consultant, master herbalist and master dowser with background in anthropology, psychology, conservation, and holistic health. He is a noted Sasquatch researcher and experiencer, and author of numerous articles and the books The Psychic Sasquatch *and* The Sasquatch People.

FATE 726

Interdimensional Paraphysical Sasquatch

Rosemary Ellen Guiley

Encountering Sasquatch was not on Joe Burcaw's radar the day he went hiking in one of his favorite areas in the Litchfield Hills in southwestern Connecticut. In fact, he had no interest in looking for Sasquatch. That day in 2012 changed everything.

It was late October, the day after hurricane Sandy had battered Connecticut. Burcaw, who lived in New York City, took a run up to Litchfield County to check on his family members who were living there. Curious to see the storm damage from the high winds and rain in his favorite haunts in the hills, he decided to go out for a hike.

Burcaw grew up near the Litchfield Hills, and had been hiking, mountain biking, and cross country skiing in the area since the 1980s. He was intimately familiar with the terrain.

He arrived at one of his favorite spots in the mid- to late afternoon. His destination was an old abandoned mining tunnel deep in the woods. The storm devastation he found was difficult to absorb. Huge, majestic cedar trees were toppled over like toothpicks snapped in half, and water floods from a river spread all over the walking trails.

The damage hindered his progress, and it took him longer than usual to reach the old mining tunnel. The woods here always felt strange and eerie—one of the attractions for him. The place had never been very active with wildlife and always gave off a sense that something invisible was watching and observing. Burcaw had experienced times when the birds and insects went from vibrant to complete silence for hours.

Today the environment felt stranger than usual. There was absolute silence, and it was uncanny, almost unsettling.

For some reason, Burcaw kept feeling the urge to look down. He did so and noticed the multitude of leaves covering the muddy path leading into the tunnel. Something struck his attention. Curious, he wiped away leaves, and uncovered what looked like a footprint—but this was no ordinary footprint.

Joe Burcaw compares his size 11 shoe to one of the mystery prints. Credit: Joe Burcaw.

His first thought was that it was not a human boot print from someone who got out there investigating before him. He took a closer look, and then knew without a doubt that the print was not human-made at all. It was much larger than his size 11 shoe, maybe a size 15. Even stranger, there were no other prints near it, just the single footprint, as though dropped from space.

Burcaw fished out his flip phone camera and snapped a few shots so that he could blow them up for a more detailed look when he got home. Seconds after he finished taking the photos, wood knocking sounded somewhere out in the distance, and a "god awful" screeching echoed throughout the entire valley. It sounded like a dog or some sort of animal in distress. Another 20 seconds later, a large tree fell over on the side of the valley opposite the screeching.

Alarmed, and not sure what was happening, Burcaw decided to get the hell out. He put his camera away and headed at a quick pace back to where he had parked his car, some distance away. He was acutely aware that suddenly dusk was closing in, and the sky was darkening rapidly. He picked up his pace, blood pumping.

The screeching continued along with the wood knocking but subsided as he drew close to his vehicle. He flung open the door and slid inside, flooded with relief and the odd thought that he was lucky to have gotten there in one piece. Never before, in all the years that he had spent time alone and with friends in these woods, had he encountered something so mysterious and frightening.

On that day, a door to an alternate reality opened for Joe Burcaw, never to close. Sasquatch had introduced itself, and it had a purpose.

Up until then, Burcaw had believed in the existence of Sasquatch, even though he had no compunction to search them out. They deserved human respect and to be left alone, in his view. Now he was on *their* radar. From then on for years, wood knocks greeted him whenever he entered the forest by himself.

In early November 2012, less than a week after his initial encounter with an unseen Sasquatch, a light snow fell, leaving behind a few inches on the ground. Burcaw was still visiting his family and decided to go back up to the woods. This time, he was fully prepared with cameras and video units. It was a reasonable idea to try to capture evidence. As he would soon learn, however, Sasquatch do not appreciate attempts at photography. They make themselves known on their own terms, not on human terms.

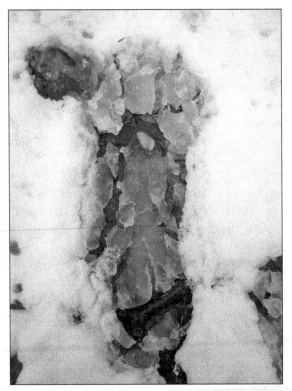

Mystery print appears to have talons. Credit: Joe Burcaw.

Burcaw arrived at the trail and had made it halfway to the old mining tunnel when he saw different tracks in the snow that he could recognize as human. The tracks were single and had no pairing whatsoever. He knew what bear and cougar tracks looked like, and these were not made by those animals. Some of the tracks looked bipedal, with large talons sticking out of the toes. Other tracks defied identification.

Burcaw pulled out his camera and took some pictures. Immediately, he was overcome by a rush of dread and a pounding headache, as though something or someone was shooting fear into his body. A thought rose in his mind that he was trespassing, and some species of Sasquatch was sending the message that it wanted him to get out on the spot. He wasted no time jamming his belongings in his pack, and then jogged back to his car.

There was no apparent pursuit—at least in physical terms. What happened next ramped up the high strangeness index in Burcaw's life.

A few nights later, he had a vision or astral projection in the early morning hours while sleeping. It was one of those intense, lucid dream-like experiences, in which a person feels awake and the experience is "real," not a dream.

"I was completely coherent and present," said Burcaw. "It was almost as though I was in complete control, yet someone else was invading my personal space, causing me to feel violated and out of control. It's hard to put into words, but it wasn't a comforting situation by any means."

An out of the ordinary scenario unfolded right before him. Burcaw found himself back in his childhood neighborhood in Litchfield County, Connecticut. He was not in his own home, but in the home of a childhood friend, and he was staring out his friend's bedroom window. An Asian woman who looked to be in her late fifties was running frantically, as though for her life, across the front lawn. Two disc-shaped craft came into view and hovered, switching from a horizontal position to a vertical position. The craft then landed behind trees across the street, close to where the woman was fleeing. Then two black SUVs pulled up close to the house, and two men stepped out of the trucks. They carried weapons that looked like old-fashioned sub machine guns beneath their long trench coats. The guns reminded Burcaw of those from the gangster era in the early 20th century.

The men—who Burcaw felt were Men in Black, wore white surgical masks on their faces, obscuring their features. He could see, however, that their skin was not human-looking, but had a blue tint. One MIB wore a beige trench coat and the other wore a black trench. They were obviously in hot pursuit of the Asian woman—they meant business.

Burcaw, still in this alternate reality, started to feel panicky and felt the urge to throw himself under a bed for cover. There was one near him in the bedroom. Just as he slid under the bed, he heard footsteps enter in the room and saw two sets of legs stand directly in front of him. His adrenaline was pumping as he wondered frantically what he should do.

The two MIB spoke to each other about the woman, and where they should search next for her. She evidently possessed information they did not want disclosed to the public. Burcaw prayed they would not look under the bed. They did not seem to be in pursuit of him, but he was certain they were aware of his existence.

The weird experience ended.

After he awakened, Burcaw puzzled over it. It seemed dream-like, but it was a "100 percent real" experience, and he was in complete control of his actions. He soon contacted author and investigator Nick Redfern, who told him that he had heard of similar experiences from others.

There was much more to come. There were no more MIB visits, but black helicopters occasionally buzzed his home. In 2015, Burcaw moved back to Connecticut, not far from where he grew up, and the helicopters continued to show up. There is no pattern to them, and as of this writing, their frequency was declining.

I asked Burcaw for his interpretation of the MIB "dream" experience. Was it a warning?

"The MIB experience was a scare tactic of what could happen to me if I pursue investigating the Bigfoot," he said. "Our government and secret government have a boat-load of information about Bigfoot that they want kept quiet from the general public."

He said he protected himself from the MIB with white light and a high spiritual energy. "The MIB have no consciousness and cannot function if confronted with the Christ figure or angelic realm," Burcaw said. "They see that world as a threat and therefore back off if someone is strong enough to deflect their harassment. I told them to f-- off and to never contact me again. I possess a stronger constitution than they thought, because I know who they are, and what they do to people with their bullshit intimidation tactics. I haven't seen or heard from them since. The black helicopters buzzing my condo have diminished, too, at least for the time being."

With the intimidation halted in the early stages, other paranormal activity with Sasquatch increased. Burcaw began having more encounters with them when he went into the woods alone. As these encounters increased, the incidences of wood knocking decreased. A new type of apparent surveillance began—white planes hovering over him when he went into the woods.

The Sasquatch are "in the astral world," Burcaw said. "I have seen 95 percent of my sightings of Bigfoot through the dream state, yet I have complete control of my body and actions while having the experience," he said. "My first sighting was of a large male hiding behind a robust oak tree, sticking its head out and peeking at me from 10-20 yards away. I was on a path leading out to a field where this single tree was located. This was an observation scenario, some sort of test to see how I would react." The field reminded him of a field behind a house in his childhood neighborhood.

On another occasion, he witnessed a "youngling" accidentally falling out of a tree. "The youngling, who I caught out of the corner of my eye, was completely embarrassed," he said. "Initially, I heard a loud tree branch snap, and then had the image of it falling to the ground with a thump. I saw a dark figure for a brief second before it phased out and disappeared. My feeling was that the youngling broke a rule by getting too close to me—a human—and had to get back home before he was reprimanded by his elders."

Sometimes the Sasquatch would phase in and out like the rippled presence of Predator in the film by the same title.

Evidently, Burcaw passed the tests with the Sasquatch, for in mid-2016, his encounters took a new and dramatic turn, involving visits to spacecraft and being in the presence of Sasquatch and aliens.

"I made communication with a male clan leader named Girdock, who asked for my help in healing his wounded father," Burcaw said. "I was aboard a spacecraft with Girdock, his life partner, and son. There were high-ranking humanoid Pleiadians with us, too, assisting in the healing. The four-foot greys were operating on the wounded Bigfoot. They wore surgical attire that was all in white, and they used rod-like devices to heal the wounds. I could sense from their thoughts that they needed universal loving consciousness for this operation to be a success. The elder leader did make it out alive and was very loving and appreciative for our help. He had white hair and reminded me of the abominable snow man. He was very weak from his surgery and wounds and needed to rest."

Burcaw said that until space craft experience, his Sasquatch encounters had been with males. The female life partner of Girdock was the first encounter he had with a female.

"I asked Girdock why I haven't seen them in the past, and he explained that they're highly protective of the female population from

Alien greys and humanoid Pleaidians heal the wounded father of Sasquatch leader Girdock aboard a UFO. Credit: Chris Forthofer.

the outside human world," Burcaw said. "You have to earn their trust as an outsider to have contact with the women, which is almost never. They're attracted to higher consciousness, and I have displayed this since I was a child."

This brings in another facet of meaningful contact with Sasquatch shared by many experiencers: a history of otherworldly experiences and contact from an early age. Some individuals have an inborn, heightened capability of attracting and interacting with beings and spirits. From childhood, they experience ghosts, visitations from the dead, spirit contact, UFO sightings, anomalous creature sightings, and more. I have seen this across the board in my research in the paranormal, cryptids, ufology, and metaphysics fields. Not everyone who has a contact experience shares this life-history trait, but a significant number do. Burcaw is in this category: a frequent experiencer of the paranormal and extraordinary from a young age.

Such individuals are described as having an "encounter-prone personality," a term put forward by Dr. Kenneth Ring, a leading near-death experience (NDE) researcher, in 1990 and in 1992 in his book *The Omega Project*. Encounter-prone individuals dissociate more easily than others, and once they have unusual experiences, are more open to having them in the future. Encounter-prone individuals also tend to have heightened intuitive/psychic and artistic abilities. Thus, they may be more open to intrusions of alternate realities, which, for them, are natural extensions of this reality.

Many experiencers feel they were chosen for contact. Do other beings and spirits take note of certain individuals, watch them, and then contact them? Burcaw is certain of that concerning the Sasquatch: They watched over him for years without him knowing it. Around 2012, he underwent a significant shift in spiritual development—and contact was initiated on that trip into the woods after Sandy.

"They have contacted me for a reason, why I am not sure as of yet," said Burcaw. "On separate occasions, I have left them fruits and cakes as a token of my appreciation and was left in return (days later) a single quartz crystal off the side of a trail, sitting on a log. I have always felt a close connection to the Sasquatch and hope someday to be able to converse with them on a consistent basis. I am not afraid but curious and hope my encounters will lead me toward more hidden discoveries. I have yet to see them face to face in this realm but hope that will change with time."

Paraphysical characteristics

Burcaw has plenty of company. While most reported Sasquatch "events" are fleeting sightings and contacts, there are an increasing number of people coming forward with accounts of paraphysical characteristics, and intelligent and meaningful interaction with sophisticated beings.

Paraphysical and paranormal characteristics of Sasquatch encounters also are widely reported in sightings and encounters with dogmen, mystery cats, assorted other cryptids, aliens and extraterrestrials, Black-Eyed People, Men and Women in Black, faeries, and even the Djinn—in short, other beings and entities that humans have encountered throughout the ages in a variety of forms. The most commonly reported are:

- Telepathic communication

- Sudden, unexplained appearance (possible materialization)

- Sudden, unexplained disappearance into thin air or into solid matter (possible dematerialization)

- Disappearance in flashes of light

- Rapid movement, including instant relocation (possible tele-portation)

- Isolated footprints, sometimes single, that suddenly end

- Observed walking in snow, but leaves no footprints

- Appears to float or glide rather than walk

- Invisibility or cloaking

- Shape-shifting, as though the form is not definite or "completely in" our dimension

- Appears to be impervious to bullets

- Deliberate eye contact that conveys intelligence and telepathic messages

And in some cases:

- Feelings of being constantly watched or tracked after an initial encounter

- Additional encounters, as though the person has been "tagged"

- Subsequent paranormal activity in the home, and/or bedroom experiences

- Synchronistic UFO sightings and activity, or other cryptid or entity encounters

These characteristics do not occur in all cases, perhaps not even in a majority of them—but they occur with enough frequency to indicate that something other than encounters with "normal" animals or species is afoot. Yet, some cryptid investigators resolutely cling to their convictions that Sasquatch and other strange entities are nothing more than "lost" or "hidden" physical Earth species, despite the fact that encounters with lions, bears, birds, and other denizens of wild Earth are not accompanied by a raft of high strangeness.

Paul Johnson, a Pennsylvania Sasquatch researcher, observes in his book *Chasing the Elusive Pennsylvania Bigfoot* (2018), "There is no doubt that the Pennsylvania Bigfoot is real…The problem is that our Bigfoot simply does not possess the same properties as the other indigenous Pennsylvania animals."

It is difficult, if not impossible, to know the true incidence of paraphysical Sasquatch contacts. Experiencers still fear ridicule, and so remain silent. And, biased researchers, including organizations, disregard or discredit reports pointing to an intelligent, interdimensional being with telepathic power and connections to UFO activity. Other researchers, looking for "politically correct" ground to stand on, offer such reports and data but take an "I don't know what's going on" position. Native Americans, on the other hand, (as discussed later on in this article) have had no discomfort accepting the existence of interdimensional, paraphysical Sasquatch.

Can science explain?

Does science have an explanation for beings such as Sasquatch, and for our experiences with them? There are two that address aspects of Sasquatch encounters, but neither offers "official" scientific proof of the existence of the beings. However, they do point in the direction of the paraphysical and interdimensional.

In physics, M Theory, also known as "many worlds," posits that there are dimensions, or "branes," stacked together in our universe, each vibrating at different frequencies. Most of the time, they are "invisible" to one another. There is interaction between branes, or parallel worlds, under certain conditions, such as leakage or bleed-throughs. These openings are "portals," akin to hot spots on the planet where all manner of sightings, encounters and paranormal activity is heightened or ongoing.

The Quantum Hologram Theory (QHT) posits that there is an underlying quantum reality that embraces both the physical and the paraphysical—they are flip sides of the same coin. Most encounters take place in a shifted or alternate reality, such as the lucid dream state.

Experiencers also describe time standing still or expanding or being thrust into some sort of "matrix reality" that is Earth but is not. Suddenly everything around them feels "weird" and there is a cessation of normal noise, including bird, insect and animal life.

The QHT provides a model for nonlocal consciousness. It holds that the universe is not a three-dimensional spatial construct, but a four-dimensional construct, including time. It is holographic in nature. When a person is in a high state of resonance with the quantum whole, extraordinary events can occur, such as telepathy, out-of-body projection, teleportation, and so on.

The UFO connection
A connection exists between Sasquatch sightings and UFO activity: The two sometimes happen in conjunction with each other, or both happen repeatedly in the same areas. This connection does not occur in the majority of Sasquatch reports, but it does happen often enough to raise questions about the meaning of it. For example, researcher Stan Gordon documented many cases of overlapping Sasquatch and UFO activity in Pennsylvania in 1973-74, as noted in his book *Silent Invasion: The Pennsylvania UFO-Bigfoot Casebook* (2010). A few years earlier, John Keel documented Sasquatch reports along with the UFO activity, encounters with ETs, and other high strangeness that occurred during the Mothman flap in Point Pleasant, West Virginia, in 1966-67.

Other leading Sasquatch researchers have also noted the connection, although few explanations have been put forward by either cryptid or UFO investigators. It's a hot potato, and few want touch it. That's understandable, given the interdimensional characteristics of UFO and ET contact: craft and beings that phase in and out of physical reality and move through solid matter; communication via telepathy; supernormal abilities exhibited by alien beings; and experiences that happen in "matrix" realities involving altered states of consciousness.

Contact for transformation
Surveys of experiencers and contactees, such as the global survey undertaken by The Edgar Mitchell Foundation for Research into Extraterrestrial and Extraordinary Encounters (FREE), released in 2015, reveal a host of paranormal and paraphysical phenomena associated with all kinds of entity and UFO contacts, including Sasquatch-like beings,

along with ETs, "energy beings," and others. Sasquatch-like beings comprise about 14 percent of the beings cited by the study experiencers. The bulk are energy beings, short and tall greys, and humanoids, followed by reptilians, and insectoids.

The implications of contact point to marked psycho-spiritual and physical changes in the experiencers that are in line with the kundalini awakenings described in yoga, which lead to enlightened states of consciousness. In fact, experiencers say the purposes of contact are the resulting transformations in themselves: a greater awareness of the connectedness of all things, and the importance of "love and oneness."

The phenomena and messages described in the FREE study are no strangers to Kewaunee Lapseritis, the leading advocate of the psychic, ET and paraphysical natures of Sasquatch, and their roles in human development. Lapseritis, a holistic health consultant, master herbalist and master dowser, was contacted simultaneously by a Sasquatch and ET in 1979. He developed psychic ability overnight and underwent a spiritual transformation. Since then, he has fostered deep relationships with Sasquatch, described in his books *The Psychic Sasquatch* (2015) and *The Sasquatch People and Their Interdimensional Connection* (2011). He stresses the importance of learning telepathy and teaches it to individuals who are sincere about having a meaningful contact. Th beings respond to those with an open heart and sincerity.

The Native American viewpoint

Lapseritis also has a close relationship with Native Americans, many of whom regard Sasquatch as paraphysical beings—spiritual or interdimensional—who have great psychic powers. Not all Native Americans see Bigfoot as interdimensional—in the Pacific Northwest, he is regarded as a physical creature. Elsewhere across North America, Bigfoot resides in another world, and enters the world of human beings to teach, protect, and warn. Bigfoot is an "elder brother" to people, not an animal, monster, or mysterious creature.

The otherworldly nature of Sasquatch is accepted by many Native American peoples, who consider Sasquatch as much a part of the Earth as humans—although they have superior abilities, such as invisibility, psychic powers, shape-shifting, and more. Such beliefs are found among diverse peoples as the Hopi, Sioux, Iroquois, Northern Athabascan, Athapascan, Lakota, and Dakota.

The Objibway and Algonquin identify Sasquatch with the Windigo or Ho-Chunk, the evil human spirit turned cannibalistic monster.

Messengers for change

According to Lapseritis, as well as Native American lore, one of Sasquatch's purposes is as a messenger to humanity, specifically to convey warnings about our destructive ways. They urge humanity to mend its ways or face disaster. Their messages include the need to have more respect for the Earth, to get rid of wicked and evil behavior, to live in peace and harmony, and to get back on the spiritual track. From that perspective, they are the spiritual protectors of the land, a concept found universally in mythology. Every people and nation have protectors who appear in times of distress to want and help restore order.

Lapseritis states that Sasquatch have been increasing their appearances worldwide since 2000 with this purpose in mind. They make use of their psychic network to communicate with humans everywhere:

> They want to sensitize the public and validate that they do indeed exist and are a part of our physical world. They have also repeatedly said that if man continues at the rate of destruction of the biosphere, with our dysfunctional and socio-political behavior and blasé attitude toward ecological issues, then all races—including humanity—are doomed. To save the planet is to save ourselves as well as our Sasquatch neighbors... The Sasquatch will help show us the way, if we would only seek out their wisdom from our hearts, not with a gun or just the intellect.

To that end, Kelly Lapseritis, Kewaunee's wife, has been working with DawahOuta LomaKatski (Sunbow TrueBrother, or Sunbow), to publish Sunbow's extensive channeled messages from Kamooh, a Sasquatch Elder Brother, which he began receiving in May 2015.

According to Kamooh, both humans and Sasquatch were bioengineered by Star Elders. Sasquatch came first, and then helped humans to adapt to this world.

We were also gifted with powerful psychic abilities that we have kept to this day including telepathy, mind reading, remote viewing, hypnosis, astral projection, dematerialization, teleportation, shape shifting and permeating consciousness. This last ability allows us to impregnate an area and surround entities with our soul. So we might be perceived as interdimensional beings, but in reality we are an incarnated species with highly developed psychic powers like none other from this home-planet.

The channelings are detailed and extensive about the history of Earth and how Sasquatch have been greatly reduced in numbers due to the actions of humans. In reaching out to select persons, Sasquatch, in concert with the Star Elders, have been providing teachings on interdimensionality through psychic experiences, dreams, astral travels and information downloads.

Lapseritis and other contactees hold that the Sasquatch will continue to avoid the "bag a Bigfoot" hunter types bristling with guns and gear, and instead seek out individuals with a more receptive and refined consciousness. According to Sunbow (December 7, 2015), Sasquatch do not seek to be photographed or have their DNA identified, because they sense, through remote viewing of humans, how this evidence will be misused and manipulated.

The only approach to study Sasquatch that really seems to bring some genuine results is to see them for who they are: an ancient highly spiritual Elder Brother. This means to stop seeing them as animals or primitive hominids that we could trick or trap for curiosity.

But the scientists and Humanity in general will never understand Sasquatch until they think outside of the box and feel existence beyond the limitating [sic] materialist mind frame. Interdimensional beings prove by their existence that there are other planes or dimensional levels of existence where other intelligent life forms dwell. It also reminds us that we too are interdimensional beings

185

but have forgotten and lost most of our psychic abilities and perceptions, getting trapped in the physical 3D because of materialism.

The supernormal abilities of Sasquatch can be mastered by human beings. As mentioned earlier, in yoga, intense spiritual development and training through meditation and spiritual practices raise the kundalini force, a psycho-spiritual energy that lies dormant in most people. When activated, it energizes the chakra system and expands consciousness. The *siddhis* are byproducts: psychic powers, psychokinetic powers (ability to influence matter), teleportation, bilocation, and the ability to make one's self invisible by changing the "vibration" of the body, to cite a few. Sasquatch is ahead of our game, having developed these abilities long before us. Developing and using these powers wisely requires advanced spiritualized consciousness.

Meaningful research and advancement of knowledge about Sasquatch will remain mired if researchers refuse to look beyond the physical for explanations. Investigators need to stop equivocating and fence-sitting when it comes to the mounting paraphysical evidence. "I don't know" is not an answer. It's doubtful we know everything—but we need to make a start. We need to put ideas, possible explanations, and hypotheses on the table, and then follow the data into new directions. For those who choose to go bravely into explorations, a wealth of discoveries awaits.

[A version of this article appeared in Woodknocks II, *published by Leprechaun Press in 2017.]*

Rosemary Ellen Guiley: FATE *Executive Editor; researcher and author of more than 65 books.*

2019

HAIRY HOMINIDS IN LATIN AMERICA

Scott Corrales

It is possible that the man-apes variously known as Sasquatch, Yeti, Ukumari, and so on constitute the greatest and best-known variety of mystery creature, and the only kind whose study has received a tacit nod from officialdom. Anthropologists have even gone as far as establishing its identity as the *Gigantopithecus*, an anthropoidal creature that may have survived into modern times by keeping clear of *Homo sapiens*. The historic record contains mentions of these beings, such as that they were used by the ancient Medes and Persians as ferocious battle animals, and that Nearchos, Alexander the Great's admiral, encountered communities of these creatures on the barren shores of the Persian Gulf. The historian Arrian, whose *Anabasis Alexandri (Indica)* was translated by E. Iliff Robson in 1933, mentions that as the Greek admiral headed westward, his galleys hugging the shore of the Asiatic landmass, he came upon a remarkable and terrifying group of natives.

When anchored by the River Tomerus (its modern location unknown), the returning Macedonians found "a lagoon at the mouth of the river" whose natives dwelt in recesses near the bank, occupying "stifling cabins." The natives, having never seen ships, took an offensive stance: Arrian states that, ignorant of metals, they nonetheless wielded fire-hardened spears. The war galleys fired a volley of stones and arrows against them, and the primitives proved no match against the Macedonians, fresh from their victories along the Indus. But what is of interest to us isn't the prowess of Nearchos' forces, but the description of the 600 or so primitives:

> *Some were killed in flight; others were captured; but some escaped into the hills. Those captured were hairy, not only their heads but the rest of their bodies; their nails were rather like beasts' claws; they used their nails (according to report) as if they were iron tools; with these they tore asunder their fishes, and even the less solid kinds of wood; everything else they cleft with sharp stones; for iron they did not possess. For clothing they wore skins of animals, some even the thick skins of the larger fishes.*

The rough technology evinced by these hirsute primitives—tropical versions of the Toonijuk or Tunnit who reputedly lived in Greenland and Bylot Island in ages past—is also found in descriptions of the Maricoxis, bestial creatures confronted by the ill-fated explorer Colonel H.P. Fawcett in the early 20th century while surveying the Matto Grosso. Fawcett's description of the Maricoxis, as "great apelike brutes who looked as if they had scarcely evolved beyond the level of beasts" would not have been out of place in Admiral Nearchos' log. The Maricoxis were considered primitive even by the standards of other primitive tribes, despite the fact that they wielded bows and arrows.

Arrian mentions that the number of primitives who attacked the Macedonians stood at approximately 600. Did the ones that escaped, assuming both males and females, retreat to the mountains of what is today northern Pakistan, moving on into what are now the modern republics of Central Asia (Kazakhstan, Turkmenistan, Tadzhikistan, etc.) to give rise to the legend of the Almasti?

Mexico's ancient hairy hominids

One of these early chroniclers of Mexico's history, Fernando Alva Ixtlilxochitl, mentions in his book *Obras Históricas* the widespread belief that the Chichimecs, the earliest occupants of what is now Mexico, had to displace an old race of giants that lived there. This echoes not only the Biblical displacement of giants from Canaan by the advancing Hebrews, but other traditions surrounding the elimination of giants from Britain by a Trojan warrior named Brutus. The presence of these ancient colossi would thus account for the persistent discovery of abnormally large remains. Ixtlilxochitl also mentions the wars between the giants known as Quinametzin and normal-sized humans.

Memory of the Quinametzin was widespread throughout Mesoamerica, as can be seen from the information gleaned by Spanish explorers and colonizers. Bernal Diaz del Castillo, who accompanied Hernán Cortés on his conquest of the Aztec Empire, wrote of a belief among the Tlaxcalan people that "their ancestors had shared the land with men and women of very tall bodies and large bones, and since they were very wicked and ill mannered, [the ancestors] slew them in combat, and what remained of them died out."

Other information turned up by early missionaries is also quite intriguing. Fray Diego Durán claimed to have seen the bones "of immense giants" excavated "out of rough places." Fray Gerónimo de Mendieta was told by the older natives that their predecessors had been forced to struggle against giants, "and after this land was won, the bones of many tall men were found." Bernardo de Sahagún, the great Franciscan missionary, would be the first to suggest that the pyramids of Teothihuacan and Cholula were the handiwork of the vanished giant race.

Wherever the conquistadors went, more stories were added to the body of information concerning these creatures. When the rapacious Nuno de Guzman reached what is today Jalisco, he demanded to know from the natives why a number of towns had been abandoned. They informed him that the towns had been inhabited by a band of giants who had come up from the south.

There was to be no peaceful coexistence between the Quinametzin and the newly-arrived humans, who called them *quinametzin hueytlacame* ("huge deformed men" or "monstrous giants"). The advancing human tribes (tentatively identified as Olmecs

189

and Toltecs) drove the giants out of their ancestral domain, causing some of them to flee to the north and others to the south, following the Pacific coastline down to Central America. Fray José Mariano Rothea, a Jesuit, sums up this belief as follows: "In very ancient times there came men and women of extraordinary height, seemingly in flight from the North. Some of them went along the coast of the Southern Sea, while others took to the rough mountainsides." Fray Andrés de Olmos, writing in the 16th century, mentions a curious detail: the Mexican giants nourished themselves on oak acorns and a variety of weeds. This detail contained in the codexes enables us to contemplate a strange possibility: could the quinametzin have survived into our present age under the guise of the tall, hirsute simian beings known as Bigfoot, Yeti, Sasquatch, and myriad other denominations? Those interviewed by the Colonial-era chroniclers explained that tradition held that those giants who were not exterminated by normal-sized humans were chased into the wilderness, where remnants of their race still endure.

Marc Dern, the French author of a number of works on the paranormal, has identified the Biblical Anakim with giant beings such as the Asian Yeti. Is there any evidence that such a race of giants actually existed south of the border?

In 1975, Mexican ufologist Pedro Ferriz visited Calvillo, Aguascalientes (on the Pacific coast, famous for its intricate mazes of unexplored man-made caves) to inspect some ancient petroglyphs on the property of local landowner Victor Martinez.

Martinez told the ufologist that he was ambivalent about the petroglyphs, which he considered unlucky, particularly since "that affair with the giants." When asked to elaborate, Martinez explained that he had stumbled upon the ancient skeletons of two extraordinarily large creatures while tilling the soil. Martinez went into Calvillo to notify the authorities about his find, only to discover that the local police believed him to have killed both giants and wanted to incarcerate him!

The farmer finessed his way out of the predicament, returned to his farm, and set fire to the bones.

The Ukumar-Zupai
Argentina's Salta region has been the focus of a number of hairy hominid sightings for many years. This rugged, mountainous region could not

differ more from the Sasquatch's forested Pacific Northwest: arid, desolate landscapes meet vast salt deserts, such as the Puna de Atacama, where rainfall is almost nonexistent.

In 1956, Dr. José Cerato and geologist Claudio Spitch discovered the footprints of a Bigfoot-like creature at an elevation of almost 16,000 feet. The prints, according to Spitch, were so large that they precluded the possibility of having been made by a human being.

Shortly after Cerato and Spitch's discovery, a muleteer named Ernesto Salitonlay (his name is also given as José Santolay by some sources) led his animals into a lowland area and was startled by "a strange being covered by dense hair" that let out piercing screams upon seeing the human, terrifying the pack beasts in the process. Salitonlay said that the bizarre creature looked more like "a large, agile monkey" than anything else. He fired his shotgun at it but missed. The hairy hominid took flight and the muleteer headed posthaste to the local police station to report the incident. Authorities looking into his claims surmised that it could have been the Ukumar Zupai described in the legends of the Coya inhabitants of the region.

From all descriptions, the Ukumar was smaller than its Himalayan counterpart. It had a pointed head and projected its body forward when it ran; the natives became accustomed to hearing its cries at dusk and in the winter months. There was also the interesting detail that locals would come across ruined condor and eagle nests, high in the mountains, which appeared to have been ransacked by a savage attacker, leaving dead and injured birds in its wake.

The creature was not seen again until a hapless prospector named Benigno Hoyos, combing the Quitillipi region for minerals, was caught by an unexpected snowstorm in the vicinity of Morro del Pilar and was forced to take shelter from the elements in a cave... which turned out to be occupied by an "unknown creature of large proportions, similar to a bear." The prospector was able to fire his sidearm at the improbable being and scored a hit: the creature's screams turned into heart-rending cries of pain.

According to anthropologist Silvia Alicia Barrios, hunters have successfully apprehended live specimens of Bigfoot's southern cousin. One such case involves the capture of a family of Ukumaris (a mother and two offspring) by Andres Olguin. The two young Ukumaris were allegedly turned over to a Paraguayan zoologist.

Ukumaris and UFOs?

Argentinean cryptozoologist Fabio Picasso, compiler of the *Manual de Criptozoología Argentina y Sudamericana* (1990), mentions the Ukumar-Zupai in his catalog of hairy hominid sightings. In July and August 1956, the *La Gaceta* newspaper began to publish a series of articles (obtained with the aid of Chilean researcher Liliana Núñez) about the creature seen in the vicinity of Nevado Macón, an Andean peak standing 5,700 meters above sea level, where "huge human footprints larger than those of an elephant have allegedly been seen."

Picasso notes that the sightings of the Andean hominids commenced shortly after a flurry of UFO sightings in the area, to which the newspaper items attest. In 1955, the year before the first hominid reports began, a strange object crashed into the slopes of Nevado Macón in full view of the residents of the villages of Tolar Grande, Caipe, and Quebrada de Agua Chuya, all in the vicinity of the Salar de Arízaro. Apparently, prior to colliding, the vehicle had flown over the region all day, making itself visible to workers at a public works shanty and members of the local gendarmerie, who took photos of it.

The Ministry of Aeronautics's Information Service received a request, says Picasso, to conduct an investigation to determine if the crashed object was either "an aircraft or an aerolite," but nothing appears to have been done in this regard. Strange, luminous artifacts continued to be seen over the Andean deserts, first hovering over the dusty villages and then giving the appearance of descending in the mountains. Author Gustavo Fernández adds the interesting detail that an official police communique revealed the crashed object was cylindrical and measured a whopping 350 meters long by 50 meters in diameter (approximately 1,000 by 165 feet) and was metallic in color with a "dark band" visible across it. Despite the fact that it was wingless, it executed sharp and sudden turns, leaving a smoky contrail that remained visible for four hours.

"This anecdote," states Fabio Picasso, "appears to contain the seeds of the oft-mentioned theory regarding the link between UFOs and Yeti-type creatures; a theory which was foreign to the specialized media and was only approached in the 1970s by Angelo Moretti, regarding South American cases involving primitive beings found amid a sweeping UFO flap. The author cautions his readers that this should not be construed as the creatures and the UFOs sharing the same origin. It is possible that the powerful crash into the mountainside drove the hominids out of their lairs."

In 1963, the village of Ranelagh in the Province of Buenos Aires was visited by a strange entity whose journalistic moniker, El Dientudo ("Toothy") de Ranelagh, came from its extraordinarily long fangs. For eight days, according to Gustavo Fernandez, residents of this unpaved shanty town, surrounded by contaminated streams, were haunted by the fearsome Toothy. This shaggy entity, standing some six feet tall, had phosphorescent eyes and was seen by a number of witnesses late at night near a small bridge.

Unlike most cases involving hairy hominids, Toothy lashed out against humans, injuring a few of them; but it saved its true rage for dogs. According to reports, the monster killed several and devoured them.

Toothy's short reign came to an end when a police officer fired his service revolver at the monster one night. The following morning it was ascertained that blood had been found next to its footprints. Police speculated that the creature, wounded to death, had fallen into Ranelagh's polluted creek. It was never seen again.

There are more recent cases of strange creature activity in Argentina: Carlos Alberto Iurchuk, editor of the *El Dragón Invisible* journal, received a letter from one Gustavo Aufnerr, owner of an estate in the municipality of Carlos Spegazzini, regarding a 1996 encounter with the unknown.

Aufnerr was walking through a forest trail one summer evening when he heard a noise behind him. Upon closer inspection, Aufnerr and a companion shone their flashlights toward the ground, only to find the carcass of a dog, eyes vacant and jaw torn off. Gripped by fear, both young men heard the noise once again. As they moved away, they came across another carcass—this time that of a cat, slain in the same gruesome fashion. They did what could only be expected in such a circumstance: they ran.

But their frantic race toward safety was interrupted by "something" that crossed their path in a sideways motion, crossing the forest trail from left to right. According to Aufnerr's description, the strange "something" was about the size of a dog, but running on two legs, with a rounded head smaller than its body, and with claws dangling from the upper part of its body.

Our unknown neighbors

Could it be possible, as many authors have suggested in past decades, that humanity is not quite alone on this planet? This question has usually been raised with regard to presence of extraterrestrial life on our world, whether visiting in passing or possessing permanent bases on it. But in this case the question is directed at the very real presence of other beings—possibly sentient—living in remote or nearly impenetrable parts of our world. Earlier articles in FATE by Paul Stonehill have suggested the existence of "hairy hominids" in the distant reaches of Asiatic Russia, and Loren Coleman's excellent scholarship on Bigfoot have made us aware that these can be found not only in all continents, but throughout the ages as well.

Scott Corrales: Frequent contributor to FATE; *editor of* Inexplicata: The Journal of Hispanic Ufology.

FATE August 2004

HOAX DEBATES

THE ICEMAN GOETH

Jerome Clark

One day in the fall of 1968 a zoologist informant alerted Ivan Sanderson to an extraordinary story: an apparently authentic Bigfoot corpse was being shown around the country as a carnival exhibit.

Sanderson, a biologist who long had been interested in unknown animals, was understandably intrigued. So was Belgian naturalist Bernard Heuvelmans, also famous for his writings on zoological mysteries. Heuvelmans was visiting Sanderson at the latter's New Jersey farm when the news came.

The two lost no time in getting to Rollingstone, Minnesota, where they met one Frank Hansen on whose farm the body, frozen in a block of ice and encased in a refrigerated coffin, reposed over the winter months during the carnival off-season. Hansen led them to a tiny trailer where the "Iceman," as it came to be called, was stored. The scientists spent the next two days studying, sketching and photographing the figure. Heuvelmans described it as follows:

"The specimen at first looks like a man, or, if you prefer, an adult human of the male sex, of rather normal height (six feet) and proportions but excessively hairy. It 1s entirely covered with very dark brown hair three to four inches long. Its skin appears wax-like, similar in color to the cadavers of white men not tanned by the sun…

"The specimen is lying on its back… the left arm is twisted behind the head with the palm of the hand upward. The arm makes a strange curve, as if it were that of a sawdust doll, but this curvature is due to an open fracture midway between the wrist and the elbow where one can distinguish the broken ulna in a gaping wound.

"The right arm is twisted and held tightly against the flank, with the hand spread palm down over the right side of the abdomen. Between the ring finger and the medius the penis is visible, lying obliquely on the groin. The testicles are vaguely distinguishable at the juncture of the thighs."

The creature appeared to have been shot in the right eye. The impact apparently knocked the left eye out of its socket and blew out the back of the head.

Sanderson and Heuvelmans were convinced the figure was what it purported to be: a body, not a model. The two averred that during their examination they even detected gas bubbles and odors from the creature's slowly decomposing remains.

Hansen claimed that the creature had been found floating in a 6000-pound block of natural ice in the Sea of Okhotsk. The men who discovered it were Russian seal-hunters. (In a later version of the tale Hansen identified them as Japanese whalers.) Eventually, according to Hansen, it turned up in Hong Kong where an agent of an anonymous California multimillionaire purchased it. In due course the purchaser rented it to Hansen who began touring the country with it in May 1967.

Finally, in an article published in a 1970 issue of *Saga*, Hansen "confessed" the "truth." He had shot the creature himself 10 years earlier while hunting in the Minnesota woods.

Sanderson and Heuvelmans seem never to have considered seriously the possibility that they might be the victims of a well-executed hoax. Heuvelmans rushed into print with a paper, published in the *Bulletin of the Royal Institute of Natural Sciences of Belgium* for February 1969, in which he gave the Iceman the scientific name of *Homo pongoides*. Meanwhile Sanderson too endorsed the Iceman in articles published in the scientific journal *Genus* and in the popular magazine *Argosy*. In the latter he wrote, "I defy anybody to fool Bernard Heuvelmans in a case like this. You just cannot 'make' a corpse like this."

Frank Hansen and the "Iceman."

Early in February 1969 Sanderson contacted an old friend, John Napier, curator of the primate collections at the Smithsonian Institution, in an effort to encourage the Smithsonian's participation in the investigation. Sanderson provided Napier with his report and diagrams.

As Napier would write in *Bigfoot* (1972), "My first reaction, based on the creature's anatomy, was extreme dubiety… On the face of it, the Iceman is some crazy sort of hybrid… [combining] the worst features of apes and none of the best features which make these two groups extremely successful primates in their respective environments." In other words, zoologically speaking, the Iceman didn't make a lot of sense.

Still, the Smithsonian tried to secure the specimen from Hansen, who said he could not provide it because the anonymous owner had taken it away. Hansen said that when he went back on tour it would be with a model that would "in many respects resemble" the original. After further investigation the Smithsonian concluded that the story and the figure were a hoax.

Over the years Hansen has toured the United States with his Iceman exhibit. He will neither confirm nor deny its authenticity. In his promotional material, however, he does quote the views of "scientists" (Sanderson and Heuvelmans) who have declared it the genuine article.

As recently as August 1981 *Washington Post* reporter Michael Kernan was willing to entertain the possibility that the Iceman was a Bigfoot corpse. "If you ask [Hansen] what we are looking at, the model or the original," Kernan wrote, "he smiles and says carefully, 'We're claiming it's a fabricated illusion.' Even while the odor of dead flesh drifts up from the coffin." Hansen went on to say that the "owner" invented the "fabricated illusion" line to discourage government efforts to examine the creature.

Over the years most persons familiar with the controversy have agreed that the affair is a hoax but an unusually complex and perplexing one. Writing of Hansen, Napier remarks, "He was always one step ahead of the rest of us... He never claimed anything for this exhibit other than that it was a mystery, which indeed it was—and still is."

It is no longer. Thanks to a curious science reporter, we know now the who, why, when and how of the Minnesota Iceman.

In August 1981 C. Eugene Emery of the *Providence* [R. I.] *Journal-Bulletin* interviewed Hansen while the latter was displaying the Iceman at a Providence shopping mall. He wrote a skeptical account, noting that two Brown University anthropologists who had seen it were sure it was fake.

Soon after the article appeared Emery got a call from Bonnie Dalzell, a Washington, D.C., artist and naturalist who was in Providence on business. She said she had first heard about the Iceman in the late 1960s from Leonard C. Sessom, Jr., a paleontologist at the Los Angeles County museum. At Dalzell's urging Emery called the now-retired Sessom.

Sessom said that more than 15 years ago a man had asked him to design and build a creature figure. The man wanted to freeze it and display it at fairs. "It was supposed to be a reproduction of Cro-Magnon man," Sessom recalled. "But I was working at the museum and it's important to have some credibility. I didn't think it would be too neat for me to go around making fake cavemen. But I think Howard Ball made it."

Howard Ball, who died several years ago, made models for Disneyland. He created the animals in the Disneyland Jungle Cruise as well as the dancing figures in the "Small World" attraction. His specialty, however, was prehistoric beasts such as the mechanical dinosaurs in the Ford exhibit at the 1964 New York World's Fair.

"He made [the Iceman] here in his studio in Torrance [California]," Ball's widow Helen told Emery. "The man who commissioned it said he was going to encase it in ice and pass it off, I think, as a prehistoric man."

Ball's son Kenneth helped his father build the figure. He says its "skin" is half-inch-thick rubber. "We modeled it after an artist's conception of Cro-Magnon man and gave it a broken arm and a bashed-in skull with one eye popped out. As I understand it, [the man who commissioned the job] took the creature to Mexico to have the hair implanted."

The Balls were much amused when they saw the *Argosy* story and recognized their creation in the accompanying photographs. "I never thought it would get so carried away," Mrs. Ball says. Kenneth remembers that the man who hired them "discussed with us some of the fun and some of the trials and tribulations with it."

Hansen admitted to Emery that Ball had made a figure for him but insisted that it "was discarded." When Emery pointed out that the Balls affirm that the figure and the one in *Argosy* are identical, Hansen replied, "They can say whatever they want to."

The Balls say there was neither a mysterious millionaire owner nor an original "real" Iceman. It "came from my dad's imagination," Kenneth asserts. "This is the original." His mother adds, "I assure you, it's a hoax."

That, one should think, is that—but it probably isn't. I think we can safely assume that the shopping malls and carnivals of America have not seen the last of the Iceman, the "fabricated illusion" that, while it may never have lived, is not likely to die very soon either.

Jerome Clark: Former longtime FATE *columnist and contributor reporting on UFOs, cryptids and paranormal topics; author of several books.*

FATE March 1982

BACK TO BLUFF CREEK

Daniel Perez

Roswell, New Mexico, will perhaps be forever linked with unidentified flying objects, as it is said a flying saucer crashed nearby in 1947. Dallas, Texas, is embedded in our minds when, in 1963, the president of the United States was assassinated—the incident caught on movie film by an unsuspecting Abraham Zapruder. His stunning footage only served to etch the memory more deeply into our psyche.

And so Bluff Creek, California, will be forever linked to a strip of Kodachrome 11 color movie film shot on a lazy Friday afternoon, October 20, 1967. It was then that the late Roger Clarence Patterson filmed the enigmatic and legendary beast, Bigfoot. Prior to this, Bluff Creek was already a storied place because numerous sightings and footprints attributed to Bigfoot were frequently reported in this heavily forested and mountainous terrain. But the imagery of a color movie film brought a whole new dimension to the Bigfoot mystery as it brought a legendary creature into the realm of almost real…but not quite.

Alleged Bigfoot captured in the Patterson-Gimlin film on October 20, 1967.

Controversy continues

I need not remind you that even today the jury is still out on what exactly is depicted on the Patterson-Gimlin movie. (Bob Gimlin, a long-time friend of Roger Patterson, was with him when this very famous movie was shot. To give due credit to Gimlin, the silent partner and one-time one-third owner in the film, the late Rene Dahinden is credited with circulating the term "Patterson-Gimlin" movie or film). Debunkers of the movie continue to insist that what you see projected on a movie screen is a man in a gorilla costume. The non-debunkers, or "believers" as they are invariably labeled by skeptics and media, insist that the film is evidence of an unknown primate popularly called Bigfoot. No matter, what is certain today is that no one, neither science nor Hollywood, has been able to duplicate the film. Taken by itself, this should speak volumes.

My first visit

I first ventured into the Bluff Creek area, some 190 miles north of San Francisco, in the summer of 1980. I was 17, and the subject of Bigfoot fascinated me. Now I am 38, and my fascination continues. What continues to stand out in my mind some 22 years later is how heavily wooded and remote Bluff Creek is. Since that time, I have made innumerable outings to the area, always hoping to catch a glimpse of our furry and ever-so-shy Sasquatch. To date I have logged a big fat zero for sightings. I have seen plenty of bears, deer, and squirrels, but they are hardly worth a mention. Colleagues have seen mountain lions, a factual animal for purposes of this discussion, but in my mind the mountain lion is a dumb old legend because I have never seen one.

Last August, Don Davis, a veteran Bigfoot enthusiast, and I made a decision to spend about a week in the Bluff Creek area, and, more specifically, to take another look at the famous Patterson-Gimlin film site. Between us, we brought in his motor home, a Suzuki 4X4 Jeep, and my truck.

The site of the sighting

I had questions worthy of asking and certainly worthy of having answered. Right from the get-go, I should remind you, is an incontestable fact: The film in question had to have been made at Bluff Creek. Major investigators

The Patterson-Gimlin site almost 35 years later. Credit: Daniel Perez.

and supporters of the film, including the late George Haas, Peter Byrne, John Green, and the late Rene Dahinden have all independently verified that such a place actually exists. Curiously indeed, I have yet to hear of one P-G film debunker who has ever been to the site. It would seem to me, at least, that they have already made up their minds that the film is bogus, so why bother paying a visit.

To the best of my knowledge no one has ever taken a GPS (global positioning system) to the site to get readings of elevation and latitude and longitude. Until now. I brought along my GPS Blazer 12 Satellite Navigator to address these questions. The P-G film site is 2,581 feet above sea level. I had Don Davis along to verify this information. Knowing elevation doesn't make the film real or fake; it's just a factual piece of data collected in the field for those questioning minds who should ask: what are the facts? With solid facts at hand, of course, one can dispense an opinion truly worth listening to.

More questions and answers

My other question addressed coordinates. The latitude of the P-G film site is: N41° 26.38'. Longitude: W123° 42.011'. A generation from now, this may be the only way to recognize this famous location as the beautiful scenery in the background of the film continues to alter in appearance.

But there were more questions. Does the subject in the movie film, often nicknamed "Patty" (after Patterson, and gender specific because of the visible breast seen on the subject) show skin which is representative of the color of her feet, or is what you see in the P-G film the sandy soil, perhaps wet, adhering to the bottom of her soles? Which is it?

Just recently, I asked Bob Gimlin, now retired and still living in Yakima, Washington, about the soil conditions on the day in question, October 20, 1967, a day he probably thinks about every day. Bob was specific with an answer: "The top layer was not damp. It was completely dry."

Therefore, it was my reasoning that some of the early frames, between numbers 61 and 72 in the 952-frame P-G movie, show an accurate representation of the skin coloring on the bottom of Patty's feet. When I was there last year doing basic research for an upcoming book on the subject, I walked many times on the film site sand bar without shoes, and at no time did the soil adhere to my sole. When I immersed my naked foot into the chilly Bluff Creek waters and then stepped into the sandy soil, it only took moments and a step or two before the soil was dislodged.

In the end, I have asked questions and answered them to my satisfaction. Perhaps someone reading this may be inspired with still more questions. That is the true spirit of science, to go forward and ask questions, no matter what the cost.

I still have memories of the late Rene Dahinden, an icon in the world of Bigfooting, who did more work on the P-G film site than anyone. Unfortunately, a lot of his work and study of the film site can't be repeated because the location has changed immensely since that 1967 day when Patty walked on it. However, he told me once or twice, "You know why I did all this damn work on the film site?" He points two index fingers at himself. "Because I wanted to know!"

Data from Bigfoot at Bluff Creek

Encounter type: Sighting (filmed), subject in film about 6'9"; footprints (filmed and plaster casts made of 10 consecutive tracks) measuring 14-1/2 long, 5-1/2" across the ball, and 4" across the heel.

Date: October 20, 1967, Friday.

Time: Anywhere from 1:15 through 1:40 P.M. (Pacific Standard Time).

Place: On a sand bar, Bluff Creek, California, United States of America (Del Norte County, Six Rivers National Forest).

Witnesses: Roger Clarence Patterson (photographer), February 14, 1933-January 15, 1972; Robert (Bob) Emory Gimlin, October 18, 1931.

First publicity: (California) "Mrs. Bigfoot Is Filmed!" *Eureka Times-Standard*, October 21, 1967, Saturday; thereafter released to the wire services.

Location verified by Rene Dahinden, John Green, Lyle Laverty, Jim McClarin, Bob Titmus, and many others.

Camera used: Cine-Kodak K-100 16-millimeter movie camera with Ektar 25-millimeter fixed lens; f1.9; magnified viewer; made from March 1955-September 1964; list price, $269; hand wound; with 100-foot film loading capability. Operation: 16-64 frames per second (fps).

Film used: Color 16-millimeter Kodachrome H; ASA 64; process K-12; 100' roll of film. Film length: 23' 9-1/4" with 952 frames. If shot at 16 frames per second, duration of film is 59.5 seconds. First part of 100-foot roll of film (76' 2-3/4) shows scenery, horses, and riders.

Film's "official" name: "Bluff Creek Bigfoot" as per copyright registration. (File 176105; serial 269982; register 158).

Closest approach to filmed subject: 25'- 30' according to Bob Titmus; 50' according to Bob Gimlin in a computer questionnaire prepared in the early 1970s.

Implication if subject in film is real: Perhaps the biggest scientific discovery of all time.

Daniel Perez: Longtime Bigfoot investigator, author and researcher; editor/ publisher of the Bigfoot Times *newsletter.*

FATE June 2002

THE PATTERSON FILM HOAX DEBATE

Loren Coleman

A dying man in British Columbia holds the key to research into what may be a species of undiscovered primate. A widow silently guards the film that is as important to Sasquatch studies as the Zapruder footage is to the JFK assassination conspiracy. At the same time, secret forces are working silently to undermine the film's credibility. What's going on?

For years, unknown to the public, a conflict has raged over the ownership of Roger Patterson's short movie of a large-breasted Bigfoot, which was taken at Bluff Creek, California, on October 20, 1967. Patterson, Robert Gimlin (who stood by, rifle ready, while Patterson filmed), and other Bigfoot trackers such as Bob Titmus were able to cast several footprints the Bigfoot left that day as corroborative evidence. Despite its role as an important cinematic piece of the Bigfoot puzzle, people have questioned the film ever since.

In late December 1998, Fox aired *World's Greatest Hoaxes: Secrets Finally Revealed*, which attempted to label the Patterson film a hoax. I took issue with several of the program's claims. As it turned out, however, *World's Greatest Hoaxes* would be only the first of three "the Patterson film is a hoax" stories that would become the talk of Bigfoot followers in early 1999.

There's more to this story than the press is letting on.

Fact or artifact?

On January 11, 1999, a news release bounced across North America, appearing in local papers and national outlets such as *USA Today*. It announced the discovery of "proof" that the Patterson film was a fraud. Cliff Crook of Bothell, Washington, and Chris Murphy of Vancouver, British Columbia, were quoted as saying that enlargements and computer enhancements of the film's frames revealed an object resembling a metal fastener hanging from the Bigfoot in one frame of the film.

"When the guy in the suit turned to look at the camera, it probably snapped loose and dangled from the fur," Crook told reporter Joseph Rose. "It's a hoax. Why would Bigfoot be wearing a belt buckle?"

Murphy says he photocopied this frame for a class project of his son's in 1995 and began questioning the movie's validity after discovering what he called an aberration in the film. Using a computer, he zoomed in tighter and tighter on the image until he found what appears to be a glimmering ornate latch in the shape of a bottle opener. But others can't see it.

When people hear "computer enhancement" they usually think of high-tech procedures used by NASA or the CIA, but it quickly became apparent that the reality in this case was much more modest. Murphy divulged that he had started with photographs of the Patterson film found in the 1990 book *Manlike Monsters on Trial*. Photo experts would later point out that the visual "noise" in a printed still from the film would be greater and much more likely to contain false information than would a frame directly from the film.

"It's like picking a sheep out of the clouds," said Western Bigfoot Society President Ray Crowe. "They've blown up the images beyond the size of recognition. So, they can pretty much see anything they imagine."

Steve Armstrong of Tampa, Florida-based Pegasus Imaging told Rose he didn't think the film would capture an object as small as a buckle. "Zoom in on an image too much, and you get a lot of blocky artifacts," Armstrong said. "Artifacts," in this sense, are shapes or images that result from imperfections in image processing.

The man in the suit

The other "hoax" story came out of Yakima, Washington, home of the late Roger Patterson. In mid-January 1999 rumors began circulating that Patterson had paid a Hollywood costume designer to make a suit and hired a big Yakima Indian to wear it for the film.

Finally, late in January, mostly through reporter David Wasson of the *Yakima Herald Republic*, the story broke under the headline "Bigfoot Unzipped—Man Claims It Was Him in a Suit."

Sparked by the "revelation" of the fastener story, Zillah, Washington, attorney Barry M. Woodard confirmed to Wasson that he was representing a Yakima man claiming to have worn the elaborate monkey suit in the Patterson-Gimlin film, and that his client had passed a lie detector test to prove it.

"Woodard described the man only as a 58-year-old lifelong resident of the Yakima Valley who approached him a few months ago after a network news program called questioning the authenticity of the 1967 film," Wasson wrote. "The man wanted help negotiating a deal for rights to his story ... as well as to explore any legal issues he might face as a result of his involvement in the hoax."

Woodard provided a statement from retired Yakima police officer Jim McCormick, a certified polygraph examiner who administered a lie detector test on Woodard's client. The 75-minute exam suggested that the man was truthful when claiming to have worn the Bigfoot suit in the 1967 film, McCormick wrote. So why weren't they coming quickly forward with details? Money. Woodard told Wasson that his client wanted to sign a contract with the tabloid *The Sun* before releasing further information.

A press conference scheduled for late February never happened. Reports began to circulate that the 58-year-old, six-foot-tall man who now weighed 200 pounds would become a laughingstock when asked to demonstrate how 30 years earlier he had been able to imitate the gait of a 1,500-pound, six-and-a-half- to seven-foot-tall Bigfoot.

The money trail

There must be a reason that the Patterson film is receiving so much scrutiny. Why now, more than 30 years after it was made, has it suddenly become the target of so many would-be debunkers? Why are the clerk at my corner store and my postal worker telling me that "Bigfoot doesn't exist" anymore?

Money. History. Copyrights. Research. And more money.

Roger Patterson died years ago and is thus unavailable to address the recent hoax revelations. Robert Gimlin, however, still lives in Yakima. He dismisses the rumors and the computer analysis as "whacko."

"I was there. I saw [Bigfoot]. The film is genuine," the 67-year-old Gimlin said in a telephone interview. "Anybody who says different is just trying to make a buck." And he hung up.

The Patterson film is at a crossroads. Two people currently own the rights to it. Patterson's widow, Patricia, owns the motion picture rights, and Rene Dahinden, the colorful Swiss-born Sasquatch hunter who has been involved in tracking Bigfoot since 1956 has the still picture rights. They share some video and CD-ROM rights. Pat Patterson has been only marginally interested in Bigfoot for years, although she now has a website and is mentioned more and more in discussions about the film. Dahinden, with whom I spoke a week before this writing, is suffering from the advance of a painful cancer.

People are circling like vultures over Dahinden, waiting for the copyright war to begin. Dahinden says he has already been offered several thousand dollars by a person in California who allegedly has one or two Canadian backers.

Dahinden, who says he has no respect for the individual in question, is angry at the situation and is in no mood to negotiate the rights away. The timing of the new hoax claims suggests why. Portraying the film as a fake would certainly lessen its value on the open market.

Let's look at the story behind the hoax claims. The fastener tale was first pushed by Chris Murphy, a stamp collector and investment manager. Murphy's interest in Bigfoot is recent, about four years old. During this time, he quickly sized up the field and approached Rene Dahinden and asked about becoming Dahinden's promoter and manager.

It's widely known that Dahinden is strong-willed and can be difficult to work with. He was the model for the Sasquatch hunter in the 1987 movie *Harry and the Hendersons*. But Murphy persisted. He republished Patterson's 1966 book, *Do Abominable Snowmen of America Really Exist?*

He distributed some books on the Russian Snowman and published a book on Bigfoot articles. He helped Dahinden get organized and developed a series of prints of the frames from the Patterson film.

But then he published a book about the "Ohio Bigfoot" with a couple of (according to Dahinden) little-respected researchers there. Most disgusting to Dahinden, the Ohio Bigfoot book suggested Murphy was an expert on the Patterson film and contained some enhancements from the film in which Murphy claimed to see some Bigfoot babies. Tempers flared and the men parted ways.

Murphy seems to have fished around for months for a partner to help push his fastener theory before finding Cliff Crook. Crook, a rival of Dahinden's for three decades and the other nonfictional person depicted loosely in Harry and the Hendersons, is a mild-mannered Bigfoot studies participant from Washington. Director of the self-styled Bigfoot Central, Crook is a true believer, having seen Bigfoot when he was a teenager in 1956. Together, with Crook talking to the media, and Murphy with a single press statement, they attacked the Patterson film and, indirectly, Rene Dahinden.

The story unfolding in Yakima appears to be more of the same. Although David Wasson was quick to note in his article who owned the rights to the Patterson film, the story that went unreported was the group outside the spotlight jockeying for positions.

The truth is that not much money has ever been made off the Patterson film. And amid the anger, feuds, looming death, and contract battles, it certainly appears that the true worth of the Patterson film—as a piece of evidence in the case for the elusive hominid—is being forgotten in the haste to make profits today.

Loren Coleman: Longtime former FATE *columnist; author and noted authority on mysterious creatures.*

FATE May 1999

BIGFOOT FILM SITE INSIGHTS

Christopher L. Murphy

The 1967 Patterson/Gimlin film of a Bigfoot creature at Bluff Creek, California, continues to intrigue us. It is certainly one of the most viewed and most controversial strips of film since the invention of motion picture cameras. Despite 35 years of research, we still cannot prove beyond a reasonable doubt that the creature seen is real or a hoax. Remarkably, the passage of time works to both prove and disprove the film's authenticity. On one hand, we can point to the lack of firm hoax evidence and say that such evidence would have surfaced by now. On the other hand, we can say that if Bigfoot is a reality, by now we should have obtained other photographic evidence as good or better than the film.

Whatever one's convictions, the film itself is certainly a reality, and the more we know about it the better we can judge its merits. We can also use such knowledge to evaluate claims by some Bigfoot researchers as to other "images" seen in the background of the film frames.

I constructed a model of the film site at Bluff Creek. The model scale is about one-inch equals nine feet. The entire model is 21 inches long

Author's model of Patterson/Gimlin Bigfoot sighting and film.

by 16.25 inches wide. Actual measurements as they relate to objects seen are presented later. To my knowledge, no one has previously attempted to build a model of this nature. Indeed, I would not have attempted it myself were it not for a "strange" document given to me some five or six years ago by René Dahinden (now deceased). The document, a photocopy of film frame No. 352, with numerous lines and symbols, was given to me without explanation. I often wondered what it was all about, but just never got around to discussing it with René.

Dahinden's diagram

René had performed a lot of measurements at the film site in the early 1970s. He drew a diagram (not to scale) of the site, which was published by Dan Perez in his book, *Bigfoot Times* (1992). Dahinden showed little circles representing trees and stumps, but what trees and what stumps? By the time I started analyzing the diagram, René had passed away, and I did not know of anyone else who would have the answers. René identified some of the objects in his sketch with Roman numerals. He had also marked various objects in photographs of the site (which he had given me) with Roman numerals. When I matched the photographs to the diagram, I started to see how the site "came together." However, the photographs showed only a few objects seen in the diagram, so I could not associate other objects.

From out of nowhere, the thought came to me to get the strange document previously mentioned. As soon as I laid it on my desk, the whole film site unfolded before my eyes. This document was the key to the diagram. The Roman numerals and other symbols matched those on the diagram so that one could see the exact placement of most of the important objects in the film frames. I started mapping out the site and before long was thoroughly engrossed in constructing a proper model.

Unfortunately, René had omitted to provide any meaningful horizontal measurements. While some of these measurements could be reasonably calculated, others had to be estimated using the film itself, photographs (including an aerial shot of the site), and old-fashioned logic. In some areas, I was able to get missing information from a rough site sketch made by John Green (also published by Dan Perez). I visited John with my first model "draft," as it were, and he showed me film footage he took of the site in 1967. I am confident the model is very close to the original scene.

In talking to John about events in 1967, he remarked that he and the other Bigfoot researchers felt it would only be a matter of months before a Bigfoot creature would be brought in. For this reason, we do not have highly detailed information on the film site. Nevertheless, what we have is sufficient, and we can thank René and John for the great work they did in this regard.

Cameras can deceive

There is an old saying that cameras do not lie. While this saying is true, cameras do something just as bad—they deceive. While objects seen in photographs are exactly as they are in real life, their relationship to other objects is a totally different matter. In the Patterson/Gimlin film frames we commonly see, we are led to believe that the creature is within a few feet of individual trees, stumps, logs, and the forest in the background. This conception is totally incorrect, as can be seen in the model photograph below.

Path of Patterson Bigfoot among trees.

The most evident deception is the position of the three trees directly in front of the creature in frame 352, together with the forest debris in the frame foreground. In the film, it is seen that the creature goes behind the first tree, in front of the second tree, and then behind the third tree. The first tree is about 48 feet away, directly toward the camera. The second tree is about 10 feet farther back from the creature's path. The third tree is about 39 feet away, again directly toward the camera. The forest debris begins at more than 30 feet from the creature's path. The first and third trees are in this debris. When Roger Patterson held his camera at eye level (around five feet), the height of the forest debris in

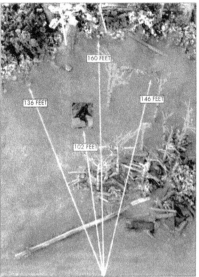

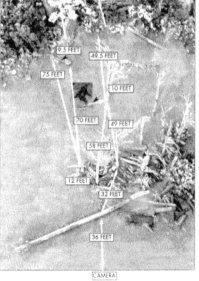

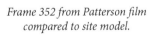

*Frame 352 from Patterson film
compared to site model.*

the foreground concealed the space between the debris and the creature.

The illustrations show the relative position of objects seen in the film frames and associated measurement.

It is highly interesting to view the model from different angles. When seen from the left, we can get an idea of what the creature saw as it crossed the gravel sandbar.

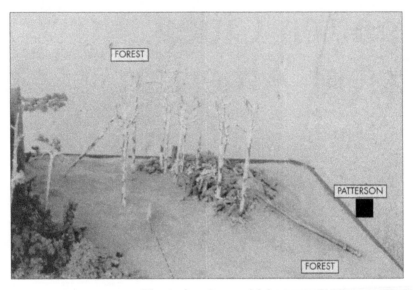

Film site from Patterson's left.

We are reasonably sure that the creature did not notice Patterson until it had reached approximately the position shown in the model. At this point, it appears that the forest to its left and directly ahead of it were about equal distance. This condition likely accounts for the fact that the creature did not dart into the forest to its left. In other words, it had an equal choice. Possibly the creature took into consideration the trees and debris to its right, on the little island as it were. This cover effectively blocked a clear view from Patterson's position. Indeed, when we view the film beyond the model boundary, we can see how difficult it would have been to get a clear rifle sighting on the creature. All of these deductions, of course, are pure speculation. However, they do justify in my mind why the creature chose to just keep moving ahead—a contentious point with some people. Do I think the creature was frightened? I think it was terrified. The expression on its face in the last clear film frame (frame 364) indicates to me that it was both terrified and a little confused as to what to do. Under the circumstances, it did what we are told to do when we are confronted with a wild animal—calmly and quickly, but without running, put distance between yourself and the animal.

Film site from Patterson's right.

Obstruction of island

Viewed from the right, the model illustrates the importance of the little "island" to the creature. Keep in mind that the island is a tangled mass of forest material. One could not run over it or through it, so it definitely put something between the creature and the intruders. The fact that Patterson and Gimlin just stayed where they were and did not pursue the creature also probably resulted in its continuing at a steady pace. Had either or both men rushed forward about 100 feet, I think the creature would have been out of sight very quickly.

Viewed from the back, we can see most clearly how Patterson and Gimlin had an unobstructed view of the creature for a considerable distance. By the same token, the creature had an unobstructed view of the men, but it apparently failed to notice them until it reached the position

Film site looking toward Patterson.

shown. Why it did not notice them earlier in its passage is difficult to explain. Nevertheless, film frames up to this point appear to show a creature with a highly preoccupied mind—a very human trait.

I believe one of the most important points presented here is that the forest behind the creature (i.e., to its left) is more than 160 feet from the camera. I do not know its exact location; however, it is beyond the farthest object measured by Dahinden. If one looks at photographs of the film frames and discovers unusual shapes in the forest that appear like little monkey faces and bodies and so forth, it must be taken into account that the object (or shape) is over 58 feet farther back than the Bigfoot creature. We can only just see general fuzzy details on the creature at 102 feet. At 160 feet, we would be able to distinguish only its overall shape, which, of course, would be much smaller in size.

Site has changed

The film site is certainly no longer like the model. Recent photographs taken by Dan Perez show that it is all overgrown. Even as early as

1972, at least three of the four trees used for measurements had fallen down. Nevertheless, I would like to see the site properly identified and preserved. When we think of the millions of people who have looked at the site in the film frames or related photographs, that little plot of land has a noted place in history—even if we never find Bigfoot.

Christopher L. Murphy: Longtime Bigfoot researcher.

FATE March 2003

IS THE PATTERSON FILM TOO GOOD A HOAX?

J. Allan Danelek

One October afternoon in 1967, self-styled Bigfoot enthusiast Roger Patterson did what no "monster" hunter had managed to do before or since. Using a small 16mm camera, he allegedly shot nearly 100 feet of color footage of the legendary Sasquatch (more commonly known as Bigfoot) as it crossed a dried creek bed and retreated into the darkened woods near Bluff Creek, California. In so doing, Patterson started a firestorm of controversy that continues to this day and likely will rage on for decades to come.

Did Patterson really film the elusive creature, as Bigfoot proponents generally insist, or did he perpetrate the greatest fraud in the history of natural science, on par with the Cardiff Giant and the Piltdown Man? Certainly, the footage looks convincing. It is reasonably clear, shot in bright sunlight, and provides a copious amount of detail. It's definitely not a bear or any other known animal native to northern California. It's not a fluke of shadows and light, nor is it a camera trick. It is either an unknown primate of considerable size or a man in a very convincing suit. Patterson's film is clear enough that it leaves no other options.

The scientific community—at least those few men and women willing to humor the cryptozoology community by looking at the footage—as a group generally considers it an obvious fraud, though some will at least allow that it is a very good one. The few scientists who take the footage seriously, most notably University of Washington anthropologist Grover Krantz, see it as too good to be a hoax. The animal's general physical dimensions are too massive and untypical of human ratios, the cranial crest, hair, and musculature too much like that of a real primate—even its gait is too different from that of either a man or an ape to be a hoax.

So which is it, beast or fraud? While we may never learn the answer with any certainty (even demonstrating the existence of a real Bigfoot would not prove Patterson's animal was real), it might be useful to look at the issue from the standpoint of a hoaxer and ascertain just what it might take to duplicate Patterson's efforts. I will examine each of the major objections commonly voiced by opponents of the Patterson film to see if they stand up rationally.

It's a guy in a monkey suit

This is, for obvious reasons, the most prevalent objection. It has to be a man in an elaborate get-up because the alternative is clearly unacceptable. This seems to be the extent of the skeptic's rationale.

The problems with the man-in-a-suit theory are many. Most obvious, of course, is the sheer size of the animal. Frame-by-frame measurements have suggested the "creature" in the film had a height of nearly seven feet, a chest circumference of over 80 inches (compare to an average adult human male chest measurement of approximately 45-50 inches), and a weight in excess of 500 pounds (as gauged by the apparent depth of footprints left in the sandy creek bed, also shot by Patterson, along with plaster castings). Even allowing that lens distortion and interpolation might reduce these measurements by as much as 10 percent, even an unusually large man in a "monkey suit" would be unlikely to approach these dimensions, with the exception of height.

Of course, a man could wear a padded undergarment designed to give the appearance of greater bulk, but then how does one account for the greater weight? Five hundred pounds of flesh and bone (as well as latex, rubber, and fur) is a lot of weight to be hauling around in the wilderness. Surely a large man in a suit weighing in at around 250-300 pounds should have been sufficient for Patterson's purposes; so why the extra unnecessary weight? (And, indeed, where did it come from?)

Additionally, considering that Patterson's friend and fellow eyewitness, Bob Gimlin, was armed and at the ready in case the animal did something unexpected, it would seem hugely irresponsible at best and insanely dangerous at worse to don such a suit (unless, of course, Gimlin was in on the hoax, a point he explicitly denies to this day). Even their verbal agreement not to shoot the creature in case of an encounter—an agreement often pointed to by debunkers as suspicious—would be no guarantee that Gimlin wouldn't fire in a moment of panic. No matter how well Patterson knew Gimlin, he could never be absolutely certain how the man would react in such a remarkable situation, and the consequences of "guessing" wrong would be catastrophic. It was simply too great a risk for either Patterson or the guy in the suit to take for any amount of fame or fortune.

Further, and I think even more important, is the question of the extraneous details the image in the film exhibits. A cranial crest—a ridge of bone along the top of the skull common to large apes—is clearly evident, as are pendulous female breasts. While the addition of the crest might be a reasonably simple addition, breasts would not. They would be an unnecessary and complicated—and possibly expensive—addition to an outfit that was going to be filmed for only a few seconds, especially when Bigfoot enthusiasts would have been equally content with a breast-less Bigfoot.

Additionally, naturalists have noted that the arms of the creature in the film are longer than those found in a human. Human hands come to about mid-thigh level, whereas the hands of the creature in the Patterson film extend nearly to the knees. This could only be accomplished through the use of arm extenders of some kind; again, another difficulty that has to be carefully integrated into the already ponderous suit.

And then there is that strange gait. As Dr. Krantz correctly points out, the Patterson creature doesn't walk like a man (or any known primate, for that matter). It walks with a continually bent knee (as opposed to humans, who lock their knees while walking) and is consistent with a creature having the type of double-jointed foot evidenced by the plaster casts Patterson made on site. (Such double-jointedness in the foot is frequently seen on the most reliable Bigfoot casts known, which are easily distinguished from hoaxed footprints that are normally nothing more than oversized human footprints.) So why the unusual, inhuman walk—a walk Dr. Krantz finds difficult and uncomfortable to mimic for any great distance? Does this sound like the sort of detail even the most clever special effects artist would dream up?

While it's true such a gait would not be impossible for a man to mimic, what would he use as the basis or "model" for such a walk in the first place? If one were to mimic a gorilla, for instance, it would be reasonable to study a real gorilla in an effort to learn and duplicate its movements as closely as possible. But what is the source of the Bigfoot "walk?" Obviously, since there are no "real" Bigfoots to study, it was invented out of thin air. Then, since the costumed man was going to get only one shot at this, he would have had to painstakingly practice the gait until he could make it appear natural. Difficult at best and an unnecessary complication for just a few seconds of hoaxed film footage. And this, of course, brings us to our second point.

SFX artists think film is fake

Debunkers of the Patterson film frequently point out that modern special effects artists usually consider the image in the film to be a suited man. Some have even maintained it was "well known" within the industry the "creature" was the work of special effects master John Chambers—a man who had considerable expertise in the field of "hairy monsters" through his work on television shows like *Lost in Space* and *The Outer Limits*.

While it is true that modern effects artists likely could reproduce the Patterson creature, it must be remembered that much has changed in the industry since 1967. Modern materials and techniques, as well as the money to put into such elaborate costumes, simply were not available 35 years ago, a point often overlooked by most debunkers today. According to Bigfoot enthusiasts Don Hunter and Rene Dahinden, the footage was shown to special effects artists at Universal Studios just weeks after it was shot. Their conclusion was: "We could try. But we would have to create a completely new system of artificial muscles and find an actor who could be trained to walk like that. It might be done, but we would have to say that it would be almost impossible."

It's not surprising then that today's special effects artists—many of whom were not even alive when Patterson shot his footage—are less impressed; they have the materials and resources available today their forebears never dreamed of. Perhaps that's why the "old school" seemed more uniformly impressed with the Patterson film; they know how difficult such a suit would have been to make in 1967, a point that today's artisans often overlook.

This point is further underscored by recent attempts to "fake" Bigfoot film for television documentaries. Such efforts routinely demonstrate that despite the significant advances in costuming available today, no one could get a guy in a fur suit to look like anything but a guy in a fur suit. One recent effort, actually shot at Bluff Creek by the BBC for Discovery Channel's television special *X-creatures*, had a man in a Bigfoot suit (inexplicably covered in long red yak fur rather than the short, coarse, black hair seen on the Patterson creature) retrace the path taken by the "thing" in the film in an effort to demonstrate how "easily" such a film could be faked. While the producers presented the spectacle as evidence of a hoax by Patterson, it more clearly demonstrates just the opposite. The remarkably unconvincing "creature" looked nothing like the Patterson creature. In fact, it was obvious to everyone—except, apparently, the producers—that it was a guy in an oversized suit. They also didn't explain why their "Bigfoot" was unable to leave footprints in the sand that showed him to weigh over 500 pounds, either.

As for the claim that special effects artist John Chambers produced the Patterson costume, some thorough research by writer Mark Chorvinsky failed to produce a single witness who could verify the claim firsthand. Evidence of Chambers' role was anecdotal, hearsay, and "general knowledge" within the industry, but no one—including Chambers himself (in a 1995 interview) —has ever admitted to producing the costume. This in itself seems remarkable, as such a confession would produce quite a sensation in the industry and immortalize its creator. Certainly, the long-since-retired Chambers had nothing to lose by admitting the hoax and, in fact, could have only enhanced his reputation as one of the greatest effects artists in history. The "Chambers Story," then, appears to be nothing more than a case of a smoking gun without a gun.

And, finally, what of the logistical problems such a shoot would entail? If one were to commission a special effects artist to produce a convincing suit and find someone large enough to wear it, why shoot the production in Bluff Creek, a full 500 air miles from Hollywood? Setting the production so far from "headquarters" would make the entire affair a logistical nightmare. First, as the suit would have been expensive to construct and maintain, it's hard to imagine its creator would have subjected it to the kind of wear and tear such a rugged locale would demand. Additionally, transporting the "ape guy" along with his hot, bulky costume—as well as several assistants (remember, our hoaxer needed someone to drive him out to the site and then pick him up again immediately afterwards)—could not be easy or inexpensive. Does it make sense to spend the time and money to drag this entire ensemble all the way to the Oregon border when they could have done the shoot much closer to home—say in the nearby Sierra Nevadas—a vast area also known for Bigfoot sightings, or, for that matter, even the forests of nearby Santa Barbara and Ventura counties, a mere two-hour drive from Hollywood? It would have made the fraud far easier and less expensive to pull off, particularly when the results would have been just as good.

Patterson had an agenda

The fact that Patterson actually made money from his film is, in the minds of some, automatically enough to dismiss the film out of hand as an obvious fake. The idea that a Bigfoot "hunter" actually found what he was searching for is looked upon with suspicion, for clearly no one could be that lucky. This deadly combination—luck and fortune—is enough, apparently, to seal its fate.

No one denies that Patterson was lucky. He set out to find a Bigfoot and actually found one. But it wasn't pure luck. He had been searching for the creature for years and pursued his quarry with considerable skill. He chose to search an area known for Bigfoot activity—a "hot spot" in modern parlance—and he further chose the perfect means of doing so: searching on horseback.

Packhorses gave Patterson a tremendous advantage in searching for a creature like Bigfoot. Vehicles make noise and would be detected by a reasonably alert Bigfoot at some distance, while horses are quiet and would be able to cover much larger areas than a man on foot. Horses might also have one other subtle advantage: Whereas a man, being bipedal, might be interpreted by a Sasquatch as an "unnatural" creature, a horse would look—and smell—more like a "natural" animal of the forest. In fact, this natural "camouflage" may be what allowed Patterson and Gimlin to get as close as they did. By the time the Bigfoot noticed the horses had human riders, it had already compromised its position.

Plus, Patterson and Gimlin were following a nearly dry creek bed—one of the few sources of water in the area—which, as a result of a particularly heavy spring runoff, now had broad, exposed banks. This would have forced any creature to cross nearly 100 feet of open space before reaching the cover of the forest. All these factors, combined with a bit of luck, are what gave Patterson his opportunity. He was simply rewarded for doing everything right—a lesson many modern Bigfoot hunters should take note of.

But what about the money? Didn't Patterson make a fortune off his film?

While it is true the man did make money from the rights to his footage, it was scarcely a fortune, and he lost most of that in later, unsuccessful Bigfoot expeditions. But even so, is that enough to question his ethics? The film, after all, was his personal property, and the expedition was undertaken at his own expense, so was he not within his rights to take advantage of the situation? He took the risks and did the work, precisely the same as does a scientist who wins a Nobel Prize. Are we to assume a researcher in the field of chemistry, for example, who receives prize money for his effort, is to be considered unethical for keeping his winnings?

Additionally, consider the personal risks Patterson ran had he hoaxed the event. He took a risk his companion wouldn't shoot the impostor (couldn't he have at least made certain Gimlin's rifle was empty before they started out?) as well as the risk the hoax wouldn't be exposed, thus subjecting himself to ridicule and possible legal action. When one considers the number of people likely involved in the fraud (at least two others besides Patterson himself, unless one assumes the guy in the monkey suit is also the designer and fabricator of the suit, which seems unlikely) what are the chances the deception would never be exposed?

It's just too good a joke to keep to oneself. And, finally, Patterson himself died in 1972 after a long illness without recanting his story. Hadn't he heard that confession was good for the soul, or did he simply have nothing to confess?

Fraud or science?

Could the Patterson film be a fraud? Of course it could. Unfortunately, that's enough to satisfy most skeptics. People tend to believe what they want, as this remarkable piece of footage vividly demonstrates. To the Bigfoot proponent, it is clear and concise "proof" that a massive, unknown primate lurks in the forests of North America awaiting imminent discovery. To the skeptic, it is a clever fraud that beautifully illustrates the gullibility of the ignorant and the naive.

J. Allan Danelek: Graphic artist and author.

FATE March 2002

RAY WALLACE: THE FATHER OF BIGFOOT

Mark Chorvinsky

On November 26, 2002, the field of strange phenomena lost one of its most colorful and controversial figures. Ray Wallace passed away. Ray, a longtime resident of Toledo, Washington, corresponded with me over a 10-year period.

Ray has been marginalized by Bigfoot enthusiasts, but his role in the creation and growth of the belief in Bigfoot cannot be overstated. He was present at Bigfoot's birth in 1958 and was most certainly one of the people responsible for the events surrounding that memorable event.

Ray Wallace was a hoaxer. Over the years he admitted to me in writing that he used fake Bigfoot feet to make innumerable tracks that were later discovered and reported as "real." In addition, he created a large quantity of highly questionable films and photos and clearly had access to several Bigfoot suits. In fact, someone in a Bigfoot suit appeared at his 50th wedding anniversary! In the early 1970s, the *Los Angeles Times* reported that Ray Wallace acquired the many fake feet that Rant Mullins had used to create tracks for the Mount St. Helens ape episode in 1924.

I would suggest that Ray Wallace is the Father of Bigfoot—that he gave birth to its modern American incarnation. Bigfoot fanatics would choose to quibble with this, but the facts mitigate in favor of Bigfoot being a cultural phenomenon. Believers are portraying Ray Wallace as a prankster and a teller of tall tales who merely distracted from the serious business of Bigfoot hunting, but in fact Wallace was much more than that.

Bigfoot believers are obviously conflicted when it comes to dealing with hoaxers like Ray Wallace. In order to keep the myth of Bigfoot alive, they have felt the need to diminish the importance of such pivotal figures. The facts are inescapable—Bigfoot as we know it today was born in 1958, and Wallace and his brother created it. Wallace should be memorialized as the man who was responsible for perpetrating the hoax that was responsible for both the name Bigfoot and its entry into the monster pantheon. Writers who portray Wallace as a harmless trickster are no better than hoaxers themselves. If Ray Wallace was the hoaxer behind the birth-of-Bigfoot case, and the self-proclaimed Bigfoot/Sasquatch experts knew this, then where did this information appear in their books and articles before I discussed Wallace in my earlier FATE magazine columns? If Wallace was nothing but a tall-tale teller, why cover up the fact that he was a central figure in the birth of Bigfoot, and that he and his brother were responsible for placing Bigfoot at Bluff Creek?

Ivan T. Sanderson, John Green, and others knew Wallace's true nature but never exposed him in their books because it would have hurt the "case for Bigfoot." Green, whose entry into the field was as a journalistic hoaxer, and Sanderson, who promoted many of the major hoaxes/canards of the latter 20th century (the Minnesota Iceman, the Patterson Bigfoot film, the Florida "Giant Penguin," the Philadelphia Experiment, the Thunderbird Photograph, etc.) both knew that Wallace had no credibility whatsoever, but they never once stated this in their books and articles.

It was only after I began to write about Wallace and his innumerable fake films, photos, and tracks that suddenly Ray Wallace was discussed, and the only way that they could deal with him at this point was to act like he was a minor figure in the scheme of things. Only John Napier, in *Bigfoot: The Yeti and Sasquatch in Myth and Reality*, devoted any space (one paragraph) to Wallace, noting that Ray was the first person who claimed to have taken a Bigfoot film, in 1957.

According to Napier, Wallace was said to have 15,000 feet of film footage of Bigfoot. In my 1983 column, I quoted Napier, who wrote, "I do not feel impressed with Mr. Wallace's story." I wrote that Wallace's films were generally held in low esteem by those who had viewed them, stating that "Many viewers have felt that the films show a man in a fur suit."

Swept under the rug

Ray Wallace is the last person in Bigfoot history who should be swept under the rug. If Bigfoot investigators and self-proclaimed cryptozoologists really cared about the truth, they would investigate every Bigfoot case that occurred in proximity to a Wallace construction site.

I have made it quite clear that the birth-of-Bigfoot case was much messier than it had been portrayed by Bigfoot proponents. While I could not come right out and call Wallace a hoaxer (he had very deep pockets and his constant threat of lawsuits meant that it was more prudent for me to imply than to state), I tried to make it quite clear that any case connected to Wallace was highly suspect, to say the least. I wrote about his wacky claims, his seemingly endless films and photos, and his connections to some of the most important Bigfoot cases.

Bigfoot was named and entered the public consciousness in 1958 when tracks and sightings in northern California led to worldwide press. Before 1958, there were some significant cases, but each has proven to be very problematic. In fact, Abominable Snowman expert Ivan T. Sanderson was shocked to hear of man-ape sightings in northern California in 1958. In his 1961 classic *Abominable Snowmen: Legend Come to Life*, Ivan T. Sanderson wrote that: "In 1958 I received a number of reports of an ABSM [Abominable Snowman] in California. At first, this sounded quite balmy even to us, and we are used to the most outrageous things…"

Sanderson wrote elsewhere that "This [account] I frankly refused to believe, mostly because I rather naturally assumed that the location as given (California) must have been a complete error or misquote. It is all very natural to have abominable creatures pounding over snow-covered passes in Nepal and Tibet. But a wild man with a 16-inch foot and a 50-inch stride tromping around California is a little too much to ask even Californians to accept."

Those of us who have grown up with Bigfoot may not realize that just 45 years ago, Bigfoot was virtually unknown in the American popular consciousness.

My research and investigation have shown that the famous 1958 case took place on a road-building site that was being worked by a construction company owned by Ray and Wilbur Wallace. Wilbur was accused of hoaxing by the local police. The Humboldt sheriff's office investigated the series of sightings and other strange occurrences surrounding the Wallaces' road crew and made accusations that Roy Wallace, Ray's other brother, had "perpetrated a hoax on his own construction job" (*The Humboldt Times*, October 14, 1958).

The Patterson connection

Since 1958, Bigfoot has become a part of the American cultural landscape, cemented by the film taken by rodeo rider Roger Patterson in 1967. The location of the Patterson film is Bluff Creek, the site of several Wallace family hoaxes including the highly tainted birth-of-Bigfoot case. In fact, Ray Wallace claims to have told Patterson where to take his film that day. Also, there are many rumors of a person in a suit. The most prominent of these rumors is that the late Hollywood makeup artist John Chambers, who worked on *Planet of the Apes,* made the Patterson suit. There are many reasons to think that this may be true, including the fact that some of Chambers' closest associates believe that he made the suit. Chambers denied involvement, but there is growing evidence to the contrary, both on and off the record. Wishful thinking by Bigfoot fans won't change the fact that there are more reasons to think that the Patterson film is a fake than to conclude that it is authentic.

At Bluff Creek, California, on the afternoon of October 20, 1967, Roger Patterson and his accomplice, Bob Gimlin, allegedly captured a Bigfoot on film, an event hailed by many as the single most important in Bigfoot history. "Roger Patterson came [over] dozens of times pumping me on this Bigfoot," Ray Wallace explained to Dennis Pilichis in 1982.

Pilichis asked, "Did Roger Patterson see your movies? Was [the Patterson Bigfoot] the same [Bigfoot] as yours?"

"Oh, sure, he's seen them," Wallace answered. "Sure, it was the same one, without a doubt. It was right down there in that same doggone country around Onion Lake. I felt sorry for Roger Patterson. He told me that he had cancer of the lymph glands and he was desperately broke, and he wanted to try get something where he could have a little income. Well, he went down there just exactly where I told him. I told him, 'You go down there and hang around on that bank. Stay up there and watch that spot.' I told him where the trail was that went down to where that big rock was. I told him where he could get those pictures down there. Just up on the hill above that doggone creek that he was on. Bluff Creek."

Corroboration

In an editorial in *Strange Magazine* 16, Fall 1995, I noted that material in *Where Bigfoot Walks*, by award-winning author Robert Michael Pyle, corroborated my theories about Ray Wallace and the birth of Bigfoot. When I called Wallace the "Father of Bigfoot" in *Strange Magazine* 13, some readers understood what I meant, while others missed the point—that there was no Bigfoot in California before Ray Wallace introduced the creature in 1958. Wallace's role is still being downplayed by Bigfoot advocates, who are now saying that they knew Wallace was a hoaxer all these years, but that there was no relationship between Wallace and the birth of Bigfoot. Was it an insignificant detail that it was Wallace's road crew that found the tracks? That the local police theorized that Ray's brother was the hoaxer? That Wallace had allegedly discussed fake track-making techniques with others?

Seattle Times article

As we go to press, the *Seattle Times* is running an article entitled "Lovable Trickster Created a Monster with a Bigfoot Hoax." I was interviewed extensively by Bob Young for this piece, and as a result of our conversations, Young contacted the Wallace family, who agreed to speak to him. The Wallace family corroborated my theory that Wallace hoaxed the birth of Bigfoot in 1958, and I think that it is safe to say that my theory has been upgraded to fact.

Wallace's nephew, Dale Lee Wallace, told Young that his Uncle Ray "…did it just for the joke, and then he was afraid to tell anybody because they'd be so mad at him." Dale said he has the alderwood carvings of the huge feet that gave birth to Bigfoot. The *Seattle Times* ran a photo of the wooden feet used to make the tracks.

Family members told the *Seattle Times* that Ray Wallace "had asked a friend to carve the 16-inch-long feet. Then he and his brother Wilbur had slipped them on and created the footprints as a prank." In addition, Michael Wallace said his father called the Patterson film "a fake." Ray's son also said that his mother admitted having been filmed in a Bigfoot costume.

Michael Wallace said family members knew about his father's hoax but never let on. "The family just sat back and grinned," he told reporter Young. "He didn't mean to hurt anyone."

For the record, the first publication to bring Ray Wallace's antics to the attention of the public was the July 1993 issue of *FATE* magazine in my column entitled "Bigfoot: Made in America:" *[see opening article in this volume]*

Significance of Wallace

In conclusion, let us not diminish the place of Ray Wallace in the cultural history of Bigfoot. It is clear now that Wallace has been casually and wrongly dismissed by Bigfoot researchers who are either more interested in promoting Bigfoot or themselves than in investigating the origin of a phenomenon that was newly born in northern California in 1958.

Mark Chorvinsky (1954-2005): Former FATE *columnist and consulting editor and founding editor of* Strange *magazine.*

FATE February 2003

The Hoaxers

Mark Sunlin

On the trail of Bigfoot

During the 1970s, books and movies turned attention to Bigfoot as never before. In 1979, on the heels of all of this, Rant Mullins, a Washington State woodsman who was born in 1896, stepped forward to tell how he had done much to promote the Bigfoot legend by his prankish hoaxing decades earlier. In fact, according to Mullins, he had all but created the Bigfoot character single-handedly...literally, the way he described it.

It all started in 1924, before the names "Bigfoot" and "Sasquatch" had caught on, and the legendary primates were known as just "apes." Mullins and a friend were hiking back from a fishing trip in Washington's Spirit Lake region when they paused to prankishly roll some stones onto a miners' cabin in the Ape Canyon region. The miners "came the following day to the Spirit Lake Ranger Station and said that hairy apes threw rocks at them," Mullins recalled with relish, adding, "they had all the lawmen up there looking for the apes."

A few years later, with this episode in mind, Mullins and friends decided to go a step further and "have some fun scaring a few city slickers from Portland who were out to pick some berries." Mullins craftily fashioned a pair of wooden "big feet" out of a split of wood made from an alder tree using his hatchet and pocket knife. One of his friends then put the big feet on his boots, snowshoe-style, and stomped a trail in the ground where the huckleberry pickers were foraging. Later, the berry pickers, upon finding the tracks, reported them anxiously to the ranger station, then hastily left the park.

Mullins eventually made eight pairs of these wooden big feet, most of which he said he sent to California, and which all but kicked off the Bigfoot legend—at least by his way of thinking. Mullin's motive in his hoaxing was pure boyish pranksterism. And while this is what we might expect is usually the case, others have different reasons for the same antics.

Stepping on toes

On several occasions beginning in 1971, Ray Dickens (a suitable name for a hoaxer) of Arden, Washington, similarly hoaxed Bigfoot tracks. But his motive was different from Mullins's, as he explains: "Well, we were sitting there having coffee in this Arden cafe when two gentlemen came in and started asking about Bigfoot. We said we didn't believe in it, and one gentlemen says, 'well, you hicks around Arden probably wouldn't.' I turned to my friend Harvey and said 'Harvey, we're hicks. What are we going to do about it? So I said, 'We're going to show them who the who the hicks are.' Then I went home and made the boots. The boots turned out to be hiking boots with wooden "big feet" attached, a la Mullins (whom Dickens probably never heard of).

Dickens donned the boots and took long, striding steps, leaving 18-inch tracks widely spaced in the woodlands which looked chillingly like the trail of some huge, bipedal ape. "By the next day there were 700 to 800 people from all over the country looking at the tracks," Dickens said with a smile. (Take that city slickers!)

Bigfoot goes to the movies

In October 1967, Roger Patterson (who had authored a book on Bigfoot) and Bob Gimlin were on a Bigfoot-hunting trip on horseback in northern

California, when they captured a one-minute film of what they said was a female Bigfoot walking along a dry stream bed. To many Bigfoot believers, this film has become enshrined as proof, or at least as a logo or mascot of the Sasquatch's existence. Like a Hollywood starlet leaving signature footprints in cement at Grauman's Chinese Theater, there were even footprints allegedly left by this northern California film queen. But to many this analogy is apt, for they see it as nothing more than an act.

The film has been widely scrutinized and both attacked and defended. "There are two eyewitnesses; there are footprints," said the late Rene Dahinden of Richmond, British Columbia, one of the foremost veteran Bigfoot believers, who shared the film copyright. "We never had anything like it previously, and anything like it since." However, this rationale is highly inconclusive, especially if it develops that the "eyewitness" had perpetuated the hoax.

Even some Bigfoot believers have criticized the film as a hoax. In 1999, Cliff Crook, a Seattle-area Bigfoot believer, announced to the media that "computer enhancements" made by fellow Bigfoot buff Chris Murphy of Vancouver, British Columbia, show what Crook sees as a costume fastener cinching a gorilla suit in place at the waist. "It was a hoax," said Crook, who nevertheless is a firm believer in Bigfoot himself, and whose home outside Seattle is a veritable museum filled with Bigfoot paraphernalia such as the obligatory plaster footprints casts and bumper stickers proclaiming I BRAKE FOR BIGFOOT. "Even though the Patterson film is a hoax," says Crook, "it doesn't mean Bigfoot doesn't exist."

Some skeptics have noted that the soles of this black-colored Bigfoot's feet are oddly white-colored, rather like 1960s tennis shoes, while the palms of the hands, like the face, are blackish. One observation I haven't heard noted is that the Bigfoot's head turns around to look at the cameraman while still walking forward. This is very surprising, since nonhuman animals, and naturalistic humans, virtually never look away from the direction in which they are walking. If they wish to look at something behind them, they will stop walking and then look. The reason, of course, is to avoid walking into something unforeseen like a tree limb. This Bigfoot's mannerism appears suspiciously like an actor in a costume giving a good showing for the camera. Likewise, most fleeing wild creatures will walk away from a threatening intruder, rather than at right angles, as this camera-friendly Bigfoot does. The Patterson-Gimlin film seems more reminiscent of a television beauty pageant contestant or Bob Hope making a strange entrance than an evasive wild creature.

While some have maintained that only Hollywood special effects props could have produced such an elaborate hoax, this is literally an example of viewers seeing what they wish to see. The film, as shown on television, and in books, has been greatly "blown up" to display the small image of the Bigfoot figure, and is consequently very hazy, for as a picture is enlarged it loses its sharpness and becomes increasingly grainy and hazy. This in turn compels viewers to fill in the details according to their own personal ideas. The figure is very unclear, and it would require no special talent to reproduce it. (Perhaps significantly, this film was made 11 days before Halloween, when all the elements needed to make such a costume were readily available for sale in drug and fabric stores—the artificial face paint, puttylike face "appliances," and fake fur.) Although I believe it is probably Bob Gimlin in the suit, I also believe he is doing the right thing by not admitting to it and thus allowing the mystery to remain entertainingly intact and mysterious. But if the Patterson-Gimlin film is a hoax, what was the motive? Was Patterson ridiculed or frustrated because of his belief in Bigfoot, resulting in the desire to prove himself? (Then again, knowing this would take a mystery out of it, wouldn't it?)

When is a hoax a hoax?

As we have seen there are many, often subtle reasons which compel hoaxers to bamboozle the anomalist (and everyone else for that matter). The anomalist's criterion of seeing an eyewitness as "reliable" ignores the possibility that the eyewitness could be a victim of a hoax, rather than a perpetrator. But hoaxing in itself is quite legal, and often entertaining— although I'm sure those on the receiving end of a hoax fail to be amused by it.

FATE August 2002

ABOMINABLE SNOWMEN

RUSSIA SEEKS THE SNOWMAN

Frank Volkmann

Diehard Russian Marxists have always maintained that the *Yeti*, or abominable snowman, is a romantic fiction dreamed up by Western statesman and used as a pretext to spy on the frontiers of Nepal and Tibet. Recently, however, they have done a sharp about face on the subject—for good reasons.

In January 1958, a Soviet scientist, Dr. Alexander G. Pronin, reported that in August of the previous year, he had seen a snowman in the Baliand-Kiik valley in the Pamir Mountains. Dr. Pronin is a senior scientist of the Geographic Scientific Institute of Leningrad University and was in this region as head of the Hydrological section of the International Geophysical Year joint expedition of the Uzbek Academy of Science and Leningrad University.

He saw the snowman, or *galub-yavanna* as they say in Russian, quite by accident. His party had been wandering for days in a wild region of mountain, thickly forested and encrusted with hardened snow. Near the top of a 1,500-foot cliff, silhouetted against the darkening sky, he noticed a strange creature.

"At first," he said, "I thought it was a bear but, having collected myself, it became clear that this was no bear but a man-like creature. It walked out of its cave for a distance of some 200 yards and then disappeared beyond the edge of the cliff."

Dr. Pronin watched the creature for about 10 minutes and would have followed it but for the difficulty of the terrain. He returned three days later, however, and observed it again.

"This time I was able to see it more clearly. It was a man-like creature walking on two feet in a slightly stooping manner and wearing no clothes. Its thick-set body was covered with reddish-grey hairs, and it had long arms," he reported.

Dr. Pronin's report provoked considerable criticism at first. Why, it was asked, had he waited a year before publishing his observations? Meteorologists who had been stationed on Glacier Fedchenko II, in the area where Dr. Pronin had worked, disclaimed any knowledge of a "man-like creature" or anything similar to one. "We do not believe Pronin's statement," *Komsomolskaya Pravda* quoted them as saying, "and we think that a true scientist would not publish a discovery until it had been verified many times."

Nevertheless, these scientists intended to return to the Pamirs at the first opportunity to search for the nonexistent beast.

Shortly after Dr. Pronin's report a well-known Chinese cameraman offered corroborative testimony for the existence of a snowman in the Pamirs. In 1954 he was filming three associates on Mount Muztahl-Atu at an altitude of 20,000 feet when he saw two snowmen. It was early in the morning, he said, and the sun had not risen high enough to impair his vision. He had a very clear view of the creatures. They were not especially tall and stooped slightly as they descended a rocky slope. They were half a mile in front of him.

More evidence of a snowman came to light in July (1958) when another Soviet scientist, Prof. B. Porshnev, reported their existence in the remote desert areas of Central Mongolia. These creatures were described as a Neanderthal-type man covered with a thin reddish-black hair.

Prof. Porshnev pointed out that similar creatures had been found in other parts of Asia linked to Mongolia by unexplored mountain ranges. Possibly, he suggested, they represent some primitive race of ape-men once common to all of Asia but now confined to inaccessible mountain regions. He got his information from a Mongolian zoologist named Rinchev. According to this scientist Mongolia's snowmen are about the same height as the native populace but have round shoulders, low foreheads and walk with their knees bent.

Subsequently a Russian newspaper, *Culture and Life*, undertook research preparatory for a joint Soviet-Mongolian search for the creatures. They turned up some important new information. To begin with they found that Mongolian histories recorded the presence of a snowman in that country as early as the 11th century. There were old legends, also, that spoke of evil, hairy men who lived in caves and came out only at night. They were often credited with magical powers, being able to transform themselves into humans, under which guise they stole human children and reared them as their own.

In 1939 during a disturbance with Japanese troops on the Mongolian-Chinese frontier, Mongolian troops shot three strange animals described as hairy, dark-skinned half-men. Several years later a Mongolian chemist encountered one such creature on a field trip. He was resting on a shelf of rock on the side of a mountain and eating some lunch. The snowman—if that, indeed, is what it was—emerged from a crevice in the rocks and started to root in the ground with its hands—much as an ape is observed to do. Occasionally it stood up and put something into its mouth, presumably a grub or root, and then bent down and resumed digging. After a while it became aware that it was not alone, and seeing the intruder, fled back to the crevice.

By 1958 Soviet newspapers and magazines began to show considerable interest in the creatures that Western statesmen had created out of whole cloth. Even scientific institutions rejected the current "legend" explanation of the snowman and suggested that more information be collected.

Then a Soviet Army colonel, Vasgen Karapetyan, came forward with a remarkable story. In 1941 he was stationed at a tiny outpost in the Daghestan Mountain region of the Caucasus where he actually examined a "wild man." It had been captured by local residents far up in the mountains where a race of such creatures had long been known to exist.

The story that Karapetyan told Russian newspaper reporters went like this: Three Daghestan hunters came upon a strange spoor near a mountain stream; being unable to identify the tracks their interest was aroused and they followed them high into the mountains. When they reached a rocky plateau near the summit they lost the spoor and split up to search the region. In about two hours one of the hunters saw the tracks again at the entrance to a narrow cleft in the side of the mountain. Beckoning his two comrades he again gave pursuit and by the middle of the afternoon came to the end of the cleft. There, crouched under a rock shelter and whimpering pitifully, was a strange creature. It was nude, barefoot and "unquestionably human." It spoke no human language, however, but chattered inarticulately and whined when it was most frightened.

"Its chest, back and shoulders," said Karapetyan, who saw it several days later in the native village, "were covered with fluffy hair of dark brown color. This wool reminded me of a bear."

The creature was prodded from its refuge by long poles and with the use of ropes and after a furious struggle was finally subdued. The creature was not vicious although it resisted strenuously, biting and clawing at its antagonists. It was uncommonly strong for its small size (it was about four and one-half feet tall) and repeatedly threw off the hunters. They immediately identified the creature as a "wild man," one of them having seen a similar creature as a youth in the same region.

Offhand this story sounded authentic enough and it certainly came from a reliable source. But why were scientists not informed of the capture of the creature when it happened? Why, indeed, was it not brought to them?

Colonel Karapetyan waved such questions aside. "It was the war. In the confusion and difficulty these things were not as easy as they seem now."

Most Soviet zoologists took him at his word and in 1959 two expeditions were organized to search the Caucasus region. The first came from Kiev University and set out early in the year. It found the peasants of Daghestan very talkative on the subject of its pursuit. They knew of the "wild men" and had seen them many times. The young ones were like normal size human beings but the adults were "giants" covered with brown hair.

While this expedition was unsuccessful in capturing a wild man, or even sighting one, it collected an extensive dossier of information. Hundreds of peasants who had allegedly seen or heard of the creature were interviewed. Old records were checked and references to "wild men who lived in caves" were found. They even examined one of these caves where they were told the creatures were supposed to live.

In general, the reports were so favorable that a second expedition was outfitted. This one came from the USSR Academy of Sciences and it re-explored the same area. Acting as a guide was the Daghestan hunting inspector, V. Leontiev, a man ideally suited for the task. In 1957, while camping in the mountains, he shot at a wild man. It was a tall, upright-walking creature that looked, for all the world, like a hairy human being.

"The night before I shot at the creature," Leontiev reported, "I heard a strange scream. It didn't resemble the roar of a lion or the howl of an animal or bird. Nor could such a sound have been made by an ordinary human."

Leontiev said that stories of "wild men" had been circulated in the Daghestan mountains since he was a child. The creatures were always "nude and barefoot, with broad shoulders and hair like a bear." They walked in the manner of a man but some of their actions were "more like an animal than a human." They were most frequently seen roaming the glaciers of the high mountain regions.

Ralph Izzard, a London newspaperman and author of the popular book, *The Abominable Snowman* (1955) reported in 1960 that the Russian Academy of Science had appointed a highly qualified panel of scientists to promote investigation of this creature and compile a dossier of available evidence. Shortly afterwards in Moscow Russian officials sponsored a "summit conference" on the subject though details of this meeting were not reported. Izzard claimed that Russians no longer regard their snowman as a "legend" but take it "very seriously."

Assuming that they exist then, what are these creatures? Are they to be identified with the Yeti of Nepal and Tibet? Or do they represent a different type? No one knows, of course, but the general consensus of scientific opinion is that they are not the same as the abominable snowman of the Himalayas but are another kind related to them. Professor Porshnev contends that they are a primitive race of "apemen" which have developed purely on an animal level as distinct from a human level.

Similar theories have been advanced by Zoologists P. Sushkia and Prof. N. Sirotinin of the Ukrainian Academy of Sciences; by Prof.

S. Obruchev, of the USSR Academy of Science, and by E. N. Pavlovsky, Russia's greatest zoologist. But despite the theories of her scientists, despite even her success in launching sputniks and producing two-headed dogs, Russia has not captured one snowman. She is still looking for them in the mountains of her eastern provinces, though; now sure that they exist she is no doubt anxious to be acclaimed their discoverer. For it seems that the snowman hunt is no longer an amiable scientific preoccupation but a tough international race. All of the participants are aware that the prize has more than scientific value.

FATE May 1961

RUSSIA SEARCHES FOR THE ABOMINABLE SNOWMAN

Timothy Green Beckley

Its rounded shoulders are broad, its head small and egg-shaped, the brow low and sloping. It has an out-thrust jaw, showing large teeth. Its nose is wide and flat. Its hands are almost human, the fingers exceptionally long. It waddles when it walks but can run swiftly. It does not talk and can apparently only mumble.

This description of the abominable snowman comes from *Nauka i Religiya* (*Science and Religion*), a respected monthly magazine published in the Soviet Union. Another Russian magazine, *Tekhnika Molodezhi* (*Technology for Youth*), also has carried lengthy articles on this legendary creature. In Russia, as in this country, speculation on the existence of the abominable snowman has been treated both with open-mindedness and skepticism by scientists.

Russian scientist Jeanne Koffman, who headed a five-year search for the abominable snowman under the direction of the USSR Geographical Society, recently publicized her findings.

She accompanied a total of nine expeditions to remote mountain regions inside the Soviet Union where the "snowman" reportedly has been seen. And as part of her government-financed project she talked with some 219 persons who claim they have seen this creature. It is called by various names in the various isolated areas: in Chechen it is called *almasti*, in Daghestan *kaptar*, in Ossetia *lahkir* and in Georgia *tkys-katsi*.

Accompanying Miss Koffman on her expeditions was a group of Soviet journalists. One of the first interviews was conducted in early 1962 with Dina Didanov who lives in the village of Zarma. As reported in *Nauka i Religiya*, he told the following story:

> *Last spring I traveled to the mountain pastures. I had supper with the shepherds and bedded down for the night in their camp. The man next to me was very restless. He would fall asleep and then wake up again and smoke. That's why I couldn't fall asleep for a long time.*
>
> *Suddenly I saw a hand parting the flaps of our tent. A strange hairy animal appeared on the threshold. It peered about cautiously, then withdrew. Terribly frightened, I nudged my neighbor and asked, "What is that?"*
>
> *"Eh," he replied, "pay no attention. If you come around here oftener, you'll see more than that. That's an almasti." And he calmly dozed off.*
>
> *But there was no sleep for me. The tent flaps parted again, and the thing entered. I lay with my eyes open…too afraid to move. After what seemed to be a wary look at us, the thing squatted beside the pots of food. Lifting the lids, it began to eat, gulping the food and glancing our way constantly to see if we were asleep. Then it stood up, silently replaced the lids on both pots and walked to a peg on one wall. Removing a bridle from the peg it inspected it carefully, returned it to its place and slipped out of the tent.*
>
> *I waited impatiently for dawn to come. With the first streak of light I jumped up and examined the pots.*

There was no doubt about it; the amount of food had greatly diminished.

'When the man next to me awoke he explained that legend had it that the almasti were evil spirits which roamed the mountains having been punished by Allah for having attempted at some remote time in the past to climb into heaven.

Shortly after this interview, while the expedition was attempting to track down reports of a snowman in a nearby community, during the night they were waked by one of the villagers who hurried into camp to announce that an *almasti* had been seen on a major road on the outskirts of the village. Despite the lateness of the hour Miss Koffman, accompanied by the reporters, immediately went to the area and talked with witnesses. One Aubekir Bekanov told, in a seemingly strained voice, that he had seen a nonhuman creature slumped near a fence as he was returning from the late show at a local movie house. He had pulled out a flashlight which he always carried and flashed the light into the creature's eyes. This seemed to stun the *almasti* which appeared to become rooted to the spot. Finally, after what seemed like minutes to Bekanov but probably was only seconds, the *almasti* bounded over the fence and disappeared in the dark.

On the following morning Miss Koffman heard the story of two young village girls who were out picking cherries in a nearby orchard when suddenly a creature they claimed was close to seven feet tall approached them, mumbling. The frightened girls had made the mistake of climbing a tree whereupon the creature had wrapped its huge hands around the tree trunk and shaken it. One of the girls, losing her grip, fell to the ground. However, her screaming frightened the monster and it took off in long strides. Miss Koffman's party was able to examine the footprints which the creature (or something) had left in the soft earth.

Still another villager reported seeing the *almasti* disappear into a field of tall corn. A total of nine witnesses were interviewed, but despite the fact that Miss Koffman's team of investigators stayed in town for five days, they themselves did not see the "wild man."

On hearing about the grave of what appeared to be a large "snowwoman" in the community of *Tkhina* the party traveled to the region of the Caucasus where long-time residents there told Jeanne Koffman a most unusual story:

> *More than 125 years before, the leader of the community had been a rich lord named Genaba. One day, after visiting with his friend Prince Achba, Genaba returned to the town with a most unusual gift—a female creature who, except for being extremely large and covered with thick dark hair, had looked almost human. Genaba called her Zana. She had been caught by a hunting party but seemed quite gentle and even learned to carry pitchers of water to the lord from a nearby stream. Although Zana never learned to talk she apparently could understand simple orders and lived well in her captive surroundings. Although her refusal to wear clothes had continued to cause comment by outsiders she became, in fact, well-liked by members of the village and several of them, still alive when Miss Koffman visited there, claimed to have attended her funeral in 1880.*

The scientists accompanying Miss Koffman examined what were claimed to be Zana's remains and declared the bones were not human but declined to say they represented the object—the "snowman"—of their search.

Late in 1963 *Literaturnaya Gazeta* published the following critical letter by Professor Valeri Avdeyev:

> *In popular science literature from time to time the question is raised of the existence of hitherto unknown wild men. An article signed by four correspondents of TASS and Nedelya has been published in Nedelya under the heading 'Do Almasti Exist?'*
>
> *The authors of the article report that they themselves chased the wild man in the Caucasian Mountains, though they never did catch up with him or get a glimpse of him. They maintain that official science is wrong in rejecting the possibility of the existence of a wild*

man-like creature, unknown to science, that is hiding in places difficult of access, because more and more testimony is being gathered to the effect that natives of the Caucasus long have known about him and some have seen him in our own time. Since the wild man, according to the authors of the article, is "nothing out of the extraordinary" to the inhabitants of the Caucasus, the various nationalities there have different names for him. A list of these names is given in the article, and all of them mean "forest man" or "wild man." The purely Russian word "leshiry" (wood-goblin), the Tatar "shurale" and others could also be added to this list. For some reason the authors of the article did not include these names, although they could have been used as "evidence" that practically all the people of the U.S.S.R. are closely acquainted with the wild men ...

'Two years ago I happened to meet Jeanne Koffman in Nalchik. I never tired of listening to her captivating stories. I would have liked to believe everything of which she was so firmly convinced, so I waited for the interesting but all too often unsubstantiated stories to be followed by facts that would immediately convince me. But no such facts were forthcoming.

The testimony of "eyewitnesses" is the main and so far the only argument on behalf of the existence of the "wild man" of the Caucasus. On the basis of this information not only has the appearance of the wild man been established but a record of meetings of modern people with him has been compiled. Kabardino-Balkaria proved to be the locale of the greatest concentration, constant habitation and propagation of these beings, with local inhabitants meeting the almasti almost every day.

But here is what strikes me as odd in all this business; neither chance "eyewitnesses" nor people who have for several years now been organizing and carrying out special searches have found the slightest material trace of their existence. Why have corpses of these creatures not been found to this day? After all, despite their extreme wariness (though how can we talk of extreme wariness if they enter homes to drink milk and eat boiled potatoes and generally don't avoid people?) some of their old ones, children or sick could have died in accidents far away from their secret recesses. Where is the hide and the hair and finally where are the bones of these creatures? If they are Neanderthals as Professor Porshnev maintains why have no traces of weapons fashioned by them or remains of their feeding ever been discovered?

It is perfectly clear that it will be possible to talk seriously of the existence of the "snowmen" only after unquestionable material traces of their presence have been found.

As to the testimony of "eyewitnesses," that can have various explanations. If one wished one could name quite a number of similar testifiers to meetings with leshirys, domoviks (brownies) and rusalkas (mermaids).

After my personal talks with her I sincerely wished—and continue to wish—Jeanne Koffman and her assistants the best of luck in their fascinating search. In the meantime, however, like many others, I do not believe in the existence of the almasti or any other goblins.

Miss Koffman's reply to Professor Avdeyev's skeptical article was quick in coming. A few weeks later *Nauka i Religiya* published her answer:

I would like to take this opportunity to comment on Professor Avdeyev's views on the so-called snowman. His ideas are shared by many others.

It is true that we do not yet possess serious material proof that man-like creatures live in the Caucasus. The stories of eyewitnesses are as yet almost the only evidence we go by.

"This means that our claims are built entirely on their accounts. But do we have any reason to question them?

You and those who think like you solve that problem very simply. All reports of wild men, whether they originate from Tibet, the Pamirs, North America or the Caucasus, are dismissed as false. Discussion thus is closed.

But there is no unanimity among you even in arriving at such an unsophisticated conclusion. Some of you think hundreds of eyewitnesses lie from a depravity inherent in human nature. Others see our informants as practical jokers, glad of the chance to put one over on the scientists. Still others consider that all our witnesses are cowards who simply see things out of fright. Kinder critics are disposed to regard them as suffering from hallucinations. Finally, there are those who consider them to be backward ignoramuses, given to superstitious fears.

Two years ago a well-known Moscow scientist, asked to look at my evidence, flatly refused to examine "old wives' tales" gathered in the marketplaces! Yet the file contained: (1) The record of a two-hour talk in one of the largest party district committees of Azerbaijan, signed by the second secretary of the committee, Dr. Kulieva, and livestock specialist Grigori Akhadov; (2) The report of militia captain Belov; (3) An affidavit by Tairov, a research worker at the Academy of Sciences of the Azerbaijanian SSR; (4) The testimony of Dyakov, a Georgian officer; (5) The testimony of Shtymov, a Kabardin, chief of the faculty of pedagogics and psychology of the Pedagogical Institute in Kustanai; (6) The statement of Lieutenant Colonel Karapetyan, of the Medical Corps, to the Academy of Sciences of the U.S.S.R.; (7) The testimony of Kardanov, a Kabardin, and deputy to the Supreme Soviet of the U.S.S.R.

Finally, in what category shall we put Marshal of the Soviet Union Rybalko, Major General Topilsky, head of the special branch of the army subunit Kolpashnikov, Professors Satunin and Baradin? And what about Professor Khokhlov, who gave a description of the unknown creature back in 1914?

257

The idea that the "wild man" is just a figure of folklore is ruled out by the testimony of witnesses not belonging to the local populations. The belief in ill-intentioned deception is incompatible with the testimony of persons who were unaware of the scientific controversy and who enjoy considerable authority among the local inhabitants. The suggestion that it is a question of hallucinations is refuted by the very nature of these hallucinations—which are the same for hundreds of people at various times and in different locations...

I agree with you that if one wishes, one can collect any number of rumors about anything. However, people not only hear but have the ability to evaluate what they hear. There is a method of ascertaining scientific truth by holding polls. A strictly worked-out system of compilation, analysis, comparative evaluation, verification and summarizing of information guarantees a definite trustworthiness of the data received...

When I left for the Caucasus some years ago to verify the first reports that had reached us I considered the possibility of "wild men" living there to be ridiculous, just as you and thousands of others do. It took a long time and hundreds of conversations before I reached the conclusion and later the conviction that I was dealing with realities.

The second stage was no less labor-consuming for me. I had to answer the questions: what, where, when and how should the search be conducted?

I consider that this stage of the work now has been completed. Today I can take a map, say of Kabarda, point to four comparatively restricted areas and say, "A well-equipped group sent to that locality is sure to sight a snowman within a year at the very most."

You underline that you don't believe in the goblins. I don't want to yield to you on this point, so I hasten to announce that I also don't believe in goblins. What is more, I don't "believe" in the abominable snowman. I possess sufficient data to simply say that he exists!

Jeanne Koffman has by no means halted her investigations. We learned that she now is heading another expedition in the Northern Caucasus.

Only time apparently will bring us a final conclusion on this. But for Jeanne Koffman and 219 witnesses, the abominable snowman is not legend but scientific fact.

Timothy Green Beckley: Author and publisher in the paranormal, UFO and cryptid fields.

FATE April 1970

YETIS OF BHUTAN

John J. Sanz

Tenzing Norkey of Nepal, the most famous of the Sherpa mountain climbers and conqueror of Mt. Everest with Sir Edmund Hillary, states the yeti is no figment of the imagination. He, too, has seen yeti footprints in the high snow country. During visits to Himalayan monasteries he has been shown the top halves of skulls of yetis, with scalp and hair still attached to the curiously pointed heads. In his autobiography, *Tiger of the Snows*, Tenzing relates the details of his father's two encounters with the fearsome snow-creatures. As a result of all he has seen and heard, Tenzing is convinced the yeti is a rare species of mountain ape.

In 1966 Bhutan, a small kingdom of about 850,000 people situated in the heart of the eastern Himalayas, issued a set of postage stamps depicting five reproductions of old historical paintings and drawings of the abominable snowman. Although these pictures vary in appearance all reports, ancient and contemporary, seem fairly consistent in their descriptions of the yeti. This is borne out in the carefully preserved manuscripts and scrolls stored in certain *dzongs,* the fortress-

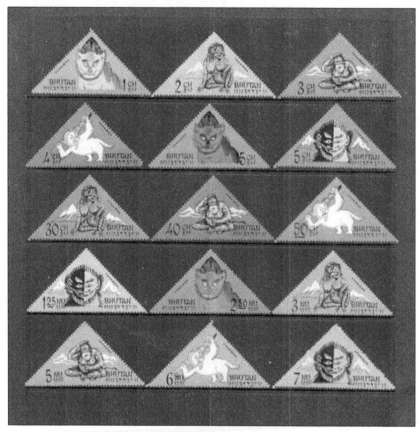

Yeti stamps from Bhutan.

monasteries of Bhutan, many of which were built by Tibetan lamas. These records are said to include lengthy descriptions of the legendary snowmen, with accounts of their appearance, behavior, habits and even their clashes with the native hillmen of the past.

A report which accompanied the stamps' issuance referred to the yeti as a "wild animal to be wary of, one which sometimes attacks cattle and yak herds and which will attack humans." Averaging only five feet in height, the report reads, the yeti is extremely hairy and muscular and has an unforgettable, pungent odor. It lives at 15 to 25 thousand feet, snowline in the Himalayas.

Although the yeti can run on all fours or walk erect like a man, it definitely is not a bear as some Westerners have suggested. Certainly, the Bhutanese "know perfectly well the difference between the animals which they have lived with for centuries."

The 1966 stamps, however, are an interesting collection of diverse artists' conceptions. One stamp pictures the yeti as an all-white, maned animal with a tail, in the act of pulling a poor native apart. Another shows a bushy-bearded, ape-like creature covered with thick body hair, much as described by most eyewitnesses. A third stamp depicts the face of a bristly-haired, devilish-looking monster, and still another shows a female with pendulous breasts, a striped body, and clawed hands and feet.

A fifth stamp shows a tiger face with a pointed hairy skull similar to the relics found in some monasteries.

Until about 15 years ago Bhutan, "The Forbidden Kingdom" lying directly south of Lhasa, was closed to Europeans much as was Tibet. No yeti hunting expedition ever has been allowed in the country although a number of unsuccessful expeditions have searched in nearby Nepal, Sikkim, and Assam. Nevertheless, the Bhutanese natives believe the elusive yetis gradually are dying out because fewer are seen each year.

It is impossible not to wonder which of the artistic representations on the Bhutanese postage stamps comes closest to looking like a real yeti. With any luck one day we shall know.

FATE April 1970

BIGFOOT RESEARCH IN THE SOVIET UNION AND CONTEMPORARY RUSSIA

Paul Stonehill

Sightings of Bigfoot-like hominid creatures have been reported for many years in rugged, isolated areas of Russia. As a consequence, numerous Soviet and Russian scientists and researchers of the paranormal have attempted to study Bigfoot.

In the Soviet Union, the beast was known as *Snezhni Chelovyek* (Snowman or Snow Person). Back in the 1950s, the Soviet Academy of Sciences had a special commission to study the "Snowman."

Expeditions to the Soviet Pamir Mountains (in Central Asia) failed to find the Snowman, and the government stopped taking its existence seriously. Yet there continued to be numerous reports of sightings of the mysterious creatures throughout the USSR.

Maya Bikova

One of the leading Russian authorities on Bigfoot was Maya Bykova, who

Bigfoot in Russia cover design specially commissioned from R. Crumb.

passed away in 1996, leaving behind a legacy of serious scientific inquiry into the phenomenon. Bykova graduated from the Moscow Agricultural Academy in 1955. For many years she studied Bigfoot (naming it Relict Hominoid), and she authored three books on the elusive creature: *A Legend for Adults*; *He Is, Though He Must Not Be*; and *Not That Frightful Thing* ...

Beginning in 1972, Bykova organized a dozen expeditions to search for traces of animals unknown to science. None of these expeditions obtained the support of official government agencies. After long years of study, she came to some interesting conclusions.

Bigfoot's appearance has been consistently described by many eyewitnesses. It looks like a man or a huge ape, its body covered in fur. Bigfoot is nocturnal and moves very fast. No one has ever seen a Bigfoot dwelling, and nobody knows the reasons for this beast's migrations.

The most stunning property attributed to Bigfoot is its ability to disappear and appear suddenly, as if dissolving into thin air. This unusual property has led to various, sometimes fantastic, hypotheses of Bigfoot's origin. Some look for its tracks in other dimensions, while others connect its appearance with UFO activities. Bykova believed that there was no basis for these suppositions. However, she carefully pointed out that we cannot supply an adequate scientific explanation of the phenomenon until we have access to the object of our inquiry. In the meantime, we can only piece together characteristics using the testimonies of as many different witnesses as possible.

Bigfoot's fur has been compared to that of an ape. However, some researchers disagree, asserting that large apes live only in warm environments. Until recently, scientists believed that apes could only live in places where the air temperature never drops below 14 degrees Celsius, and where there are no sharp temperature fluctuations. Yet Bigfoot has been encountered across the globe, from burning deserts to areas inside the Arctic circle.

The snow monkey

The diversity of nature suggests a few possible explanations. There are several well-known mammals that can live in conditions which are seemingly unsuitable for any kind of life. One example is the snow monkey (*Macaca speciosa*) found in sparsely populated regions of northern Japan. Unlike their close relatives, who live in the tropics, the snow monkeys have thick fur. They are larger and live in mountainous terrain where snow covers the ground four months out of the year. They find their food—grass, young sprouts, leaf buds and tree bark—under the snow. Bykova and her colleagues were very interested in the peculiarities of the snow monkeys' fur, the structure of their skin, and their behavior.

Scientific studies on polar bear fur, such as those conducted at Northeastern University in Boston, Massachusetts, may offer vital clues to the Bigfoot enigma. Despite its whiteness, the fur of the polar bear is capable of converting 90 percent of the sun's energy it catches into warmth. Bigfoot specimens inside the Arctic Circle have fur of the same color. Experiments showed that when a portion of polar bear fur is placed under the glass of a solar collector, the efficiency of the apparatus increases by 50 percent and more.

Despite such facts some zoologists and researchers refuse to discuss the possibility of Bigfoot living inside the Arctic Circle.

Maya Bykova's explanation for Bigfoot's sudden disappearances is that the creature camouflages its biofield (aura) to become invisible. This phenomenon has been noted in Bigfoot encounters in the Himalayas.

Tibetan monks say that the Yeti possesses control over its will— it can stop the activity of its brain to become invisible. Monks themselves can do this—indeed, it is a necessary part of their spiritual practice. The red-hatted monks believe that the Yeti is the only creature on Earth that has preserved the ability to become completely invisible. The monks say that Europeans have often observed Bigfoot as a real object and even followed it. Each time they were left disappointed. Bigfoot disappeared every time—right into thin air.

Bykova thinks this is a case of "psychological suggestion." It is directed not outward, but inward, at itself, as proposed by Professor Porshnev in his 1974 book *About Early Human History*. This does not produce complete physical disappearance, but invisibility vis-à-vis the observer. Professor Porshnev concluded that humans have lost this and similar abilities as a result of the increasing complexity of the human psyche.

In the course of evolution, humans have gained much, including the power of speech, but have lost something else at a certain stage of our evolution. Bigfoot, who has not attained the capacity for speech, may be a creature parallel to *Homo sapiens*, a member of the same order and by no means our ancestor.

Fanciful guesses

The mystery surrounding Bigfoot has led to many wild guesses by people who never seriously worked to investigate the phenomenon. The voices of psychics and parapsychologists are the loudest in this out-of-key chorus. Bykova was quite convinced that analogues of this creature's properties should be sought on Earth, not in wild fantasies. This, Bykova said, is the only sensible approach to the subject.

Bigfoot's ability to adapt to vastly different environments and its mysterious defense mechanisms make the creature extremely elusive. But in Bykova's assessment, the facts were amazingly simple: this creature can do everything that *Homo sapien's* ancestors could do at the preverbal stage of their evolution. These are the things humans strive to recover and which we admire when we encounter signs of our evolutionary past in gifted individuals: telepathic communication, the ability to find a lost person, extraordinary vision of situations that occur on the other side of the globe (or inside the Earth), and so on. Bykova believed that Bigfoot's behavior was of no less interest than its natural gifts. Eyewitnesses speak of encounters that lasted only seconds, a minute at the most.

Bigfoot is never encountered face to face. And despite its ability to vanish in front of human eyes, Bykova feared that the species might be dying out.

Human hunger for knowledge, accompanied by loss of interest in the Earth and its inhabitants, leaves Bigfoot with poor chances for survival, said Bykova. She apparently was not aware of ecological defense movements in the West (which are now taking root in the East as well). But she went on to say that there are those in Russia who are impatient and tired of waiting for reliable data of the creature's real existence. They are ready to shoot the obstinate creature at the first opportunity, and so put an end to this mystery once and for all. Others believe that Bigfoot's corpse will somehow bring them the Nobel prize.

Bigfoot's powerful set of defense mechanisms offers it a natural advantage in the face of this adversity. Some eyewitnesses say that it has the ability to influence people, filling them with an unusual fear just short of complete paralysis. Bykova was convinced that this stemmed from a form of ancestral memory that binds humans' fears to notions of Bigfoot.

During a 1992 expedition, Bykova's guide, Maksim, discovered a dozen footprints no less than 1.5 meters apart. The tracks ran down the stony slope of a hill. The stony slope descended at an angle of 30 degrees; only the foolhardy would attempt to go down. The tracks ran among shaggy fir trees, which grow close together in the taiga. Nights are pitch-black here, especially between 3-4 AM, more so when it is raining. Sometime later more footprints with well-marked toes were seen not far off, an inch longer than a European size-29 boot.

Encounters have frequently occurred on a lake inside the Arctic Circle where Bykova often led her expeditions. During one incident at this location, which occurred at the beginning of this century, a local Saami met the creature by a river that flows into the lake. Taking pity on the Bigfoot, he left it some food. Ever since that first encounter in the winter, the Saami looked after his dependent. When the Saami was dying, he asked his daughter to continue giving the creature food.

This is what Bykova called an "advanced contact." They are quite rare, but two such contacts are said to be taking place in Russia now: one is in the Arkhangelsk region, the other near Vologda. Similar relations have been reported between Bigfoot and local people of the Caucasus region, where population density is higher than in the North. Local hunters have informed Bykova and her colleagues that all the big game has left the area. This exodus has been caused by geological prospecting and tourist routes, which pass right through the remote, hidden settlements and sacred places of the Saami people.

Casualties of a distant war

There is an interesting episode in the Soviet digest *Tainy XX Veka* (Moscow, 1990). Professor Porshnev, mentioned in the beginning of the article, presented a lecture about the Snowman to the workers of the Moscow V. I. Lenin auto plant. After the lecture was completed, one of the attendees stood up and told the following story.

His last name was Kolpashnikov. In 1939 he participated in battles in the Klakhin Gol river area in Mongolia. The Soviets were fighting the Imperial Japanese army. Kolpashnikov was commander of the special section (KGB) of the 8th Motorized Brigade. Sometime in the end of August he was informed that two Japanese spies had been killed. He went to the area to verify the report and found two corpses lying in the sand. They were of average human size. Kolpashnikov identified the bodies as those of two anthropoid apes. They were covered with reddish or brownish hair. The hair that covered their bodies was uneven. Their hands were disproportionately long. Mongolian soldiers told him that they had observed silhouettes of the two people close to dawn. These people walked, quite unhurriedly, along the apex of the sand hill *(barkhan)*. After repeated warnings to stop, the sentry shot both of them.

Kolpashnikov knew nothing about Snowman back then, but he did know that there were no anthropoid apes in Mongolia. Then a local denizen, an old Mongol, told Kolpashnikov that the creatures shot that night were wild men. They lived in the mountains. Kolpashnikov ordered that a statement be recorded, and the corpses be buried. The statement, he added, was in the Soviet archives still.

Another important case, revealed by a Soviet lieutenant colonel of the medical corps, deserves our attention.

V.S. Karapetian stated that the military unit he had served with was transferred to a mountainous area in Dagestan (Caucasus Mountains), sometime around October or December 1941. Karapetian was asked by local authorities to look at a man captured in the mountains and help determine if he was a masked enemy agent.

The doctor observed a male, naked and barefoot. His chest, his back, and his shoulders were covered with thick, dark-brown hair. He was quite large, broad shouldered, full of muscles. His gaze was obscure; it was devoid of meaning, like that of an animal. This person would not eat anything in captivity, or drink, and sweated profusely. The authorities did not know what to do with him, and finally let him go, and he went back to the mountains.

Lake Tonee

Alexei Sitnikov and his team of researchers reported a very strange encounter that took place in 1993, while on their way to Lake Tonee. Their plan was to determine the optimal time to conduct an expedition to search for proof of a gigantic serpent in the region. There have been numerous reports about the existence of such a serpent in the far eastern part of Russia.

The explorers had been planning to study the area for several years but had been unable to do so because of a lack of resources and the wretched state of the Russian economy. In 1993 Sitnikov and his colleagues decided that no matter what, the Lake Tonee area had to be explored. Too many disturbing reports were coming from the area to be ignored. The group had barely begun their trek when they had encountered a creature known to the locals as a "Snowman." They were crossing the river on a raft, and on the other bank of the river noticed a man who was covered with reddish fur. The explorers recalled that they felt no fear. The creature turned around, made a grunting sound, and then disappeared in the thicket. A few seconds later the raft had reached the shore, and Sitnikov and a colleague chased the creature. Their fellow explorer Sergei guarded the raft. They did not find the creature and came back to the river. Sergei did find a barely visible footprint at the site where they first sighted the Snowman.

Sitnikov recalls that the creature was only three meters away when they saw it, and it was plainly visible. The weather was sunny and clear. The creature was about two meters in height; its fur was of a dark hue, and not thick. Its head was somewhat triangular in shape, widening toward its base. The creature had small eyes, wide nostrils, a broad chest, and a slit in place of a mouth. The neck was not visible.

Lake Tonee is full of mysterious, anomalous phenomena. Sitnikov had collected many descriptions of the Snowman and has gathered statements from the local populace, including hunters who have encountered it in the wilds. However, Russia has neither the financial means nor the will to explore the taiga in the current era of chaos and near-anarchy. There are many areas in that part of the taiga that have been concealed from human eyes for millennia. Secret settlements have been found deep in the thick woods. For centuries, reports about strange creatures and rituals have leaked from the taiga. The Russian Snowman could be yet another creature hidden deep in the impenetrable forests.

Dr. Septunov's research

Valentin Septunov is a doctor of biological sciences who resides in St. Petersburg, Russia. For years, Dr. Septunov has conducted research on Bigfoot, and he has headed a number of important expeditions. Dr. Septunov reported the results of his expeditions in the summer of 1995 in *Anomaliya*, a Russian newspaper dedicated to covering anomalous phenomena. He is one of the few courageous scientists who continue with this controversial research, although they themselves are on the edge of poverty. No funds are being allocated for any significant research, and Dr. Sapunov is fearful for the future of Russian cryptobiology. Being a true scientist and patriot, Dr. Sapunov cares for the ecological well-being of his country. Yet he has noticed that science is being dreadfully neglected in today's Russia.

And still the scientists carry on their work, collecting data about the mysterious Snowman. Ties that had been severed when the Soviet Union disintegrated are slowly being restored. Information is now coming into Petrograd (as its denizens like to call St. Petersburg) from the Baltic counties and Central Asia. Some information has been exchanged with American researchers, too. The Caucasus Mountains have been cut off from research because of armed conflicts, but research in the Parnir Altai Mountains, the Urals, and in the Russian Northwest goes on.

In the summer of 1995, Dr. Sapunov and his colleagues took part in an expedition of the Center for Ecological Safety. The area of operation was the Viborgsky region of the Karelsky Isthmus (a 90-mile-long isthmus in Karelia, northwest Russia, between the Gulf of Finland and Lake Ladoga). Dr. Sapunov was also a participant in the exploration work of the Kriptobiologiya Society in the Sortavelsky and Olonetsky regions of Kareliya; the area is known for the absence of human inhabitants. Dr. Sapunov has studied a number of reports of a huge being stalking the area. Russian military border guards have confirmed that they have tried to capture the mysterious creature, but to no avail.

In June 1995, Dr. Sapunov visited Riga, Latvia. He had been invited by his Latvian colleagues to help open a Snowman exhibit in the Museum of Nature. During this visit, Dr. Sapunov participated in the planning of an expedition to find the Snowman in the Parnir-Altai. (The Altai Mountains are in Central Asia, Northwestern China, and West Mongolia.)

Use of pheromones

The scientists had worked out a scheme to lure the Snowman by using the sexual pheromones of female apes. A pheromone is any of various chemical substances secreted externally by certain animals that convey information to and produce specific responses in other individuals of the same species. Dr. Sapunov was not able to join the expedition, but his Riga colleagues under the scientific leadership of M. Kudryavtsev, a biologist and criminologist, were able to explore the mountainous route.

In the mountains of the Altai, the Snowman approached the camp, growled, and breathed heavily on three consecutive nights, attracted by strong sexual secretions from female apes. Each time, it left its memorable footprints; the scientists had no trouble identifying them. The scientists tried to take pictures of the creature, having brought along a special camera for the job. But every time the creature appeared, strong and well-armed men were stricken with panic. Dr. Sapunov himself has reported feeling such fear on many occasions while pursuing the elusive creature.

On July 30, 1995, at 11 AM Igor K., a technician from Petrograd, was walking in the forest, near the Vaskelovo village. He recalls suddenly becoming very disoriented. Igor knew the area quite well, yet he kept "walking in circles." Finally, Igor came to a clearing in the forest. He noticed a giant, silver-furred man at a distance. The three-meter tall creature made a few steps toward Igor, then disappeared in the trees.

Dr. Sapunov was unable to personally investigate the area until September. Sergei Turkin, another Bigfoot researcher, came along with him. The ground where the sighting took place was dry and covered with grass. No ground traces were detected. However, some dried-out trees nearby had a strange type of damage to their bark. A creature with thick, chisel-like nails had torn away the bark, up to a height of three meters. Whatever it was, it apparently had a taste for the larva of bark-eating insects.

Dr. Sapunov has made many important findings about the Snowman. The creature is an ecological antipode to *Homo sapiens*. It prefers those areas that have a lower anthropogenetic load. That is why the Snowman has been sighted in forbidden, closed-off areas— the borderlands, nature reserves, and similar places. For example, in the southern part of the Ural Mountains, there have been many recent encounters with the Snowman. This area was closed off for a long time because of radioactive pollution. Once the radiological toxicity had diminished and the environment was healed to some extent by nature, the anthropogenetic pressure remained low, and the Snowman seems to have made its way there. If the same processes take place around Chernobyl, it is natural to suppose that the Snowman may eventually appear there as well. Areas where snowman encounters are most frequently reported tend to offer the creature an ecological advantage.

The Russian sports industry has paid attention to the scientists' findings; the military-industrial complex has perked its ears up as well. The Snowman embodies progressive biological solutions for the adaptation of humankind to its habitat. What humans get from material culture, the Snowman has obtained in the course of biological progress. There has been research in Russia on the creature's movements (based on available photographs and films). Back in 1994, a Russian military college began studying the movements of the Snowman, hoping to use the creature's survival techniques in military applications.

Not far from Moscow

In November 1992, Anatoly Dobrenko, who lives in the village of Samoryadovo (Dimitrovsky District, Moscow Region), was walking his Alsatian dog near the sanatorium where he worked. Suddenly, the dog bristled up and snarled angrily. Anatoly then saw a two-legged hairy monster about a hundred meters away. The creature was moving toward the forest. The man says that he could make out "rusty-colored matted hair on the creature's back." When Dobrenko's son, Igor, an army captain, learned about the encounter, he visited the area of the sighting, accompanied by some employees from the sanatorium. Igor found some well-preserved prints of huge bare feet in the mud that were nearly 50 centimeters long and 15 centimeters wide at the broadest part. The participants treated the prints like material evidence, covering them for better preservation. Later Igor reported his findings to a newspaper, and the newspaper arranged a thorough examination. Local dwellers were interviewed, some of whom had seen signs of the unusual guest's presence before. The search party discovered the place where the creature had spent at least one night: the attic of an abandoned summer cottage. Not one but two creatures seemed to have been there. The second set of tracks evidently belonged to a female; the feet were smaller. The investigation of this case has not ended.

Russian sightings

There have been interesting sightings in the Arkhangelsk Region as well. In the autumn of 1989, Professor of Medicine Dr. N. Aleutsky flew to the local taiga to gather some herbs. He was on the bank of a river when a bear cub came up to him and yelped. The professor heard the cub's mother roaring nearby. Dr. Aleutsky had a knife with him but felt it would be a poor defense against an angry beast. The doctor hastily abandoned his basket of mushrooms and raced back to his boat. Suddenly he heard a blood-chilling scream from behind. Turning his head, the doctor saw a gorilla-like creature holding the bear in its hands. The beast was 2.5 meters tall, its body covered with thick, brown fur. It was a female, and its large teeth were bared. Holding the bear by the hind legs the creature tore the animal in two without any visible effort. The whole episode lasted just a few seconds.

Dr. Aleutsky told his bizarre story to two of his companions. They decided it would be wise to forget the event and not tell anybody about it. Only after some time had passed did they decide to report the story. Luckily the eyewitnesses had a sound biological background. But as more time passed, Dr. Aleutsky couldn't help but doubt the earthly existence of the creature he had sighted.

Yet another sighting took place on January 24, 1992, in the village of Sosnino six kilometers from the ancient Russian town of Kargopol. Two creatures covered with long, grizzly hair entered the barrack of an army unit engaged in road construction. One was enormously tall, about 2.5 meters; the other was half that size. Circumstantial evidence suggests that the larger one was a female, and the other one was its child.

The baby jumped onto the soldiers' night table while its mother stopped by the stove, waved its long arms, and gave a series of short cries in a very low voice. Then the strangers, who encountered neither understanding nor approval, ran away and hid in the forest.

During this incident, a dozen people sighted the strange creatures. More soldiers had seen the creatures a short time before, but they did not believe their eyes. After the incident some soldiers felt ill and went to consult the unit's doctor. One witness could not utter a word. His speech returned several days later. The strangers left behind some tufts of hair (they have not been identified so far, a drop of coagulated blood and large footprints. The footprints were 50 centimeters long, 15 centimeters wide and 20 centimeters deep; the snow was knee-deep for humans.

No record of the Russian studies of Bigfoot will be complete without mentioning Mikhail Sergeyevitch Yeltsin (no relation to the former President of Russia). In the early 1980s his underground report circulated in the USSR among researchers of anomalous phenomena.

Yeltsin was a journalist and the deputy science chief of the Gissar-82 expedition. This expedition, which has studied the Snowman phenomenon since 1974, was organized with the help of *Komsomolskaya Pravda* newspaper. Since 1981 the Gissar expedition has explored the Pamir Mountains, and Pravda has reported its findings.

There were many people in the old USSR who were quite interested in the subject. Major publications such as *Tekhnika Molodezhi* (1966, 1969, 1978) and *Nauka y religiya* (1964, 1968), as well as many newspapers and magazines, featured articles about the Snowman. Many eyewitnesses said that near areas where these apelike creatures were sighted, strange giant footprints (50-60 centimeters) were often found.

A joint research expedition

In 1994 my colleagues from the Yaroslavl UFO Group (Yuri Alexandrovich Smirnov and others) took part in the Gissar-94 expedition. In the Pamir Mountains, the Yaroslavl researchers met with expedition head I.F. Tatzl. He summarized for them his experiences and knowledge of the Snowman. In his view, the Snowman is an objective reality. Tatzl has studied the creature for many years. He points out that apelike creatures study humans, just as we study them. The Snowman, according to Tatzl, possesses a powerful biofield (aura). It feeds on berries. Sometimes it attacks sheep, but it eats only their liver. The Snowman does not eat much, relative to its massive size.

As a rule, the Snowman leaves no traces of its death. In some cases, people have attempted to shoot the creature. These individuals reportedly died afterwards under mysterious circumstances. It is very difficult to catch a glimpse of this elusive hominoid. Bigfoot hates bright lights because it is a nocturnal creature. It can hide under any stone, it sees very well at night, and it is very careful. Human beings can always sense when the apelike creatures look at them. Sometimes Bigfoot throws pebbles at humans. However, should big stones be tossed, one had better leave immediately. As a rule, stones tossed by Bigfoot do not hit humans; it generally aims at other nearby targets, such as campfires. No one has ever been confronted by an aggressive Snowman.

Tatzl believed Bigfoot knows all there is to know about humans. There have been reported cases of Bigfoot helping people who were in danger, and sometimes it warns humans of impending danger. In 1982,

Communism Peak, highest in the Pamir Mountains.

a group of tourists camped at Bolshoi Igizak Ravine (Tadzik SSR) were frightened away when stones began hitting their campfire. Seconds later a landslide buried their camp—but the tourists managed to escape unharmed.

Epilogue

M.S. Yeltsin resides in Bulgaria. The current whereabouts of I. F. Taztl are not known. He has a priceless archive of research papers, sketches, maps and findings about Bigfoot.

They have no funds to study Bigfoot, and there are currently no Gissar-type expeditions to explore the Altai-Parnir Mountains.

I have written much about the strange giants of the Caucasus Mountains and the mysterious giant underwater hominoids of Siberia. The Caucasus area is now closed to us by warfare and terrorism. As for Siberia, I have not received any reports from my colleagues there in two years. Huge societal changes have rocked Russia in its tortured economic and political transition. Let us hope the search for the Snowman is not forgotten.

Paul Stonehill: A native of Kiev; author, lecturer, consultant, broadcaster, and freelance journalist on UFO, paranormal and cryptid topics; frequent contributor to FATE.

FATE January 2003

HALF-HUMAN, HALF-APE

Paul Stonehill

A "chimera"—originally the fabulous Greek mythological creature with a lion's head, a goat's body, and a serpent's tail—has come to mean any hybrid of two or more creatures.

Chimpanzees are believed by many scientists to be the closest relatives of humans. The genetic difference between the two species is estimated to be about 1.7 percent at the DNA level (less than that between horses and zebras). Recent progress in studies of DNA sequences, the fossil record, and brain functions support the idea that there is a sizeable gap separating chimpanzees and monkeys, but not chimpanzees and humans.

Many years ago, according to the recently declassified Soviet documents, a famous scientist tried to close the gap between Homo sapiens and Pan troglodytes.

Human-ape hybrids

Ilya Ivanovich Ivanov was born in 1870. In 1898, he established several zoological laboratories in Moscow, where he studied the reproductive processes of farm animals. In 1901, he established the world's first center for artificially impregnated horses. Before and after the Bolshevik revolution, Ivanov applied his practical technique to other domesticated species. Several million cattle and sheep were artificially inseminated by the mid-1930s; the Soviets needed strong animals for their monumental transformation of the economy. Ivanov also tried to preserve some endangered species using artificial insemination.

In 1927, the Russian émigré newspaper *Russkoye Vremya* published articles concerning shocking experiments in which Ivanov allegedly tried to artificially inseminate human and ape females with the other species' sperm. Few people, however, believed these reports. Many in the West at the time were supporting the "progressive" Soviet Republic.

Proof came after the fall of the Soviet Union, according to Alexander Potapov, who published his research in *Na Grani nevozhmozhnogo* newspaper (issue 335/4, 2004). A document was discovered in the state archives of the Russian Federation reporting the findings of a special commission created in 1929 to evaluate Ivanov's proposed anthropoid interspecies hybridization experiments. These experiments were considered to be of "great scientific importance," and the report indicated that they were to be continued in the Sukhumi Monkey Colony, a Soviet primate center.

The hybridization experiments (the artificial insemination of human females by anthropoid sperm) were to be conducted only with the written agreement of the female. She would accept the risk and obey the required strict isolation regime. The experiments were to be conducted with all necessary safeguards, including preclusion of natural insemination. The trials were to be conducted on as many human females as possible, but in no case, fewer than five.

Why would the luminaries of Soviet science laud Ivanov's uncanny research? According to Potapov, the Bolshevik elite wanted to destroy the belief in God, and subject nature to serve the new Soviet Man. As a former Soviet citizen myself, I can affirm that neither general ethical concerns nor Judeo-Christian beliefs would be of any interest to Soviet Marxists. Stalin, whose bloody star was rising in the crimson world of Soviet politics, would get hybrid slaves who would be completely obedient. The gulag and its network of concentration camps would not be a necessity for the hybrids.

Ivanov and the Socialist Motherland were interested in another result of crossbreeding, referred to as hybrid vigor, or heterosis. Heterosis levels tend to be higher as a result of crossbreeding, meaning that the vigor of the hybrids is greater than that of the parental lines.

I am sure that Stalin and his henchmen would have found another use for the chimeric anthropoids designed by Ivanov. Today we call it biological warfare.

Guinea

Ivanov decided that an expedition to Africa would help him achieve the necessary results. He put in a request and received an approval from the Soviet government. He also was given a financial support in the amount of $291,912, a huge amount of money for the impoverished Socialist state.

Ivanov believed that he would have no problems inseminating African women with chimpanzee sperm. But he was wrong. Local women refused to crossbreed with apes. The Russian scientist would not give up and made an agreement with physicians in a local hospital to conduct the intramural hybridization experiments. The governor of the province did not object to the experiments on the condition that the patients would agree to it. But the women of Guinea categorically refused to be any part of the lurid experiments of the Soviet scientist.

Ivanov was arrested on December 13, 1930 and sentenced to a concentration camp for five years. The OGPU (the forerunner of the KGB) commuted his sentence to a five-year exile in Kazakhstan, and finally, Ivanov was released from prison in 1932. He died just a few months later, on March 20. But our story does not end here.

USSR

In 1974, Belgian zoologist Bernard Heuvelmans and Soviet scientist Boris F. Porchnev published a fascinating book entitled *L'homme de Néanderthal est toujours vivant*. This book contains the account of a Russian doctor who escaped from the Soviet concentration camps, and in 1952 or 1953 met a trusted friend of Heuvelmans. The doctor claimed that he was arrested because he refused to obey the orders from his superiors. He was to conduct artificial insemination of Oriental women by the sperm of male gorillas. The experiments were conducted in the medical department of the Soviet forced labor camps. The doctor claimed that a race of apemen was created. They were extremely strong and covered with fur, worked tirelessly in the salt mines, and grew larger than the humans—but they could not reproduce.

Did the Soviets create an apeman in their secret labs, a creature that later escaped to be mistaken in Russia and Eurasia for a "snowman," or a relict hominoid?

People's Republic of China

The noted British novelist, screenwriter and director Stephen Gallagher revealed an interesting bit of information during an address given at the Wellcome Institute's symposium on the topic "Do Artists Demonize the New Genetics?" on March 23, 1995.

Gallagher had heard of a doctor in Shenyang, in northeast China, who claimed to have achieved success with the artificial insemination of human sperm to a female chimpanzee, only to have the three-month-old fetus destroyed by Red Guards who came in and smashed up his laboratory.

Scientists in China have created embryonic chimeras, hybrid embryos that contain human and rabbit DNA. On September 7, 2001, a report in *Beijing Youth Daily* stated that Professor Chen Xigu in the Experimental Animal Center of Sun Yat-sen University had transferred a skin cell nucleus from a seven-year-old boy into a rabbit's denucleated egg and created an embryo. The aim of his research, according to the paper, was to use cloning to develop cures for such illnesses as diabetes and Parkinson's disease.

Apparently, with the growing numbers of scientists and medical centers engaged in similar experiments in China (such as the Shanghai Second Medical University), there is also a growing debate over the ethics of cross-species reprogramming.

Italy, 1987

A very interesting article headlined "New breed of half-ape 'slave' thought possible," was published in the May 14, 1987, issue of the *Houston Chronicle*. Brunetto Chiarelli, dean of anthropology at Florence University, claimed that he had knowledge of a secret experiment in which a chimpanzee egg was exposed to human sperm with the result that an apparently viable embryo was created. The experiment was interrupted at the embryo stage because of ethical considerations. "Scientific information is numerous but reserved. Maybe at the end of the year we will have an idea of what has been achieved," Chiarelli said. Apparently, the cell proceeded to divide; it was the beginning of a routine developmental process that could potentially have resulted in a human-chimpanzee hybrid.

Italy, 1990s

Another fascinating document from the declassified Soviet archives confirms that noted endocrinologist Sergey Voronov conducted experiments on great apes in the 1920s. Voronov lived in a special facility in Grimaldi, Italy, a center he established known as "The Simian Castle." This animal preserve could contain 100 animals at a time. Voronov was searching for a formula to enable him to slow down the process of aging. He also conducted experiments to increase male virility and researched organ transplantation. Voronov published a book about sexual cell transplantation from apes to humans.

Ventimiglia is a small Italian town on the Ligurian Sea and the Italian Riviera, near the French border. In nearby Grimaldi are grottoes in which prehistoric remains have been found. Strange creatures were sighted in this area in the 1990s, resembling the crossbreed of a primitive man and a gorilla. They were naked and stood two meters tall, with long hair, human-looking heads, large hypnotic eyes, and wrinkled skin.

Did Voronov create chimeric creatures whose descendants wander in the wilderness around the Italian Riviera? There is little available information about the enigmatic Russian surgeon. Did he know of Ivanov and his research? Italian sources state that the Russian scientist tried to "graft bodies of animals on human ones."

United States

According to an article in the October 27, 2003, issue of *U.S. News and World Report* ("Mixing species – and crossing a line?"), US scientists have placed human neural stem cells into the brains of fetal monkeys to see how well these cells formed brain tissue. The cells thrived and migrated through the brain. The experiment drew little notice at the time. Nell Royce, the author of the article, wrote that today the experiment would spark more debate.

Scientists in Advanced Cell Technology, an American biotechnology company in Massachusetts, had previously (1998) mixed human cells and cow eggs in an attempt, similar to the Chinese experiments described above, to make hybrid embryos as a source of stem cells. The genes activated, and the egg began to divide in the normal way up to the 32-cell stage at which it was destroyed. According to a number of American newspapers, those experiments were not successful.

Ethical concerns

Nowadays the use of genetic engineering raises a number of concerns. By far, the greatest public concern is over the mixing of human and animal genes. After all, both cell fusion and recombinant DNA techniques allow species barriers to be readily overcome.

Human beings are changing the world at an ever-increasing pace. New crops appear almost every day. It is certain that we will be using genetic manipulation to change life forms themselves in the coming decades. Of course, we should be more alarmed about manipulation of animals than of vegetation and microorganisms.

There is a threshold of cross-species research that must never be stepped over, lest we walk into a minefield. We must not create situations where humans make life or death decisions without reference to God. We must be cautious not to create interspecies chimeras that would be able to replace or destroy Homo sapiens.

Paul Stonehill: A native of Kiev; author, lecturer, consultant, broadcaster, and freelance journalist on UFO, paranormal and cryptid topics; frequent contributor to FATE.

FATE April 2005

About FATE Magazine

65+ years of covering the strange and unknown

Six decades before the AMC's *Walking Dead*, SyFy's *Paranormal Witness*, late-night radio's *Coast to Coast AM*, and countless websites, blogs, books, and movies began captivating audiences with true tales of the paranormal—there was FATE—a first-of-its-kind publication dedicated to in-depth coverage of mysterious and unexplained phenomena.

FATE was a true journalistic pioneer, covering issues like electronic voice phenomena, cattle mutilations, life on Mars, telepathic communication with animals, and UFOs at a time when discussing such things was neither hip nor trendy. Today FATE enjoys a rare longevity achieved by only a select few US periodicals.

Where it all began: The birth of the modern UFO era

The year was 1948. The Cold War was in its infancy, and the Space Age was still a dream…but across the nation and around the world, people observed strange objects flying through the skies.

Two Chicago-based magazine editors, Raymond A. Palmer and Curtis B. Fuller, took a close look at the public's fascination with flying saucers and saw the opportunity of a lifetime. With help from connections in the worlds of science fiction and alternative spirituality, they launched a new magazine dedicated to the objective exploration of the world's mysteries. They gave their "cosmic reporter" the name FATE.

FATE's first issue, published in Spring 1948, featured as its cover story the first-hand report of pilot Kenneth Arnold on his UFO sighting of the previous year, an event widely recognized by UFO historians as the birth of the modern UFO era.

FATE's role in creating a new genre: The paranormal

Other topics covered in this and subsequent issues included vanished civilizations, communication with spirits, synchronicity, exotic religions, monsters and giants, out-of-place artifacts, and phenomena too bizarre for categorization. This mix of subjects set a template that the magazine would follow for six decades and counting. In many ways, FATE magazine created the genre that is now known as "the paranormal."

Palmer's and Fuller's judgment of FATE's potential proved correct, and as demand for the magazine grew its publication frequency increased quickly from quarterly to bimonthly to monthly. Palmer sold his share of the magazine in the late 1950s, and Fuller brought his wife, Mary, aboard to help run the growing business.

FATE's success spawned scores of imitators over the years, but none lasted very long. Through the decades FATE kept going, doggedly promoting the validity of paranormal studies but unafraid to reveal major events as hoaxes or frauds when it was warranted. Among the famous cases debunked by FATE were the Philadelphia Experiment, and the book and movie versions of the Amityville Horror.

Relevant today

So how does FATE still stay relevant after all this time? Especially in a fast-paced, high-tech world that is often short on attention span and long on cynicism, how does a magazine like FATE continue to thrive? Editor-in-Chief Phyllis Galde says, "FATE allows readers to think for themselves by providing them with stories that mainstream publications don't dare touch. The truth is, reality does not conform to the neat and tidy box that many people would like to wedge it into. Our world is a bizarre and wondrous place and our universe is filled with mystery—it is teeming with the unknown. People are longing for something more than the mundane transactions of everyday existence. FATE feeds the soul's appetite for the enigmatic, the esoteric, and the extraordinary."

Subscribe to FATE

FATE is published in intervals throughout the year in a popular digest size. Join the family of subscribers by visiting the FATE website at www.fatemag.com.

About Rosemary Ellen Guiley

Rosemary Ellen Guiley, executive editor of FATE magazine, is a leading expert in the metaphysical and paranormal fields, with more than 65 books published on a wide range of paranormal, UFO, cryptid, spiritual and mystical topics, including nine single-volume encyclopedias and reference works. Her work focuses on interdimensional entity contact experiences of all kinds (spirit, alien, creature), the afterlife and spirit communications, psychic skills, dreamwork for well-being, spiritual growth and development, angels, past and parallel lives, and investigation of unusual paranormal activity. She has worked full-time as an investigator, researcher, author, and presenter since 1983, and spends a great deal of time in the field doing original research.

Rosemary is president and owner of Visionary Living, Inc., a publishing and media company. She makes numerous appearances on radio and in documentaries, docudramas and television shows.

A personal note from Rosemary

I have been privileged to be part of the FATE family since 1991-92. Dennis Stillings, the publisher of *Artifex* magazine, brought me to the Minneapolis area to give a lecture on vampires—my book *Vampires Among Us* had just been published. In the audience were Phyllis Galde and David Godwin, editors of FATE. They invited me to contribute to FATE, and a lasting friendship was struck.

I started as a columnist for FATE; my column was called "Gateways." I joined the prestigious company of other FATE columnists and regulars, among them John A. Keel, Mark Chorvinsky, Loyd Auerbach, Antonio Huneeus, and Loren Coleman.

Phyllis and David purchased FATE from Llewellyn in the early 2000s. David passed in 2012, and FATE remains under Phyllis's ownership. The economic upheavals in publishing, combined with rapid changes in the delivery of information, have impacted FATE. One a monthly magazine, it is now published several times a year—still delivering the same varied and insightful content.

I went from columnist to consulting editor, and in 2016 became Executive Editor, taking on more editing responsibilities. Phyllis and I entered into a partnership to bring you a series of books on the best from the archives of FATE on timeless topics of ongoing interest. FATE has thousands of excellent articles in its vaults, written by the best of the best, and I am pleased to make them available again.